GETTING STARTED WITH ANGULAR JS
RAHUL SAHAY

Contents

Getting Started with Angular JS

ISBN: 1515037681

ISBN-13: 978-1515037682

Contents

Getting Started with Angular JS

CONTENTS

Contents

Getting Started with Angular JS

Contents

Getting Started with Angular JS

Contents

Getting Started with Angular JS

Contents

Getting Started with Angular JS

Hello and welcome to Getting Started with AngularJS. JavaScript has come a long way since its inception. It used to be client-side validation language than full featured web framework. JQuery has done many changes on the top of JavaScript in order to stabilize the cross browser issues especially. However, JQuery has been written with a different intention. It has been crafted for DOM manipulation. However, JQuery was unable to provide key concepts like modularity, testability, reusability and other basic stuffs, which developers need on day-to-day basis. Each JQuery project looks very different from each other, as there has not been any mandate to stick to the conventions.

AngularJS fills this gap very nicely by providing a wrapper around JQuery on the top of DOM especially in the areas of writing boilerplate code and making application more maintainable, reusable and testable. AngularJS been written by keeping testing in mind. Hence, it ensures that each piece of AngularJS is testable. AngularJS fits in all the scenarios where in basic stuffs like Data-Driven programming, Declarative programming, and Modular programming is required. AngularJS is evolving very rapidly. Their development team and community are adding tons of useful features to this library to make the same more robust and useful.

WHO THIS BOOK IS FOR

This book is for anyone who wants to get started with AngularJS development. However, I do expect from readers that they should have basic knowledge of JavaScript before getting started with AngularJS. This book will be starting from angular introduction to advanced topics like directives, services, testing and many more things. Hence, sit back, take a deep breathe, relax and then start systematically. Skipping any chapter in between is not advisable for beginners.

FROM THE MANAGER'S DESK

Today, no web developer worth his salt can afford to ignore learning concepts and tools required to develop SPA applications. There is a need today more than ever before to develop applications faster, modular, so large distributed teams with diverse skill sets can work in parallel to create an application that can provide the best of user experience and yet be performant, maintainable, extendable and testable. AngularJS is the framework to go to achieve all the above goals.

This book is an excellent resource for anyone beginning to learn Angular. Rahul has been extremely diligent in coming up with examples that are real world like and yet do not take away the reader's attention from angular concepts he is trying to explain. The concepts are first clearly explained followed by code for building a moderately complex application. Each area of

Getting Started with Angular JS

Angular is thoroughly dealt with including the tools in Angular eco system such as WebStorm, Visual Studio Code, Karma, and Yeoman. Overall, it is an enjoyable and informative read.

SITA, T

Senior Manager

Dell

FOREWORD

AngularJS has come a long way since its inception in 2009. Its initial success was spectacular when it helped to reduce 17,000 lines of code to 1,500 lines of code at Google in the Google Feedback project. Hevery, a developer in the Google Feedback project, could rewrite the code that was written over 6 months in flat 3 weeks using the AngularJS framework. Moreover, the product that was built in 3 weeks was also of a better quality in terms of ease of testing. This initial success of this platform made many Googlers support continuous development of this open source framework.

This book has done an excellent job in introducing this able platform to software developers. Rahul Sahay, the author has built an example web application, which has helped to reinforce the concepts of the project through practical implementation. The book will serve as a good tutorial and a good reference for all the developers who want to leverage the enormous capability of the AngularJS framework. With Single Page Applications and other associated frameworks such as Node.js getting popular and popular, this book is being released at an apt time. Enjoy the technical feast!

Piram Manickam

Senior Architect

Dell

Getting Started with Angular JS

HOW THIS BOOK IS STRUCTURED

Chapter 1, Getting Started

Starts by explaining what is Angular, why it is needed? How it fits in web application. You will also learn the overview of AngularJS. Then, you will understand how to build Single Page App.

Chapter 2, Controllers & Markups

In this chapter, you will learn scope and controller, which is the nerve of any ng app. Then, writing your first controller. Here, you will be using different ng pieces to display the info on the page via controller. You will also see directives, filters, and expressions in action. Then, in the end, you will be able to do client side validation for the page.

Chapter 3, Services

Services are very important ingredient in angular application. You will begin this section, by learning what are services, how do you create them and then how to register the same with angular app. After that, you will be using some built-in angular services and writing custom services for specific scenarios. Here, I have also introduced AngularJS Graph to visualize the app in console.

Chapter 4, Routing

Routing is the place, where you actually convert your angular app into Single Page App. You will learn how to configure the routes. Then, you will also learn how to configure Parameterized routes. Last but not the least you will be using location service with routes.

Chapter 5, Creating Custom Directives

In this section, you will learn how to get started with custom directives design. Why do you need them in any angular app? How it enhances the reusability and maintainability of the code? You will also learn how to encapsulate elements. Then, you will learn how to isolate the scope from the parent scope and many things that are more relevant which is required on day-to-day basis for any angular app.

Chapter 6, Testing Angular

Getting Started with Angular JS

In this chapter, you will learn how to get started with Angular Testing. First, you will learn how to setup the development environment to launch the Karma Test runner. Then, you begin this section by writing simple controller tests. Afterwards, you will be learning how to write different kinds of tests and in the end, there will be a bonus section, where in you will learn how to inspect and troubleshoot your angular app.

Chapter 7, Getting Started With Angular 2 & TypeScript

This is the last chapter of the book where you will get the feel of upcoming Angular 2.0 version. Here, you will get started with new angular features. Then, we will see how to get started with angular 2.0 with simple demos using Typescript, ES6 and ES5 as well. After understanding TypeScript basics, we will build one small Movie-Review version with TypeScript & Angular.

ACKNOWLEDGEMENTS

Again, this book would not have been possible without the loving support of my wife Nivi, who had to take over much of the household responsibility apart from her teaching activities. Appreciation also goes out to my Mom and Dad for believing in me and always keeps on encouraging me to complete the book in a best possible way. Moreover, I would also like to thank Sita and Piram for sharing their views on the book. In addition, I would also like to thank Arun and Mayank for doing the technical review and suggested few changes around it.

In the end, you know how it is, you pick a book and flip to Acknowledgement's page and find that author has once again dedicated the book someone close to him, not to you. Not this time. I would like to thank all the readers whole-heartedly for choosing the book. Finally, I would like to thank readers of my blog (http://myview.rahulnivi.net). Many of you have contributed by asking questions, providing feedback, and inspiring and encouraging me in everything, I do.

Getting Started with Angular JS

WHAT DO you find in this CHAPTER?

- Introduction
- MVC (Model-View-Controller)
- Angular Architecture
- Angular JS Advantages
- Comparison with JQuery
- Modules
- Pre-requisites
- Angular Movie App Overview
- Angular Skeleton Project
- Download Code
- Summary

INTRODUCTION:-

Hello and welcome to AngularJS world. In this section, we will get started with AngularJS. As per google, AngularJS is a superheroic JavaScript framework. They say this because AngularJS does so much heavy lifting for us, which we need in any web app on day-to-day basis. It provides a consistent scalable architecture that makes it easy to develop large web application out of the box. The best part of AngularJS is, everything done in the AngularJS library itself. Hence, it does not mandate to learn any other programming language. However, AngularJS is derived from certain basic programming standards that is MVC or MVVM, which we will be discussing next.

MVC (MODEL-VIEW-CONTROLLER):-

The Core concept behind AngularJS is MVC Architectural Pattern. MVC stands for Model-View-Controller. MVVM (Model-View-ViewModel) also similar to MVC, just a design pattern to separate the units of responsibility in different containers. This kind of design pattern gives developers a sense of architectural thinking that how they want to separate the different layers of their web application. MVC design pattern splits the app into three distinct pieces. They are-

Getting Started with Angular JS

- **Model**: - Model is nothing but data repository for the application usually fetched from the server and served on the web page via controller. Hence, any web application that is not static, which is getting data is coming via model only.

- **View**: - View is nothing but the presentation layer of web application. You can also think view as generated HTML. Views are basically dynamic in nature as it entirely depends on the data being fetched from the server and how it is finally presented.

- **Controller**: - Controller is the central processing unit of any app that is based on MVC design pattern. Once user requests the page, that is getting intercepted by controller and then controller decides where to pick the data from and finally pick which template.

As a result, each unit is responsible for one and only thing. Model means data, View means UI and controller is the business logic. Moreover, each unit is independent of each other, which makes angular more robust, unique and easy to maintain.

ANGULAR ARCHITECTURE:-

In this section, we will learn more about AngularJS architecture. However, before discussing angular architecture, let us discuss conventional web application architecture in brief. As you can see in the below diagram, whenever you make a request it is going to server and fetching the entire asset time and again which is very resource intensive, hence puts pressure on the bandwidth, on the server and end result is site response time is slow.

Getting Started with Angular JS

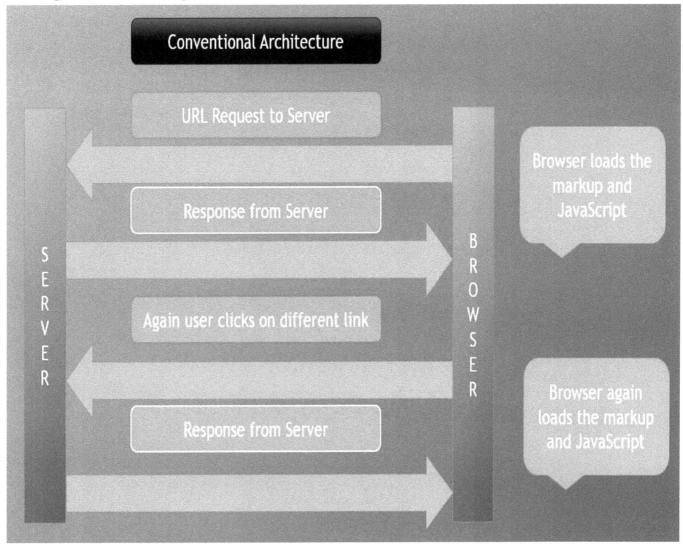

However, in case of angular, it loads all the assets and required components in the first load only. Then, whenever next request comes for any different link on the page, it only replaces JSON there. This way, angular makes any app very lightweight and fit for any device.

Getting Started with Angular JS

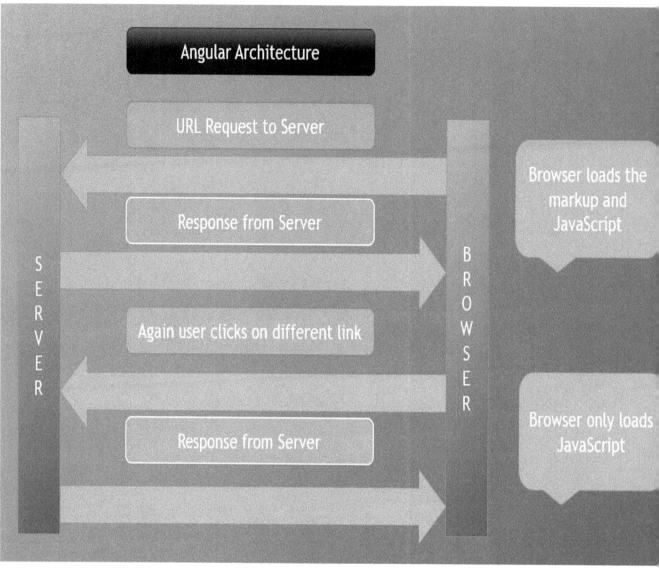

One more point to note here that modern day apps needs that universal architecture support which means you write once and use everywhere like shown below.

Getting Started with Angular JS

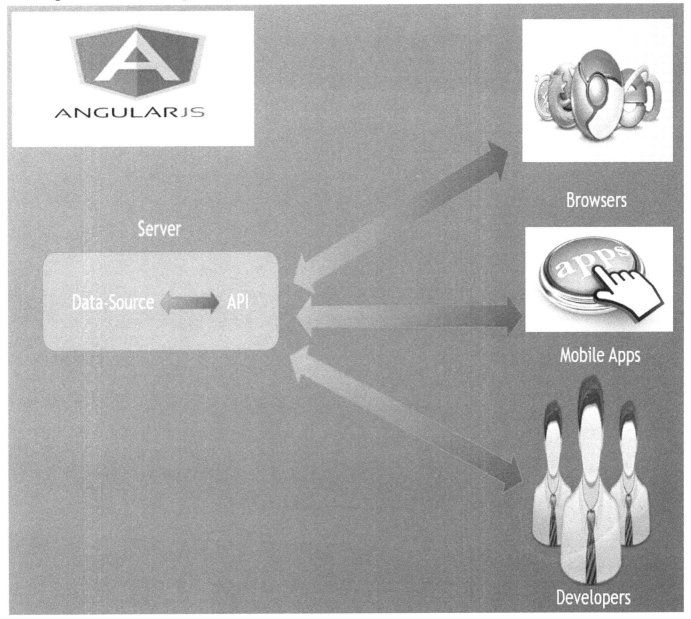

ANGULAR JS ADVANTAGES:-

In this section, we are going to discuss the AngularJS benefits. However, from the previous section, you might have got the glimpse of benefits of angular.

- AngularJS is SPA (Single-Page-Application) framework with client side templating and heavy usage of JavaScript throughout the app. As I said initially, AngularJS does all the heavy lifting required to make a web app up and running, so that we can focus on core functionality.

Getting Started with Angular JS

- Since, there are many things already built in AngularJS framework, hence it needs only proper API implementation to get the functionality running rather than using JQuery.
- As, I said, Angular is built on the top of MVC design pattern. Hence, it helps keep your code modular, maintainable, reusable and testable.
- AngularJS declarative nature gives a snapshot to developer by just looking at the code that what would have been intention behind writing this code.
- AngularJS supports many third party libraries, which people need as to style the app, notify the users and many other use cases that people need on day-to-day basis.

COMPARISON WITH JQUERY:-

In this section, we will do a brief comparison between JQuery and AngularJS. I have mentioned detailed side-by-side comparison between the two in below table.

Features	jQuery	AngularJS
Abstract The DOM	Y	Y
Animation Support	Y	Y
AJAX/JSONP	Y	Y
Cross Module Communication	Y	Y
Deferred Promises	Y	Y
Form Validation	N	Y
Integration Test Runner	N	Y
Unit Test Runner	Y	Y
Localization	N	Y
MVC Pattern	N	Y
Template	N	Y
Two-way Binding	N	Y
One-way Binding	N	Y
Dependency Injection	N	Y
Routing	N	Y
Restful	N	Y

However, JQLite is already built-in in angular. Hence, you do not need to explicitly use JQuery for any DOM manipulation. You can use JQuery stuffs by calling like **angular.element()**.

MODULES:-

Modules in AngularJS are one of the key reasons for keeping application modular. Below is the simple diagram of modules briefly.

Getting Started with Angular JS

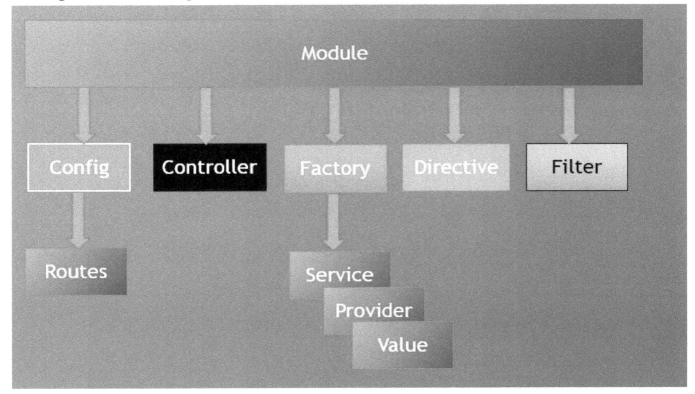

As you can see in the above screen shot, modules let you create all underlying pieces. All these pieces we will understand piece by piece in coming chapter. One more point to understand an angular application can have as many modules as required and all of these are dependent on each other like shown below.

Getting Started with Angular JS

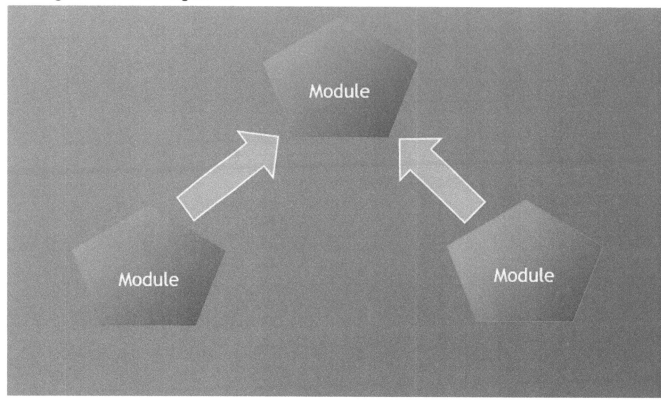

Hence, if your app module is dependent on some other module, then that dependent module can be injected before executing the actual app module. We will see all these things in detail in coming chapters.

PRE-REQUISITES:-

As far as pre-requisites are concerned, there are actually no pre-requisites except basic knowledge of JavaScript. However, few things that I would like to tell here; I am mean which I have used while writing the app.

Editor: - My choice for writing JavaScript app is WebStorm. You can get the same from here (https://www.jetbrains.com/webstorm/). This is the best JavaScript editor, I have used so far. However, there is no such mandate to use the same. You can use any of the editors listed below-

- Visual Studio
- Eclipse
- Visual Studio Code
- Brackets
- Sublime and many more

Getting Started with Angular JS

ANGULAR MOVIE APP REVIEW:-

I always like talking about the application, which you will be building here, with app snapshots, first. Below is the home page of the application.

Getting Started with Angular JS

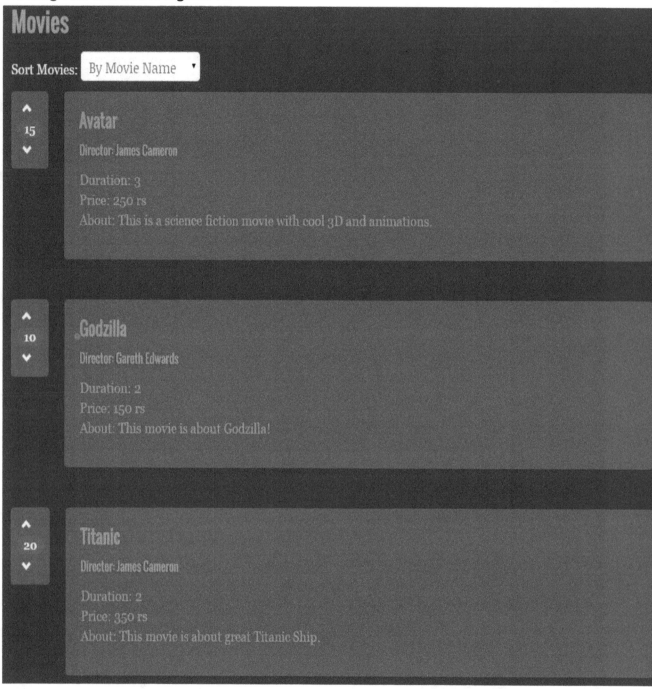

Now, when you click on any of these movies, it will take you to the corresponding pages as shown below-

Getting Started with Angular JS

Getting Started with Angular JS

Learn Live with examples how to get started with Angular JS with complete demo

MOVIE REVIEW

Date:- 1/6/2014	Address:
Time:- 10:30 am	IMAX
	Bangalore,

Director:- James Cameron	Rating:- 5
Release Year:- 2009	Reviews:- 400

Movie Review - © Rahul Sahay

Chapter 1: Getting Started

Getting Started with Angular JS

MOVIE REVIEW

Date:- 1/6/2014   Address:
Time:- 10:30 am   IMAX
                           Bangalore,

Director:- Gareth Edwards   Rating:- 5
Release Year:- 2014   Reviews:- 100

Movie Review - © Rahul Sahay

Getting Started with Angular JS

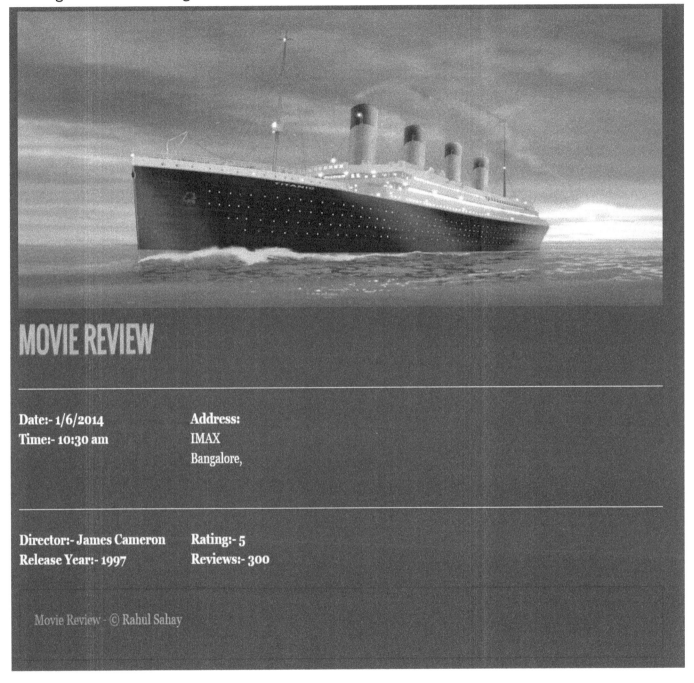

MOVIE REVIEW

Date:- 1/6/2014	**Address:**
Time:- 10:30 am	IMAX
	Bangalore,

Director:- James Cameron	**Rating:-** 5
Release Year:- 1997	**Reviews:-** 300

Movie Review - © Rahul Sahay

Similarly, you can post new movie like shown below.

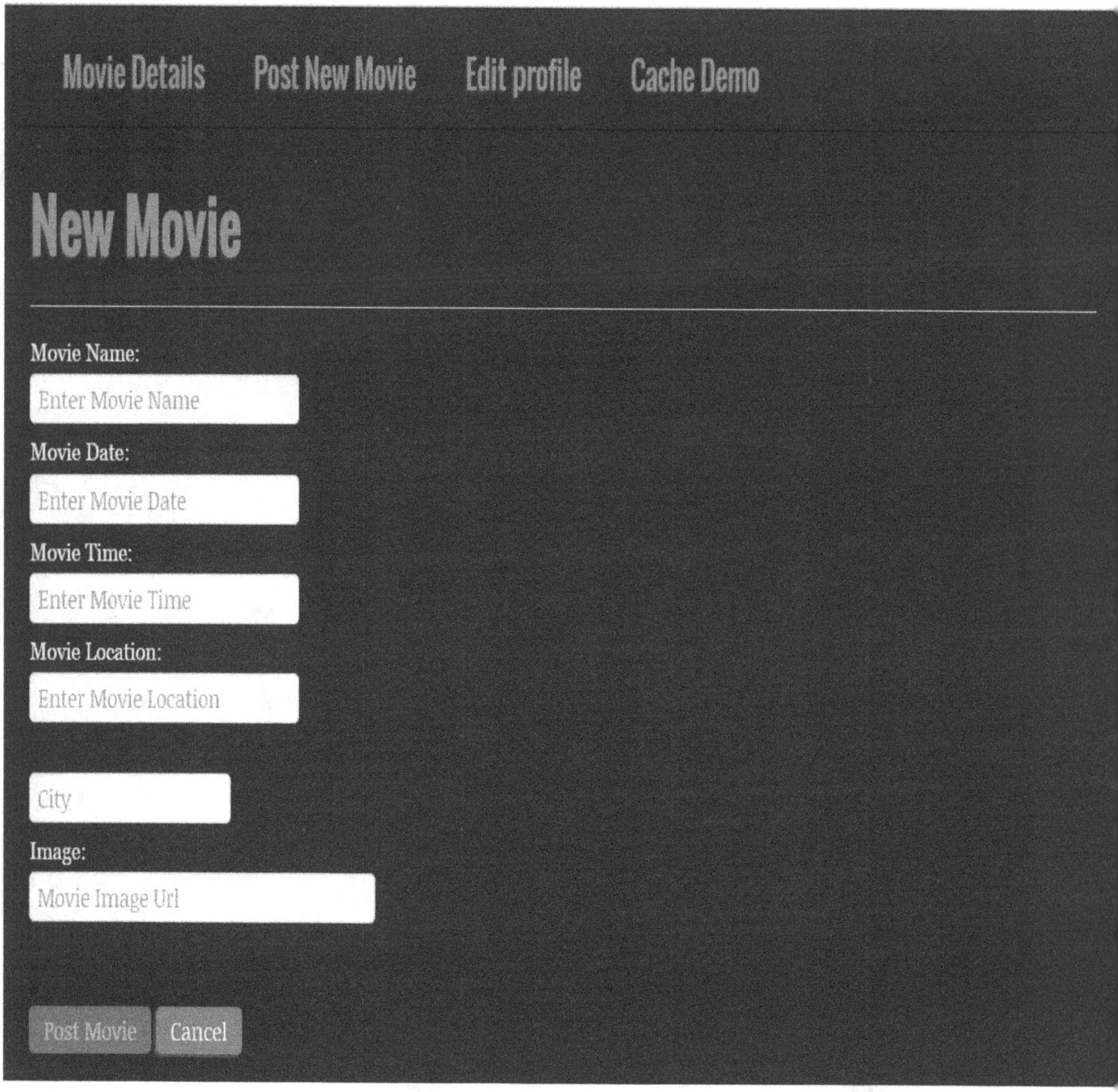

Getting Started with Angular JS

You will also learn how to write client side validation like shown below.

Getting Started with Angular JS

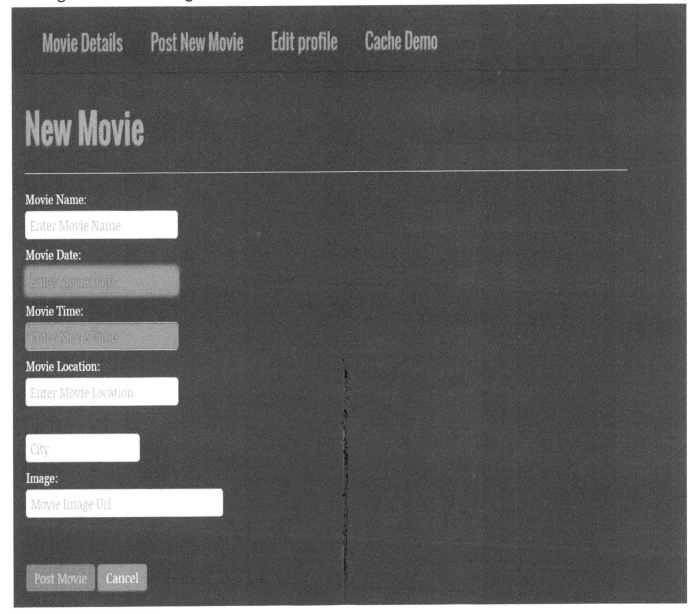

Moreover, when everything goes well, then Post Movie button will enabled as shown below.

Getting Started with Angular JS

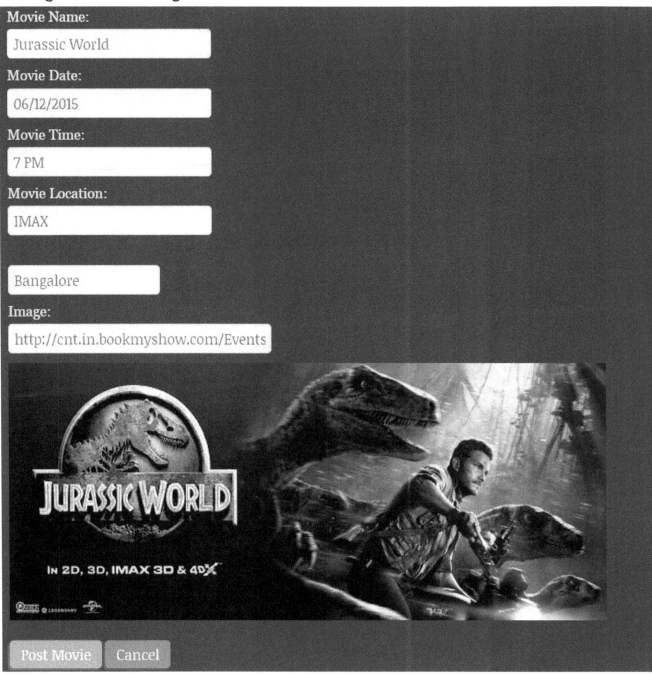

As you can see that, once image URL pasted there, it produced the relevant image. This is called data binding, which you will learn in coming chapters. Then, when you click Edit profile, it will produce the below screen.

Getting Started with Angular JS

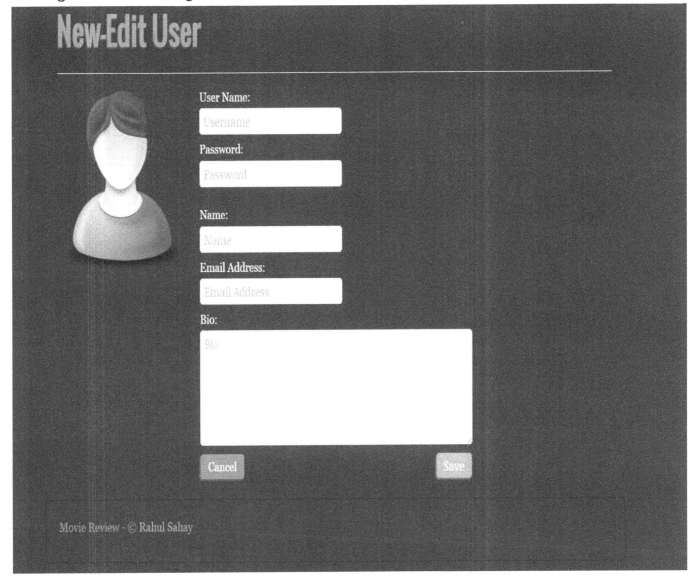

Here, you will learn the power dynamic data binding on the fly using AngularJS. Like, when I type my email id in email address box, it will fetch my image as shown below.

Getting Started with Angular JS

Similarly, when you click on the last link, then this will produce the below page.

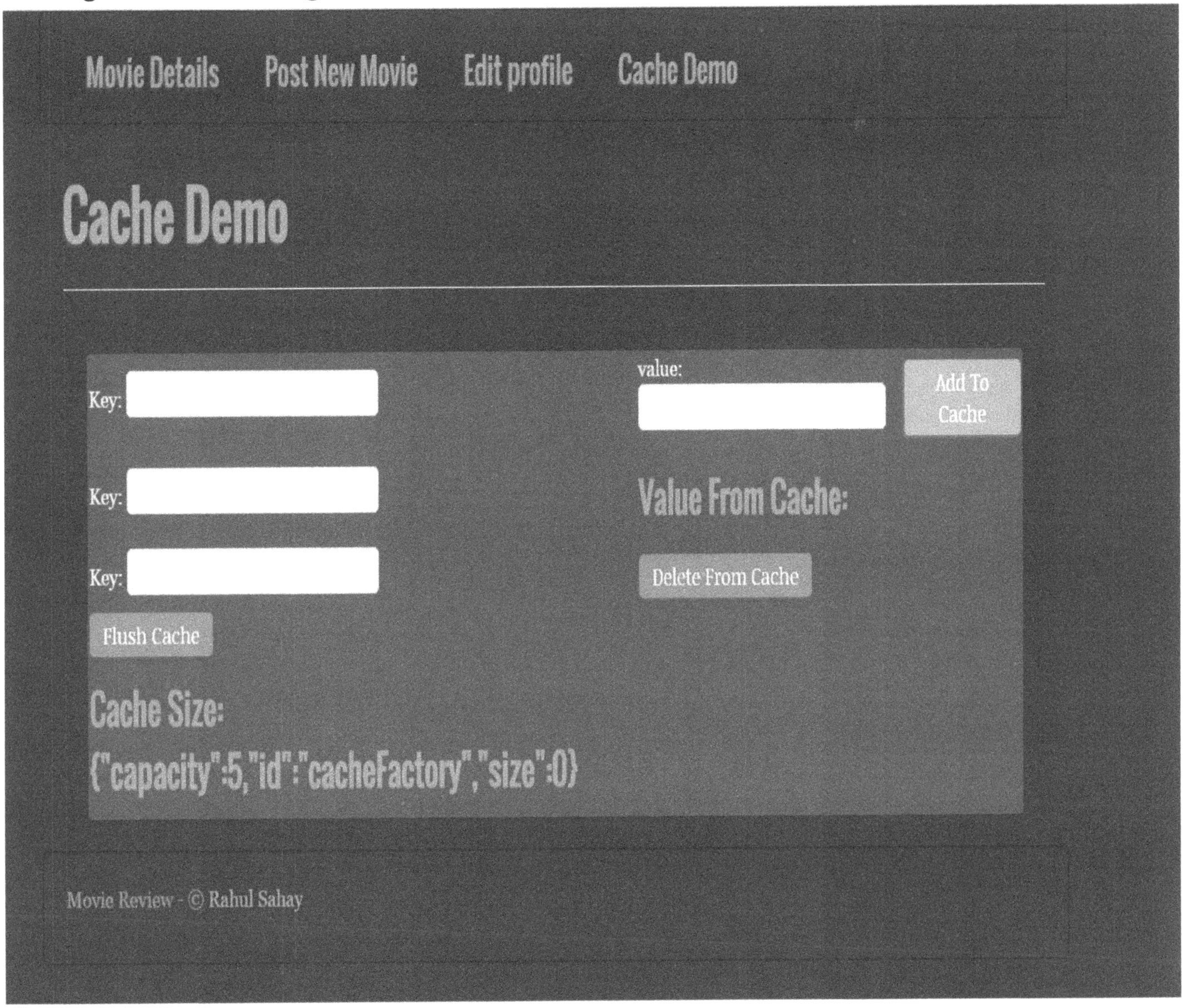

Getting Started with Angular JS

Hence, let us suppose if we enter values as shown below in the screen shot, respective cache size value also being changed.

Getting Started with Angular JS

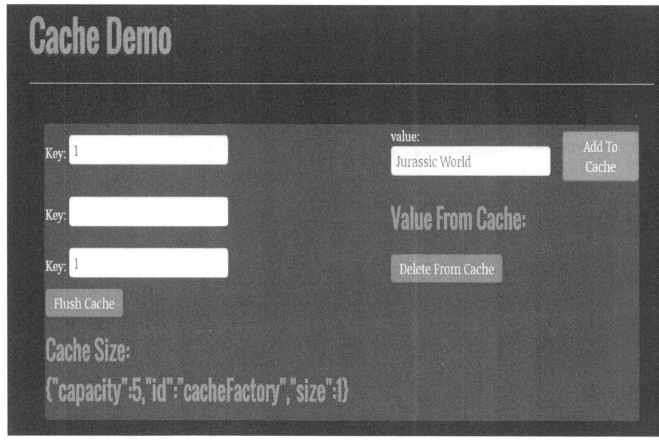

Then, you can retrieve the same by providing key as shown below.

Getting Started with Angular JS

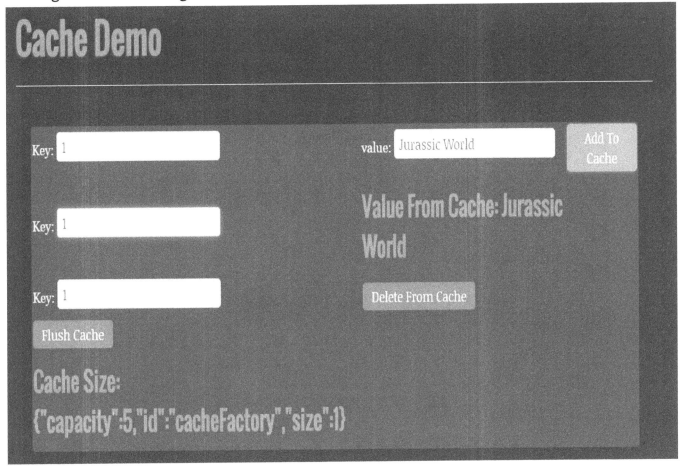

Similarly, you can delete the same based on key or flush entire set. We will discuss all these terminologies in coming chapter. We will go through complete list of directives we generally use on day-to-day basis. However, one directive that I used recently in one demo wanted to show here. This directive is used for embedding you tube videos in your angular application, angular way. Below is the glimpse for the same.

Getting Started with Angular JS

I have also explained normal authentication service by enabling user to do registration on the site and then login accordingly as shown below.

Getting Started with Angular JS

Getting Started with Angular JS

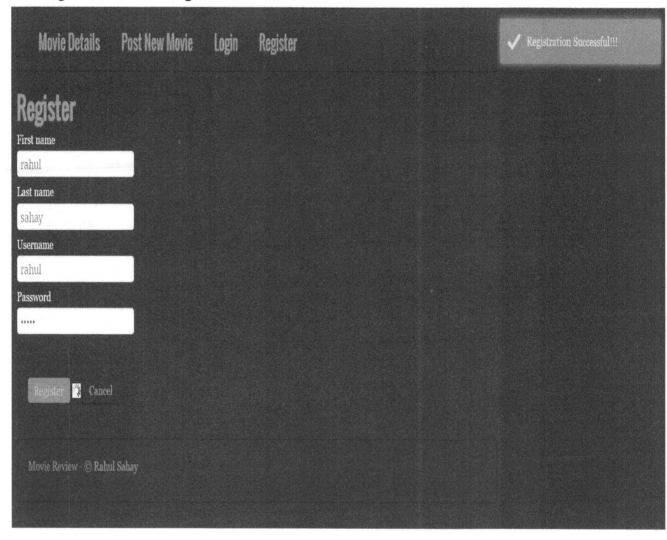

Getting Started with Angular JS

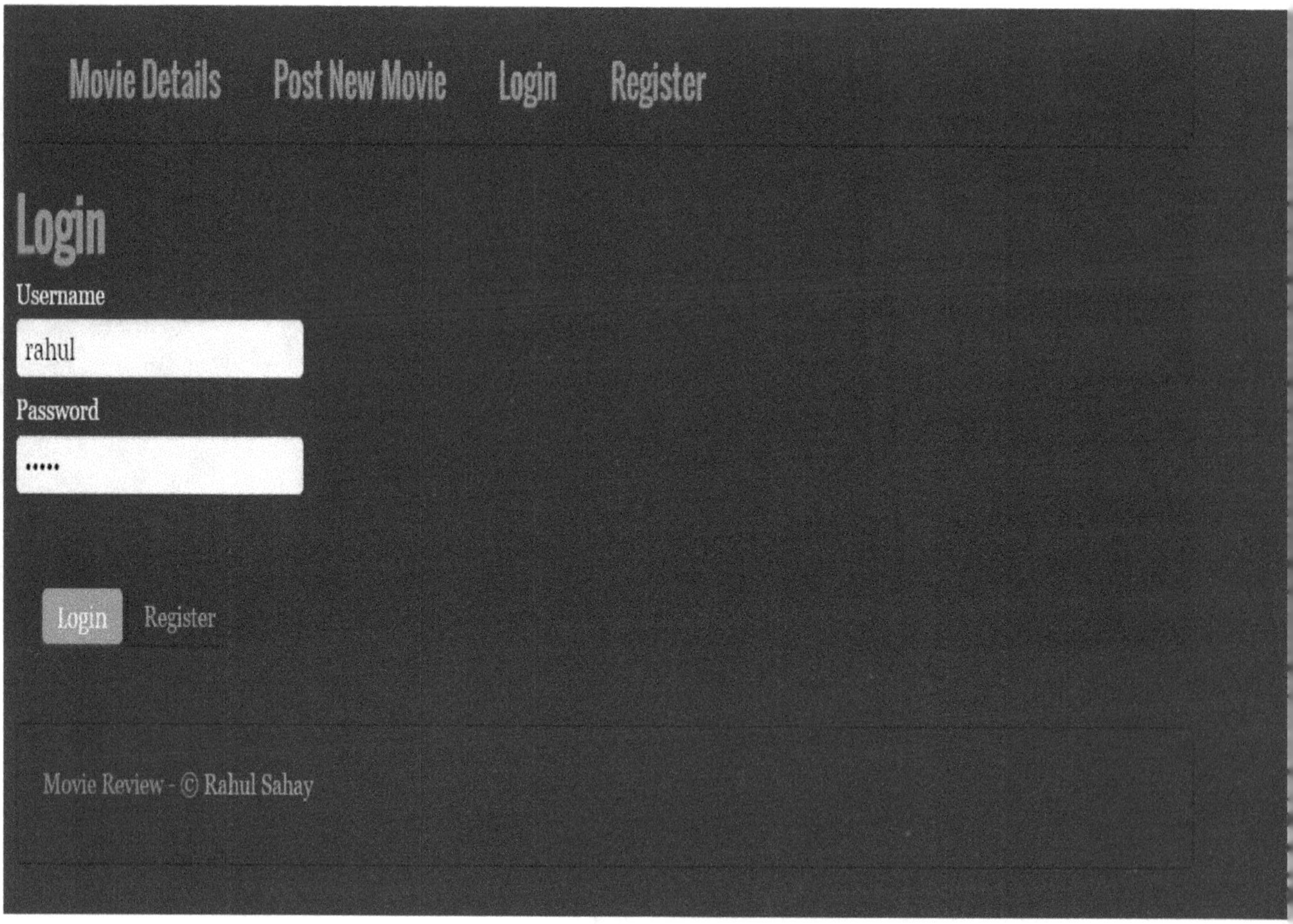

Getting Started with Angular JS

Movie Details   Post New Movie   Login   Register

Login

Username

rahul

Password

•••••

Login   Register

Movie Review - © Rahul Sahay

Getting Started with Angular JS

Apart from this, I have also explained how to get started with yeoman scaffolding template generators for angular and other required dependency. You will learn the same in coming chapters. However, below is the short glimpse for the same.

Getting Started with Angular JS

HTML5 Boilerplate

HTML5 Boilerplate is a professional front-end template for building fast, robust, and adaptable web apps or sites.

Angular

Getting Started with Angular JS

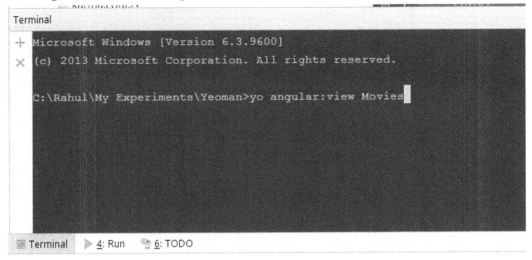

After doing improvisation on the generated code, app will look like as shown below.

Getting Started with Angular JS

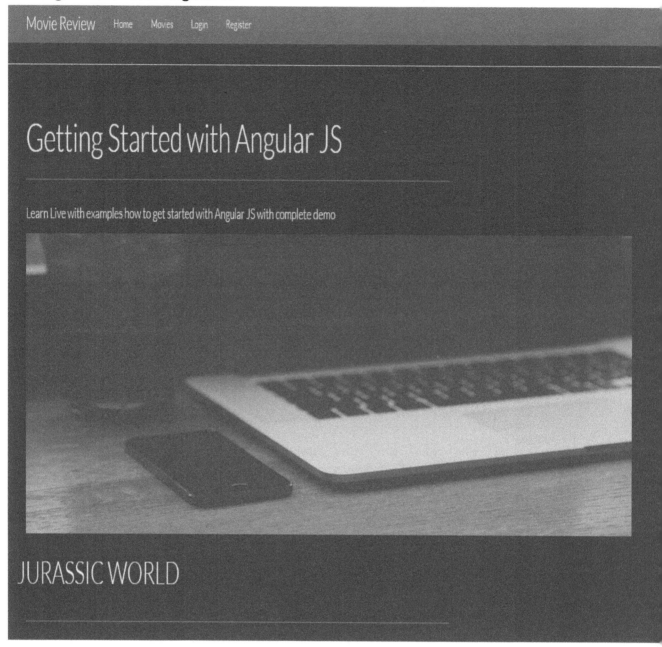

Getting Started with Angular JS

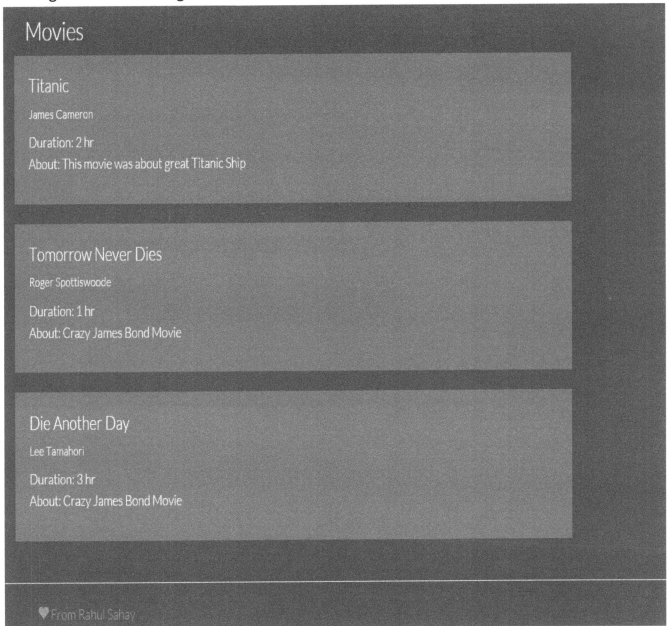

Getting Started with Angular JS

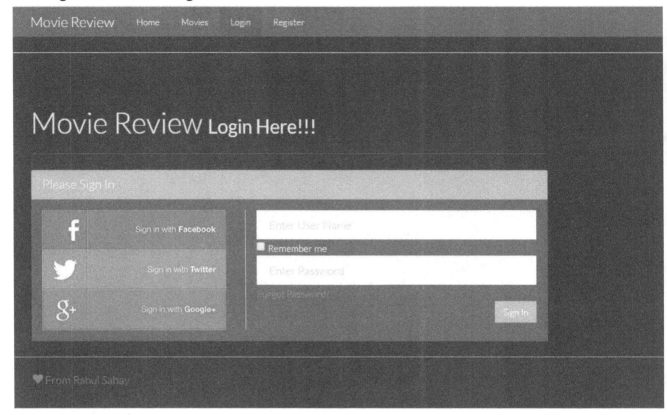

Getting Started with Angular JS

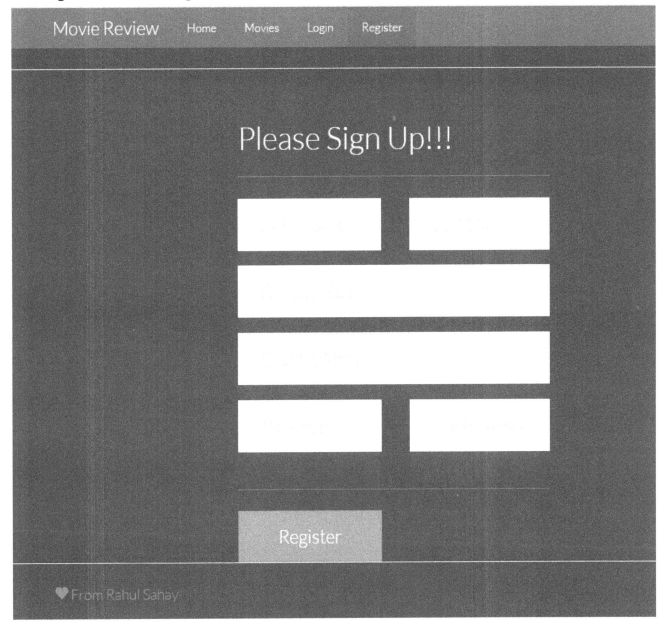

I have also discussed about Angular2 Features in the last chapter. Then how start with TypeScript and write the angular app using that. Below is the glimpse of the same.

Getting Started with Angular JS

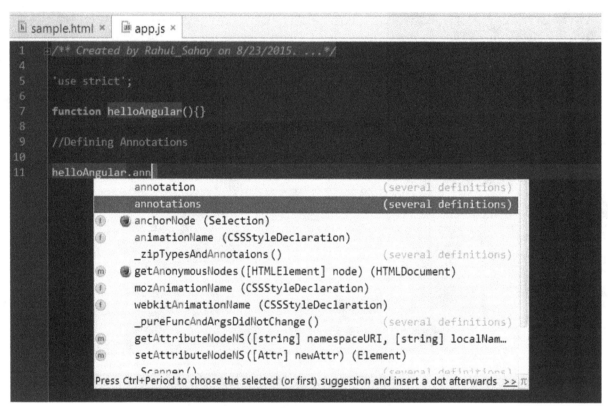

Getting Started with Angular JS

```
1  class Movie{
2      directorName;
3      movieName;
4      releaseYear;
5      noOfReviews
6      constructor(directorName,movieName,releaseYear,noOfReviews)
7      {
8      //define the props
9      this.directorName=directorName;
10     this.movieName=movieName;
11     this.releaseYear=releaseYear;
12     this.noOfReviews=noOfReviews;
13     }
14     }
15     var movie = new Movie('James Cameron','Avatar','1997','200');
16
17     console.log(movie);
```

Below is the corresponding JavaScript generated code.

```
1  'use strict';
2
3  function _classCallCheck(instance, Constructor) { if (!(instance instanceof Constructor)) { throw new TypeError('Cannot call a class as
4
5  var Movie = function Movie(directorName, movieName, releaseYear, noOfReviews) {
6      _classCallCheck(this, Movie);
7
8      //define the props
9      this.directorName = directorName;
10     this.movieName = movieName;
11     this.releaseYear = releaseYear;
12     this.noOfReviews = noOfReviews;
13  };
14
15  var movie = new Movie('James Cameron', 'Avatar', '1997', '200');
16
17  console.log(movie);
```

This also produced me the required output at the bottom of the screen in JSON format.

{"directorName":"James Cameron","movieName":"Avatar","releaseYear":"1997","noOfReviews":"200"}

Then, how to get started with TypeScript with simple TypeScript workflow discussion.

I hope you have enjoyed the app glimpse. Hence, without wasting time let us get started.

Getting Started with Angular JS

ANGULAR SKELETON PROJECT:-

In order get started with AngularJS, you can download the skeleton project from here (https://github.com/rahulsahay19/Movie-Review-Angular-Skeleton) , if you want to code along with me on the same study. However, it is not necessary to follow this convention. You can surely apply the angular techniques in any angular project that you want.

DOWNLOAD CODE:-

You can also download the full finished version from here (https://github.com/rahulsahay19/GettingStartedWithAngularJS).

SUMMARY:-

In this chapter, we have started with AngularJS overview. We started with basic understanding of angular then we also had a glimpse of MVC structure on which Angular is laid upon. Then, we discussed angular architecture in detail by comparing the same with conventional web-app architecture. We have also done concise comparison with JQuery, in order to understand how AngularJS fits in modern day web architecture. Then, we summarized this chapter by giving brief overview of the application, which you will be building along.

Getting Started with Angular JS

WHAT DO you find in this CHAPTER?

- Introduction
- Controllers & Scope
- Writing First Controller
- Displaying Repeating Information
- Handling Events
- Built-in Directives
- Event Directives
- Other Directives
- Expressions
- Filters
- Custom Filters
- Two Way Binding
- Validation
- Summary

INTRODUCTION:-

In this section, we are going to look at markup and controllers. We are going to start with controllers and scope. We are going to create first controller in this section and then we will look at how controllers and scope interact. Next, we will look how to tie up the controller in the page and how markup display data on the page with binding. We will also see how to receive events from users and how to use expressions with bindings. Then, we will look at filters. We will first see basic usage of filters then we will write some custom filters. Lastly, we will see how to work with validations in angular. Now, in order to get started with this, I want you to download the skeleton code from github (https://github.com/rahulsahay19/Movie-Review-Angular-Skeleton). Once, you downloaded the same, you can open the project in any IDE you want. Nevertheless, for this project, I prefer to use **WebStorm** as shown below in the screen shot.

Getting Started with Angular JS

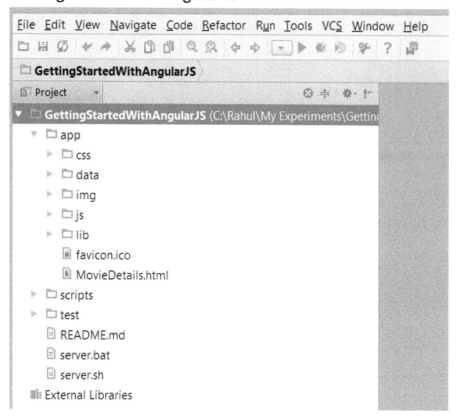

However, here I am working with a different version of same project, as this will be the finished version of the skeleton project. Therefore, if you see the app folder, it contains other important folders like css, data, img etc that has all the required components to get started with AngularJS. Then, it has scripts folder as well, which is having all the third party scripts like angular, bootstrap etc. Then, we have a test folder, which contains test scripts for my application. Hence, without wasting time let us get started with AngularJS.

CONTROLLERS & SCOPE:-

In this section, we are going to talk about controllers. However, we cannot talk about controllers without knowing scope. Therefore, let us look at the relationship between controllers and scope. A controller's primary responsibility is to create scope object. However, scope object communicates with the view. Scope communicates with the view through two-way communication. A view can bind the properties and results of function on the scope and events on the view can call method on the scope.

Getting Started with Angular JS

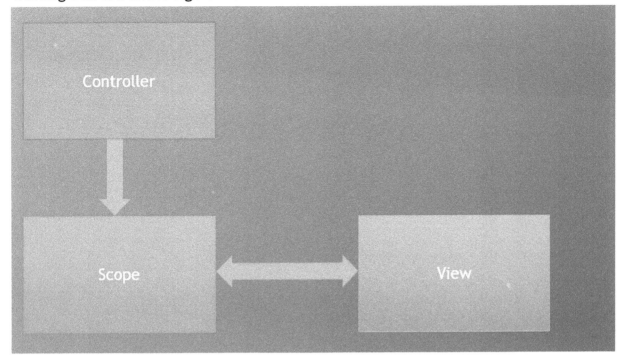

Hence, Data passes in this way from controller to scope and from the scope back and forth to view. Scope is used to expose the model to view. However, scope is not model. The model is the data, which is put in to the scope. However, if we want to modify the model, we can put methods on the scope, which can use two way binding to modify the model. In this way, users can do modifications to the model or in plain English can make modifications to the data.

WRITING FIRST CONTROLLER

In this section, we are going to write our first controller. However, before that, we are going to design our markup first. However, markup we already have from our skeleton project. Below is the snippet for the same. Therefore, as you can below in the snippet, I have referenced all the required script files. Now, the first three is there, just in case if I need them. However, last three I need to run my app.

```
<!doctype html>
<lang="en" ng-app="moviesApp">
<head>
    <meta charset="utf-8">
    <title>Movie Review</title>
    <link rel="stylesheet" href="css/bootstrap.min.css"/>
    <link rel="stylesheet" href="css/app.css"/>
</head>
<div class="container">
    <div class="navbar">
        <div clas="navbar-inner">
            <ul class="nav">
```

Getting Started with Angular JS

```
            </ul>
          </div>
      </div>
    <div ng-controller="MovieController">
        <div class="row">
          <div class="span11">
      {{show.name}}
          </div>
      </div>
      <br />
      <div class="row">
          <div class="span11">
      {{show.date}}
       </div>
      </div><br />
      <div class="row">
          <div class="span11">
      {{show.time}}

      </div>
      </div><br />
    </div>
</div>

<script src="lib/jquery.min.js"></script>
<script src="lib/underscore-1.4.4.min.js"></script>
<script src="lib/bootstrap.min.js"></script>
<script src="lib/angular/angular.js"></script>
<script src="js/app.js"></script>
<script src="js/controllers/MovieController.js"></script>
</body>
</html>
```

Now, if you look closely at the snippet, in the lang section I have included my app with the keyword **ng-app**. This is just a way to tell angular to include the required app on the page, to make this app Angular driven app. Do not worry about these directives now; we will have detailed discussion about the same later in the book. However, if you open app.js file as shown below.

```
'use strict';

var moviesApp = angular.module('moviesApp', []);
```

You will see that, here I have created the app module with **angular.module** with the **name** and **empty bracket**. Now, by nature, angular is **Dependency Injection** driven. Since, this module is currently not dependent on any other module; hence, empty bracket is kept there. Then, in the div, I have mentioned to include **MovieController** on the page with the directive **ng-controller**.

Getting Started with Angular JS

Now, **ng-controller** tells the angular to include particular controller on the page. Then, I have created the required controller as shown below in the screen shot.

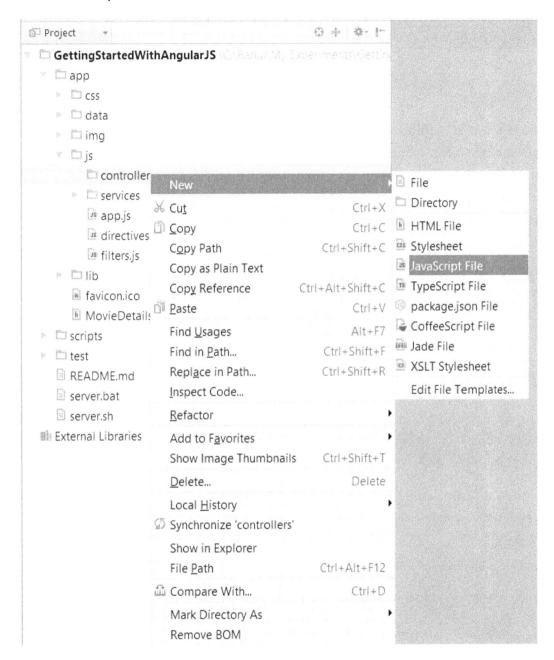

Getting Started with Angular JS

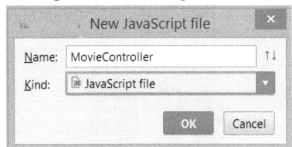

As you can see in the below snippet, I have created the controller with scope in it. Having said earlier, scope is the glue between view and controller. Hence, scope will take the element from controller and supply the same to the view. Therefore, here I have created one show object with few properties in it. Moreover, the same show, I am using in the view for data binding. In real world application, I will be pulling the same info from server. Nevertheless, this is ok for basic understanding.

```
/**
 * Created by Rahul_Sahay on 7/5/2015.
 */

'use strict';

moviesApp.controller('MovieController',function
MovieController($scope){
    $scope.show ={
        name: 'Jurassic World',
        date: '12/06/2015',
        time: '07:30 pm'
    };
});
```

With the above change in place, when I go ahead and run the app in browser, it will produce the below result.

localhost:63342/GettingStartedWithAngularJS/app/MovieDetails.html

Jurassic World

12/06/2015

07:30 pm

Therefore, if you analyze the markup code, you will see that whatever is there inside double curly braces ({{}}) is considered as angular expression. Hence, this is telling angular take this expression and replace the same with corresponding value on the page. Therefore, under this

Getting Started with Angular JS

div, scope item will be available which nothing is but show here, hence **show.propertyname.** Now, let us go ahead and make some bootstrap beautifications to the page. Below is the modified snippet for the same.

```html
<!doctype html>
<lang="en" ng-app="moviesApp">
<head>
    <meta charset="utf-8">
    <title>Movie Review</title>
    <link rel="stylesheet" href="css/bootstrap.min.css"/>
    <link rel="stylesheet" href="css/app.css"/>
</head>
<div class="container">
    <div class="navbar">
        <div class="navbar-inner">
            <ul class="nav">
                </ul>
        </div>
    </div>
    <div ng-controller="MovieController">
        <div class="row">
            <div class="span11">
        <h2>{{show.name}}</h2>
            </div>
        </div>
        <br />
        <div class="row">
            <div class="span3"><strong>{{show.date}}</strong></div>
            <div class="span3"><strong>{{show.time}}</strong></div>

        </div><br />
    </div>
</div>

<script src="lib/jquery.min.js"></script>
<script src="lib/underscore-1.4.4.min.js"></script>
<script src="lib/bootstrap.min.js"></script>
<script src="lib/angular/angular.js"></script>
<script src="js/app.js"></script>
<script src="js/controllers/MovieController.js"></script>
</body>
</html>
```

With the above changes in place, it will look like as shown below.

Getting Started with Angular JS

Ok, now let us go ahead and make some more information to it. Let us add location address to it. Therefore, here I will add location object, which contains addresses for the same. Below is the modified controller snippet.

```
/**
 * Created by Rahul_Sahay on 7/5/2015.
 */

'use strict';

moviesApp.controller('MovieController',function
MovieController($scope){
    $scope.show ={
        name: 'Jurassic World',
        date: '12/06/2015',
        time: '07:30 pm',
        location:{
            address:'IMAX',
            city:'Bangalore',
            province:'KA'
        }
    };
});
```

Moreover, here is the corresponding markup change.

```
<!doctype html>
<lang="en" ng-app="moviesApp">
<head>
<meta charset="utf-8">
<title>Movie Review</title>
<link rel="stylesheet" href="css/bootstrap.min.css"/>
<link rel="stylesheet" href="css/app.css"/>
</head>
<div class="container">
<div class="navbar">
    <div class="navbar-inner">
        <ul class="nav">
        </ul>
    </div>
</div>
</div>
<div ng-controller="MovieController">
    <div class="row">
```

Getting Started with Angular JS

```html
        <div class="span11">
    <h2>{{show.name}}</h2>
        </div>
    </div>
    <br />
    <div class="row">
        <div class="span3">
            <div><strong>{{show.date}}</strong></div>
            <div><strong>{{show.time}}</strong></div>
        </div>
        <div class="span4">
        <address>
            <strong>Address:</strong><br/>
            {{show.location.address}}<br/>
            {{show.location.city}},{{show.location.province}}
        </address>
        </div>
    </div><br />
</div>
</div>

<script src="lib/jquery.min.js"></script>
<script src="lib/underscore-1.4.4.min.js"></script>
<script src="lib/bootstrap.min.js"></script>
<script src="lib/angular/angular.js"></script>
<script src="js/app.js"></script>
<script src="js/controllers/MovieController.js"></script>
</body>
</html>
```

As you can see the expression for address, it is not single line formatted; means it is in the same form what we have mentioned in JavaScript code. Again all these things taken care by angular itself. Moreover, this makes sense as well. With the above change in place, when I go ahead and refresh the page, then it will produce the below output.

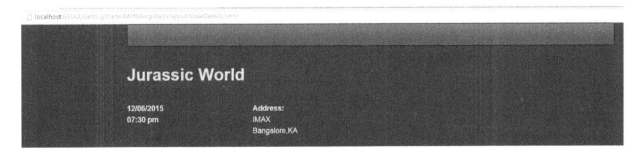

Now, let us go ahead and add image to the page. Below, is the modified controller and markup code. Here, I have added one movie image to the img folder.

```
/**
 * Created by Rahul Sahay on 7/5/2015.
```

Getting Started with Angular JS

```
*/

'use strict';

moviesApp.controller('MovieController',function
MovieController($scope){
    $scope.show ={
        name: 'Jurassic World',
        date: '12/06/2015',
        time: '07:30 pm',
        location:{
            address:'IMAX',
            city:'Bangalore',
            province:'KA'
        },
        imageUrl:'img/movie-background.jpg'
    };
});
```

```
<!doctype html>
<lang="en" ng-app="moviesApp">
<head>
<meta charset="utf-8">
<title>Movie Review</title>
<link rel="stylesheet" href="css/bootstrap.min.css"/>
<link rel="stylesheet" href="css/app.css"/>
</head>
<div class="container">
<div class="navbar">
    <div class="navbar-inner">
        <ul class="nav">
            </ul>
    </div>
</div>
</div>
<div ng-controller="MovieController">
    <img ng-src="{{event.imageUrl}}" alt="{{event.name}}"
style="width:1000px;height: 300px;"/>
    <div class="row">
        <div class="span11">
        <h2>{{show.name}}</h2>
        </div>
    </div>
    <br />
    <div class="row">
        <div class="span3">
            <div><strong>{{show.date}}</strong></div>
        <div><strong>{{show.time}}</strong></div>
        </div>
        <div class="span4">
```

Chapter 2: Controllers & markups

Getting Started with Angular JS

```
        <address>
            <strong>Address:</strong><br/>
            {{show.location.address}}<br/>
            {{show.location.city}},{{show.location.province}}
        </address>
        </div>
    </div><br />
</div>
</div>

<script src="lib/jquery.min.js"></script>
<script src="lib/underscore-1.4.4.min.js"></script>
<script src="lib/bootstrap.min.js"></script>
<script src="lib/angular/angular.js"></script>
<script src="js/app.js"></script>
<script src="js/controllers/MovieController.js"></script>
</body>
</html>
```

You can see here that for parsing image, I am using **ng-src** attribute. This is just an angular way to produce the image on the page. With the above change in place, it will produce the below result.

DISPLAYING REPEATING INFORMATION

In this section, we are going to talk about repeating information. Consider a scenario, where in you have bunch of data, and you want to display the same on the page.

```
 * Created by Rahul Sahay on 7/5/2015.
```

Chapter 2: Controllers & markups

Getting Started with Angular JS

```
*/

'use strict';

moviesApp.controller('MovieController',function
MovieController($scope){
    $scope.show ={
        name: 'Jurassic World',
        date: '12/06/2015',
        time: '07:30 pm',
        location:{
            address:'IMAX',
            city:'Bangalore',
            province:'KA'
        },
        imageUrl:'img/movie-background.jpg',
        movies:[
            {
                name:'Titanic',
                directorName:'James Cameron',
                duration:'2 hr',
                about:'This movie was about great Titanic Ship'
            },
            {
                name:'Tomorrow Never Dies',
                directorName:'Roger Spottiswoode',
                duration:'1 hr',
                about:'Crazy James Bond Movie'
            },
            {
                name:'Die Another Day',
                directorName:'Lee Tamahori',
                duration:'3 hr',
                about:'Crazy James Bond Movie'
            }

        ]
    };
});
```

Therefore, for displaying the above info on the page, I will make use of **ng-repeat** directive as shown below in the code. In addition, one great thing I would like to show here, that webstorm is smart enough to project the properties name as well while writing the markup as shown below in the screen shot.

Getting Started with Angular JS

Below, is the modified snippet for the markup.

```html
<!doctype html>
<lang="en" ng-app="moviesApp">
<head>
<meta charset="utf-8">
<title>Movie Review</title>
<link rel="stylesheet" href="css/bootstrap.min.css"/>
<link rel="stylesheet" href="css/app.css"/>
</head>
<div class="container">
<div class="navbar">
<div class="navbar-inner">
   <ul class="nav">
      </ul>
</div>
</div>
<div ng-controller="MovieController">
<img ng-src="{{show.imageUrl}}" alt="{{show.name}}"
style="width:1000px;height: 300px;"/>
<div class="row">
   <div class="span11">
<h2>{{show.name}}</h2>
   </div>
</div>
<br />
<div class="row">
   <div class="span3">
      <div><strong>{{show.date}}</strong></div>
   <div><strong>{{show.time}}</strong></div>
   </div>
   <div class="span4">
   <address>
      <strong>Address:</strong><br/>
      {{show.location.address}}<br/>
      {{show.location.city}},{{show.location.province}}
   </address>
   </div>
```

Getting Started with Angular JS

```
</div>
<hr />
<h3>Movies</h3>
<ul class="thumbnails">
    <li ng-repeat="movie in show.movies">
        <div class="row show">
            <div class="well span9">
                <h4 class="show-title">{{movie.name}}</h4>
                <h6 style="margin-top: -10ox;">{{movie.directorName}}</h6>
                <span>Duration: {{movie.duration}} </span>
                <p>About: {{movie.about}}</p>

            </div>

        </div>
    </li>
</ul>
</div>
</div>

<script src="lib/jquery.min.js"></script>
<script src="lib/underscore-1.4.4.min.js"></script>
<script src="lib/bootstrap.min.js"></script>
<script src="lib/angular/angular.js"></script>
<script src="js/app.js"></script>
<script src="js/controllers/MovieController.js"></script>
</body>
</html>
```

As you can see in the above snippet, I am looping through the movies object with the help of **ng-repeat** directive and producing the same in the form of list as shown below in the screen shot.

Getting Started with Angular JS

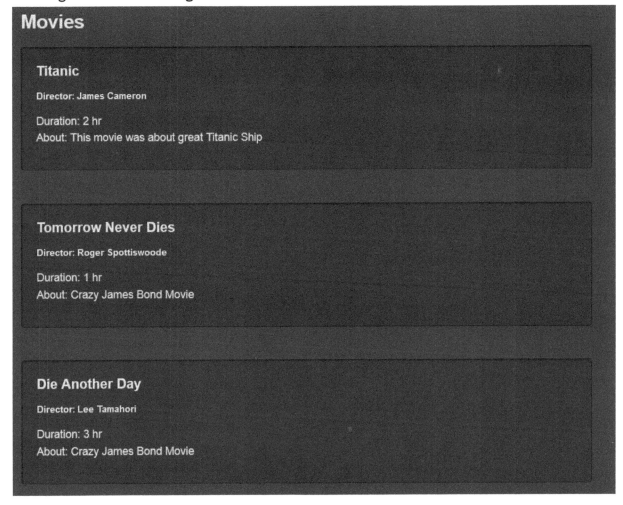

Wow, this looks awesome. Now, our Movie Review app is getting shape.

HANDLING EVENTS:-

Now, we are able to render data on the page, now let us see how to handle the events. One of things, which I like to do, is to allow the people to vote for popular movie. Hence, let us go ahead and add one simple property as shown below in the snippet for voting. Moreover, as you can see, I initially set the same as zero.

```
/*
 * Created by Rahul_Sahay on 7/5/2015.
 */

'use strict';

moviesApp.controller('MovieController',function
MovieController($scope){
    $scope.show ={
        name: 'Jurassic World',
```

Getting Started with Angular JS

```
        date: '12/06/2015',
        time: '07:30 pm',
        location:{
            address:'IMAX',
            city:'Bangalore',
            province:'KA'
        },
        imageUrl:'img/movie-background.jpg',
        movies:[
            {
                name:'Titanic',
                directorName:'James Cameron',
                duration:'2 hr',
                about:'This movie was about great Titanic Ship',
                voteCount:0
            },
            {
                name:'Tomorrow Never Dies',
                directorName:'Roger Spottiswoode',
                duration:'1 hr',
                about:'Crazy James Bond Movie',
                voteCount:0
            },
            {
                name:'Die Another Day',
                directorName:'Lee Tamahori',
                duration:'3 hr',
                about:'Crazy James Bond Movie',
                voteCount:0
            }

        ]
    };
});
```

Once, I have added the same in the controller. I need a way to increment the same, so for that I need to modify the markup as shown below.

```
<!doctype html>
<lang="en" ng-app="moviesApp">
<head>
    <meta charset="utf-8">
    <title>Movie Review</title>
    <link rel="stylesheet" href="css/bootstrap.min.css"/>
    <link rel="stylesheet" href="css/app.css"/>
</head>
<div class="container">
    <div class="navbar">
        <div class="navbar-inner">
            <ul class="nav">
            </ul>
```

Chapter 2: Controllers & markups

Getting Started with Angular JS

```html
            </div>
        </div>
        <div ng-controller="MovieController">
            <img ng-src="{{show.imageUrl}}" alt="{{show.name}}"
style="width:1000px;height: 300px;"/>

            <div class="row">
                <div class="span11">
                    <h2>{{show.name}}</h2>
                </div>
            </div>
            <br/>

            <div class="row">
                <div class="span3">
                    <div><strong>{{show.date}}</strong></div>
                    <div><strong>{{show.time}}</strong></div>
                </div>
                <div class="span4">
                    <address>
                        <strong>Address:</strong><br/>
                        {{show.location.address}}<br/>
                        {{show.location.city}},{{show.location.province}}
                    </address>
                </div>
            </div>
            <hr/>
            <h3>Movies</h3>
            <ul class="thumbnails">
                <li ng-repeat="movie in show.movies">
                    <div class="row show">
                        <div class="span0 well votingWidget">
                            <div class="votingButton">
                                <i class="icon-chevron-up icon-
white"></i>
                            </div>
                            <div class="badge badge-inverse">
                                <div>{{show.voteCount}}</div>
                            </div>
                            <div class="votingButton">
                                <i class="icon-chevron-down icon-
white"></i>
                            </div>
                        </div>
                        <div class="well span9">
                            <h4 class="well-title">{{movie.name}}</h4>
                            <h6 style="margin-top: -10ox;">Director:
{{movie.directorName}}</h6>
                            <span>Duration: {{movie.duration}} </span>

                            <p>About: {{movie.about}}</p>
```

Getting Started with Angular JS

```
                </div>

            </div>
        </li>
    </ul>
    </div>
</div>

<script src="lib/jquery.min.js"></script>
<script src="lib/underscore-1.4.4.min.js"></script>
<script src="lib/bootstrap.min.js"></script>
<script src="lib/angular/angular.js"></script>
<script src="js/app.js"></script>
<script src="js/controllers/MovieController.js"></script>
</body>
</html>
```

As you can see in the above snippet, I have used voting widget for allowing user to vote for the session. It is straightforward. Now, with the above change in place, let us refresh the browser and see the change.

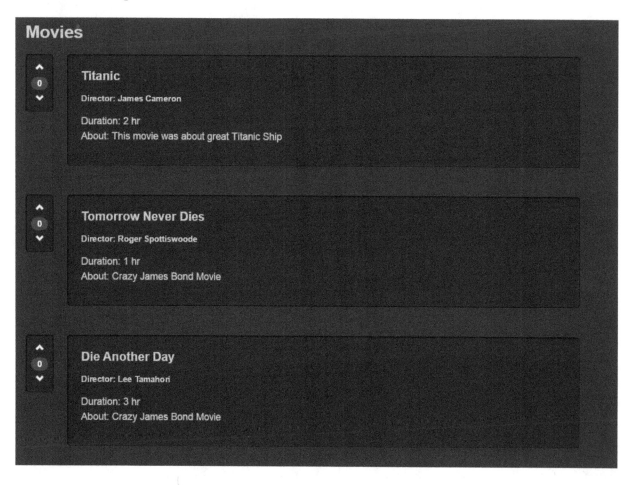

Getting Started with Angular JS

Here, on the left hand side we got our voting button. However, if I go ahead in my controller and change vote count to different numbers, then it will take effect instantly as shown below.

```
/**
 * Created by Rahul_Sahay on 7/5/2015.
 */

'use strict';

moviesApp.controller('MovieController',function
MovieController($scope){
    $scope.show ={
        name: 'Jurassic World',
        date: '12/06/2015',
        time: '07:30 pm',
        location:{
            address:'IMAX',
            city:'Bangalore',
            province:'KA'
        },
        imageUrl:'img/movie-background.jpg',
        movies:[
            {
                name:'Titanic',
                directorName:'James Cameron',
                duration:'2 hr',
                about:'This movie was about great Titanic Ship',
                voteCount:10
            },
            {
                name:'Tomorrow Never Dies',
                directorName:'Roger Spottiswoode',
                duration:'1 hr',
                about:'Crazy James Bond Movie',
                voteCount:11
            },
            {
                name:'Die Another Day',
                directorName:'Lee Tamahori',
                duration:'3 hr',
                about:'Crazy James Bond Movie',
                voteCount:12

            }

        ]
    };
});
```

Chapter 2: Controllers & markups

Getting Started with Angular JS

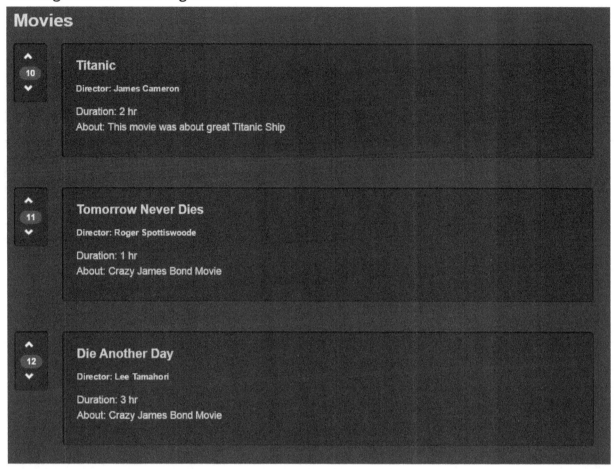

This looks great. However, this is static data and we need a way so that user can change the same. Hence, we need a click event to respond to change. With angular achieving this is very easy. Here, I will be using **ng-click** directive for the same.

```
<!doctype html>
<lang="en" ng-app="moviesApp">
<head>
    <meta charset="utf-8">
    <title>Movie Review</title>
    <link rel="stylesheet" href="css/bootstrap.min.css"/>
    <link rel="stylesheet" href="css/app.css"/>
</head>
<div class="container">
    <div class="navbar">
        <div class="navbar-inner">
            <ul class="nav">
            </ul>
        </div>
    </div>
    <div ng-controller="MovieController">
        <img ng-src="{{show.imageUrl}}" alt="{{show.name}}"
```

Getting Started with Angular JS

```html
style="width:1000px;height: 300px;"/>

        <div class="row">
            <div class="span11">
                <h2>{{show.name}}</h2>
            </div>
        </div>
        <br/>

        <div class="row">
            <div class="span3">
                <div><strong>{{show.date}}</strong></div>
                <div><strong>{{show.time}}</strong></div>
            </div>
            <div class="span4">
                <address>
                    <strong>Address:</strong><br/>
                    {{show.location.address}}<br/>
                    {{show.location.city}},{{show.location.province}}
                </address>
            </div>
        </div>
        <hr/>
        <h3>Movies</h3>
        <ul class="thumbnails">
            <li ng-repeat="movie in show.movies">
                <div class="row show">
                    <div class="span0 well votingWidget">
                        <div class="votingButton" ng-
click="upVoteMovie(movie)">
                            <i class="icon-chevron-up icon-
white"></i>
                        </div>
                        <div class="badge badge-inverse">
                            <div>{{movie.voteCount}}</div>
                        </div>
                        <div class="votingButton" ng-
click="downVoteMovie(movie)">
                            <i class="icon-chevron-down icon-
white"></i>
                        </div>
                    </div>
                    <div class="well span9">
                        <h4 class="well-title">{{movie.name}}</h4>
                        <h6 style="margin-top: -10ox;">Director:
{{movie.directorName}}</h6>
                        <span>Duration: {{movie.duration}} </span>

                        <p>About: {{movie.about}}</p>
                    </div>
```

Getting Started with Angular JS

```
                </div>
            </li>
        </ul>
    </div>
</div>

<script src="lib/jquery.min.js"></script>
<script src="lib/underscore-1.4.4.min.js"></script>
<script src="lib/bootstrap.min.js"></script>
<script src="lib/angular/angular.js"></script>
<script src="js/app.js"></script>
<script src="js/controllers/MovieController.js"></script>
</body>
</html>
```

In addition, I need to add these two ng-click methods in my controller as shown below.

```
/**
 * Created by Rahul_Sahay on 7/5/2015.
 */

'use strict';

moviesApp.controller('MovieController',function
MovieController($scope){
    $scope.show ={
        name: 'Jurassic World',
        date: '12/06/2015',
        time: '07:30 pm',
        location:{
            address:'IMAX',
            city:'Bangalore',
            province:'KA'
        },
        imageUrl:'img/movie-background.jpg',
        movies:[
            {
                name:'Titanic',
                directorName:'James Cameron',
                duration:'2 hr',
                about:'This movie was about great Titanic Ship',
                voteCount:10
            },
            {
                name:'Tomorrow Never Dies',
                directorName:'Roger Spottiswoode',
                duration:'1 hr',
                about:'Crazy James Bond Movie',
                voteCount:11
```

Chapter 2: Controllers & markups

Getting Started with Angular JS

```
        },
        {
            name:'Die Another Day',
            directorName:'Lee Tamahori',
            duration:'3 hr',
            about:'Crazy James Bond Movie',
            voteCount:12
        }

        ]
    };
    $scope.upVoteMovie=function(movie){
        movie.voteCount++;
    };
    $scope.downVoteMovie=function(movie){
        movie.voteCount--;
    };
});
```

Now, with the above change in place, I can go ahead vote against the movie as shown below in the screen shot.

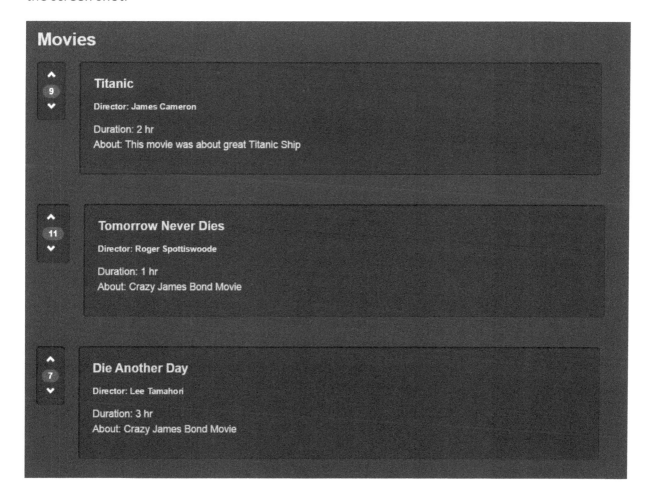

Getting Started with Angular JS

Now, what is nice about angular it will consider the particular movie under that section by default, it does not need any kind of id specifically to identify the movie.

BUILT-IN DIRECTIVES:-

In this section, our whole focus will be on Angular Directives. According to Angular documentation, Built-In directives are nothing but adding new functionalities to HTML. Essentially angular parses directives and takes action accordingly. Therefore, in case of ng-click, it registered click handler event on DOM object. There are four ways to apply directive.

- Using Tag: - In this case, we can use custom tag itself like **<ng-form />.**
- Using Attribute: - In this case, we apply directive using attribute like **<div ng-form />.**
- Using Class: - Third way of using directive is via class like **<div class="ng-form" />.**

One more way of writing HTML directives and that is nothing but in the comments section. Since, this is not oftenly used, hence not covering this piece here. However, you can always refer the same in Angular documentation.

EVENT DIRECTIVES:-

First set of directives, which we are going to look here, is the event directive. We have already seen **ng-click** in action. However, we are also going to cover

- ngDblClick
- ngMouseDown
- ngMouseEnter
- ngMouseLeave
- ngMouseMove
- mgMouseover
- ngMouseUp
- ngChange

Therefore, all these directives excluding last one are mouse events. These events functioning are similar to ng-click, only event name will change. **ngChange** will pick the change done anything with the html input. However, this is coupled with **ng-model** directive. For instance, I have a text box and in that, I want to predict item change in it, then I can make use of **ng-Change** directive. We will be covering ng-model and other required stuffs in two-way binding section separately.

Getting Started with Angular JS

OTHER DIRECTIVES:-

Apart from above mentioned directives, we have many other directives, which are equally useful and heavily used in any angular application. They are-

- ngApp
- ngBind
- ngBindTemplate
- ngBindHTML
- ngHide
- ngShow
- ngCloak
- ngStyle
- ngClass
- ngClassEven
- ngClassOdd

Here, we have already seen **ngApp** directive, we will some more examples on the same in coming section. Let us see bind in action. So far, we have been using expressions to evaluate elements. However, it can be achieved by using bind as shown below.

```
<div class="row">
    <div class="span11">
        <h2 ng-bind="show.name"></h2>
    </div>
</div>
```

In addition, this will produce the same result as shown below.

Getting Started with Angular JS

Similarly, we can use bind template. Bind Template will accept expression, but here we can provide multiple expressions as shown below.

```
<div class="row">
    <div class="span11">
        <h2 ng-bind-template="{{show.name}} {{show.date}}"></h2>
    </div>
</div>
```

Hence, this will produce the below output.

Chapter 2: Controllers & markups

Getting Started with Angular JS

Now, let us look at bind HTML directive. In order to demonstrate the same, we need to include one more file angular sanitize file as shown below.

```
<script src="lib/jquery.min.js"></script>
<script src="lib/underscore-1.4.4.min.js"></script>
<script src="lib/bootstrap.min.js"></script>
<script src="lib/angular/angular.js"></script>
<script src="lib/angular/angular-sanitize.js"></script>
<script src="js/app.js"></script>
<script src="js/controllers/MovieController.js"></script>
```

Once, we included this reference; then we need to include the same in app via dependency injection as shown below.

```
'use strict';

var moviesApp = angular.module('moviesApp', ['ngSanitize']);
```

The above line means that it is going to load sanitize module before it loads our module. Then, again, I need to modify the markup as shown below.

```
<div ng-bind-html="junkCode">Dangerous</div>
```

As you can see, here I have one div with some content in it that I will replace with "**junkCode**" variable content. Now, this value will come from controller as shown below.

```
$scope.junkCode='<span style="color:red">Junk HTML</span>';
```

With the above change in place, when I refresh the browser, then it will produce the below output.

Getting Started with Angular JS

However, here it does not set the foreground color to red. Now, if I inspect the HTML in chrome browser, will produce the plain span as shown below.

```
▶ <div class="navbar">…</div>
▼ <div ng-controller="MovieController" class="ng-scope">
    <img ng-src="img/movie-background.jpg" alt="Jurassic World" style="width:1000px;height: 300px;" src="img/movie-background.jpg">
  ▶ <div class="row">…</div>
    <br>
  ▼ <div ng-bind-html="junkCode" class="ng-binding">
      <span>Junk HTML</span>
    </div>
  ▶ <div class="row">…</div>
    <hr>
    <h3>Movies</h3>
  ▶ <ul class="thumbnails">…</ul>
  </div>
  ::after
```

This is what sanitize does. It removes any thing, which sanitize find dangerous. Hence, it removed style attribute from HTML and emitted as plain text. Now, let me explain show and hide directive based on bool value. Let us set one value in controller.

```
$scope.checkValue=true;
```

Moreover, corresponding change in markup will look like as shown below.

```
<h2 ng-show="checkValue">Show This</h2>
<h2 ng-hide="checkValue">Hide This</h2>
```

With the above change in place, when I refresh the browser, it will produce the below output.

Now, when I inspect the HTML, it will produce the below result.

Getting Started with Angular JS

```
▼<div class="container">
   ::before
 ▶ <div class="navbar">...</div>
 ▼<div ng-controller="MovieController" class="ng-scope">
     <img ng-src="img/movie-background.jpg" alt="Jurassic World" style="width:1000px;height: 300px;" src="img/movie-background.jpg">
   ▶ <div class="row">...</div>
     <hr>
     <h2 ng-show="checkValue" class>Show This</h2>
     <h2 ng-hide="checkValue" class="ng-hide">Hide This</h2>
   ▶ <div class="row">...</div>
     <hr>
     <h3>Movies</h3>
   ▶ <ul class="thumbnails">...</ul>
   </div>
   ::after
</div>
```

As long as Boolean value is true, hide directive value will hide the value and show directive will show the value. However, if we flip the value to false, then it will produce the other result as shown below.

```
$scope.checkValue=false;
```

```
    ::before
 ▶ <div class="navbar">...</div>
 ▼<div ng-controller="MovieController" class="ng-scope">
     <img ng-src="img/movie-background.jpg" alt="Jurassic World" style="width:1000px;height: 300px;" src="img/movie-background.jpg">
   ▶ <div class="row">...</div>
     <br>
     <h2 ng-show="checkValue" class="ng-hide">Show This</h2>
     <h2 ng-hide="checkValue" class>Hide This</h2>
   ▶ <div class="row">...</div>
     <hr>
     <h3>Movies</h3>
   ▶ <ul class="thumbnails">...</ul>
   </div>
   ::after
</div>
```

Chapter 2: Controllers & markups

Getting Started with Angular JS

The next directive, which we will look here, is the cloak directive. This directive will hide the portion or the entire page, until angular has a chance to run and go through and parse the HTML and replace the directives and bindings with the actual values, which are supposed to display. Hence, here first I will add the cloak directive in the body tag then, add one css rule in the app.css as shown below. This special rule you can get from angular documentation.

```
<body ng-cloak>
```

And then,

```
[ng\:cloak], [ng-cloak], [data-ng-cloak], [x-ng-cloak], .ng-cloak, .x-ng-cloak{
    display: none;
}
```

Unfortunately, this is difficult to demonstrate, because on the powerful machines, that HTML flash is so quick that is difficult to catch. All right, next directive is the style directive. This is very easy to understand. First, I will add style in markup code as shown below.

```
<h2 ng-style="customStyle" ng-bind-template="{{show.name}}
{{show.date}}"></h2>
```

Then, I will add this custom style in controller code as shown below.

```
$scope.customStyle ={color:'blue'};
```

With the above change in place, when I refresh my page, then it will produce the below output.

Jurassic World 12/06/2015

As you can see that h2 tag emitted in blue color, so custom style applied to it. Now, associated to this there are other directives as well, they are **ngClass, ngClassEven and ngClassOdd**. Class even and class Odd are just like class, only difference is that under ngRepeat directive, they apply to even or odd elements. For instance, let me introduce one variable as shown below in the snippet.

```
$scope.myClass="red";
```

Getting Started with Angular JS

Then I go back to my css and add the equivalent rule for the same.

```
.red{
    color: red;
}
```

Moreover, then small markup change.

```
<h2 ng-class="myClass" ng-bind-template="{{show.name}}
{{show.date}}"></h2>
```

Hence, with the above change in place, it will produce me the below output.

Now, there are certain other directives, which are equally useful when it comes for form validation. These are

- ngDisabled
- ngChecked
- ngMultiple
- ngReadonly
- ngSelected

These directives will either add or remove their respective directives, when you set them to true or false value. So, let us look at example of this. I have added one line of code to display the button on the page as shown below.

```
<button class="btn btn-info">Disabled Demo</button> <br /><br />
```

Getting Started with Angular JS

However, at this stage, this button is clickable not actually disabled. Nevertheless, with angular directive as shown below I can go ahead and make it disabled.

```
<button class="btn btn-info" ng-disabled="btnDisabled">Disabled
Demo</button> <br /><br />
```

I also need to modify corresponding controller as shown below.

```
$scope.btnDisabled=true;
```

Now, with the above change in place, when I refresh the page, it will produce me the below result.

Getting Started with Angular JS

Therefore, here button got disabled. Hence, if I change the value from true to false, button will be enabled. Similarly, other directives are equally on the same lines. However, the next directive, which I would like to discuss here, is the **nonBindable** directive. This is very easy to illustrate. Below, is the section of the code that is simply adding two numbers and producing the result.

```
<div>{{1+1}}</div>
```

Getting Started with Angular JS

Jurassic World 12/06/2015

2
12/06/2015
07:30 pm

Address:
IMAX
Bangalore,

However, if you do not want the result to be produced on the page, you can simply instruct angular with nonbindable directive as shown below.

```
<div ng-non-bindable>{{1+1}}</div>
```

Jurassic World 12/06/2015

{{1+1}}
12/06/2015
07:30 pm

Address:
IMAX
Bangalore,

With this, we have looked at the majority of directives present in angular. However, we will see many other directives as we progress with our application design.

Now, let us discuss one more directive, which is recently released. This directive is used for embedding YouTube videos angular way. Best way to install this dependency with bower

Getting Started with Angular JS

command as shown below. One point to note here, this demonstration is not done in movie review project. This is part of independent solution.

bower install ng-youtube-embed

Once, the component is installed then, you need to include the file in index page as shown below.

<script src="bower_components/ng-youtube-embed/ng-youtube-embed.js"></script>

Then, you need to add the dependency as shown below.

```
angular
 .module('yeomanApp', [
  'ngYoutubeEmbed'
 ])
```

After that, you need to put the same in controller logic as shown below

```
angular.module('yeomanApp')
 .controller('MainCtrl', function ($scope) {
  $scope.link = 'https://youtu.be/aHGmj_fqPLE';
});
```

Once, controller piece is done, and then you need to put the same in template as shown below.

```
<div>
 <ng-youtube-embed
  url="link"
  width="800px"
  height="500px"
  autohide="true"
  theme="light">
 </ng-youtube-embed>
</div>
```

With the above change in place, it will display the video as shown below.

Getting Started with Angular JS

EXPRESSIONS:-

In this section, we are going to discuss expressions in angular. Expressions are like JavaScript code snippets, which you can put inside the html of the page. Let us look at examples of expressions. As if initially I explained addition example, similarly we can do string concatenation like shown below.

```
<div>{{'Hello'+' Angular!'}}</div>
```

Getting Started with Angular JS

Now, let us create, array, and access the same from there itself.

```
<div>{{['Hello','Angular','Javascript','World'][3]}}</div>
```

As you can see expressions in angular are powerful. Therefore, having good knowledge of angular expressions can make your life really simpler.

Getting Started with Angular JS

FILTERS:-

In this section, we are going to learn about filters. Filters are way of modifying output. Filters can do three main things. First is formatting like making strings lowercase or uppercase, printing date or time in a particular format. Second thing is like sorting, so once data is rendered, and then you can apply sorting on the same. Last but not the least filters can filter the dataset based on your input. Now, let us see filters in action. In order to use the filters, we need to use pipe (I) symbol as shown below.

```
<h2 > {{show.name | uppercase}}</h2>
```

This will produce the below result.

Similarly, we can apply lowercase filter as well. Angular also provide number filter and currency filter.

```
<div>
    Number with 3 decimal digits: {{27.1234567 | number:3}}
</div>
```

With the above filter in place, it will produce the below output.

Getting Started with Angular JS

Similarly, we can use currency filter. Let us introduce one price variable as shown below in controller.

```
/**
 * Created by Rahul_Sahay on 7/5/2015.
 */

'use strict';

moviesApp.controller('MovieController',function
MovieController($scope){
    $scope.btnDisabled=true;
    $scope.show ={
        name: 'Jurassic World',
        date: '12/06/2015',
        time: '07:30 pm',
        location:{
            address:'IMAX',
            city:'Bangalore',
            province:'KA'
        },
        imageUrl:'img/movie-background.jpg',
        movies:[
            {
                name:'Titanic',
                directorName:'James Cameron',
                duration:'2 hr',
                about:'This movie was about great Titanic Ship',
                price:250,
                voteCount:10
```

Getting Started with Angular JS

```
        },
        {
                name:'Tomorrow Never Dies',
                directorName:'Roger Spottiswoode',
                duration:'1 hr',
                about:'Crazy James Bond Movie',
                price:350,
                voteCount:11
        },
        {
                name:'Die Another Day',
                directorName:'Lee Tamahori',
                duration:'3 hr',
                about:'Crazy James Bond Movie',
                price:150,
                voteCount:12

        }

    ]
  };
  $scope.upVotemMovie=function(movie){
      movie.voteCount++;
  };
  $scope.downVotemMovie=function(movie){
      movie.voteCount--;
  };
});
```

Now, let us use the same in markup as well.

```
<div class="well span9">
    <h4 class="show-title">{{movie.name}}</h4>
    <h6 style="margin-top: -10ox;">Director:
{{movie.directorName}}</h6>
    <span>Duration: {{movie.duration}} </span><br />
    <span>Price: {{movie.price | currency}} </span>
    <p>About: {{movie.about}}</p>
</div>
```

With the above change in place, it will produce the price with default currency as shown below.

Getting Started with Angular JS

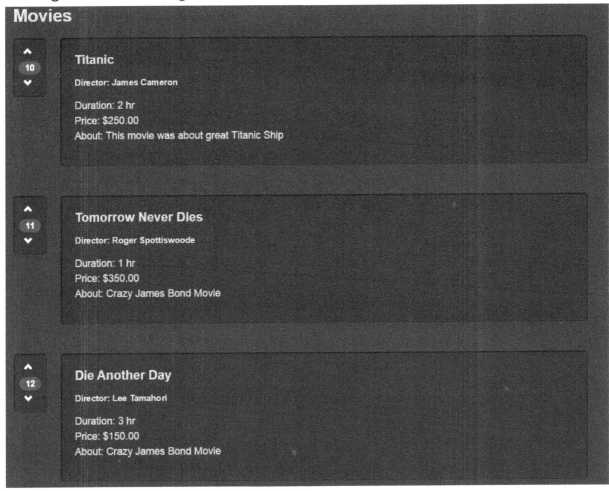

However, if I would like to print currency in specific locale, for instance in Indian Rupee, then for that I need to use angular localization feature, which we will see later in this book. Now, let us see date filter in action. For that, I will use JavaScript date format as shown below.

```
date: new Date("June 12, 2015 07:30"),
```

Then, corresponding markup change as shown below.

```
<div><strong>{{show.date | date:'medium'}}</strong></div>
```

Now, with the above change in place, it will produce me the below output.

Getting Started with Angular JS

Similarly, if I use short date format, then it will produce the following output.

```
<div><strong>{{show.date | date:'short'}}</strong></div>
```

Like this, there are variety of formatting options available. You can check all these on AngularJS site. Next filters which we are going to look at usually used with ngRepeat directive. Let us look at orderBy directive first. Below, is the markup change for the same.

```
Sort Movies:
<select ng-model="sortMovie" class="input-medium">
    <option selected value="name">By Movie Name</option>
```

Getting Started with Angular JS

```
        <option value="-voteCount">By Vote</option>
</select>
<ul class="thumbnails">
    <li ng-repeat="movie in show.movies | orderBy:sortMovie">
        <div class="row show">
            <div class="span0 well votingWidget">
                <div class="votingButton" ng-
click="upVotemMovie(movie)">
                    <i class="icon-chevron-up icon-white"></i>
                </div>
                <div class="badge badge-inverse">
                    <div>{{movie.voteCount}}</div>
                </div>
                <div class="votingButton" ng-
click="downVotemMovie(movie)">
                    <i class="icon-chevron-down icon-white"></i>
                </div>
            </div>
            <div class="well span9">
                <h4 class="show-title">{{movie.name}}</h4>
                <h6 style="margin-top: -10ox;">Director:
{{movie.directorName}}</h6>
                <span>Duration: {{movie.duration}} </span><br />
                <span>Price: {{movie.price | currency}} </span>
                <p>About: {{movie.about}}</p>
            </div>

        </div>
    </li>
</ul>
```

Here, I have done couple of things, first thing is I have used orderBy filter and there I have assigned the variable whose value I am setting from the dropdown. Then based on the input whether it is movie name or votes count it is sorting accordingly. I have also introduced the scope variable in the controller as well. Below is the change for the same.

```
$scope.sortMovie = 'name';
```

With the above change in place, it will produce the below output.

Getting Started with Angular JS

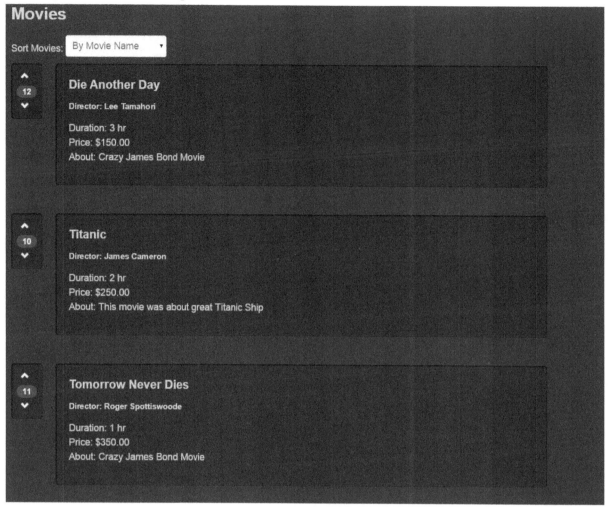

CUSTOM FILTERS:-

In this section, we will see how to write our own custom filters. I am going to write **rupeesFilter**. It will accept incoming integer value and it will produce custom string value. Here, I am going to use **filters.js**, which is already there in the project under js folder. Below is the snippet for custom filter.

```
'use strict';

moviesApp.filter('rupeesFilter',function(){
    return function(rupees){
        switch (rupees){
            case 150:
                return "150 rs";
            case 250:
                return "250 rs";
            case 350:
                return "350 rs";
        }
```

Chapter 2: Controllers & markups

Getting Started with Angular JS

```
    }

});
```

Now, in order to wire up the filter, we need to go the markup and change the following things. Here, I have included the physical file.

```
<script src="lib/jquery.min.js"></script>
<script src="lib/underscore-1.4.4.min.js"></script>
<script src="lib/bootstrap.min.js"></script>
<script src="lib/angular/angular.js"></script>
<script src="lib/angular/angular-sanitize.js"></script>
<script src="js/app.js"></script>
<script src="js/controllers/MovieController.js"></script>
<script src="js/filters.js"></script>
```

Then, I have applied the custom filter as shown below.

```
<span>Price: {{movie.price | rupeesFilter }} </span>
```

With the above change in place, it produced me the following output.

Getting Started with Angular JS

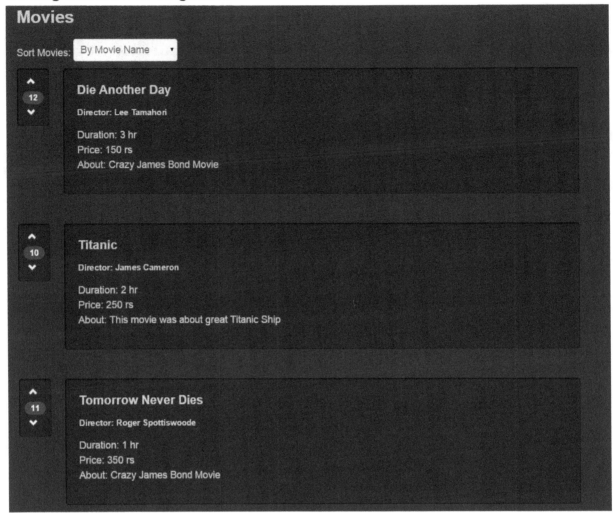

TWO WAY BINDING:-

In this segment, we are going to look at two way binding in detail. Let us walk through example by adding two way binding in our application. We are going to add new page in our application, which allow users to create new shows.

Getting Started with Angular JS

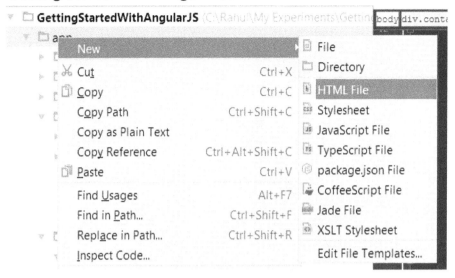

Below is the markup that I have created for posting new movie.

```
<!doctype html>
<lang="en" ng-app="moviesApp">
<head>
    <meta charset="utf-8">
    <title>Movie Review</title>
    <link rel="stylesheet" href="css/bootstrap.min.css"/>
    <link rel="stylesheet" href="css/app.css"/>
</head>
<body>
<div class="container">
    <div class="navbar">
        <div class="navbar-inner">
            <ul class="nav">
                <li><a href="MovieDetails.html">Movie Details</a></li>
                <li><a href="NewMovie.html">Post New Movie</a></li>
            </ul>
        </div>
    </div>

    <div ng-controller="PostMovieController">
        <div class="container">
            <h1>New Movie</h1>
            <hr />
            <form>
                <fieldset>
                    <label for="movieName">Movie Name:</label>
                    <input id="movieName" type="text" ng-
model="show.movieName" placeholder="Enter Movie Name"/>
                    <label for="movieDate">Movie Date:</label>
                    <input id="movieDate" type="text" ng-
model="show.movieDate" placeholder="Enter Movie Date"/>
                    <label for="movieTime">Movie Time:</label>
```

Chapter 2: Controllers & markups

Getting Started with Angular JS

```html
                        <input id="movieTime" type="text" ng-
model="show.movieTime" placeholder="Enter Movie Time"/>
                        <label for="movieLocation">Movie Location:</label>
                        <input id="movieLocation" type="text" ng-
model="show.movieLocation" placeholder="Enter Movie Location"/>
                        <br>
                        <input id="showCity" type="text" class="input-
medium" ng-model="show.showCity" placeholder="City"/>
                        <label for="movieImageURL">Image:</label>
                        <input id="movieImageURL" type="url" class="input-
xlarge" ng-model="show.movieImageURL" placeholder="Movie Image Url"/>
                </fieldset>
                <img ng-src="{{show.movieImageURL}}" />
                <br><br>
                <button type="submit" class="btn btn-success">Post
Movie</button>
                <button type="button" class="btn btn-
danger">Cancel</button>
            </form>
        </div>
    </div>
</div>

<script src="lib/jquery.min.js"></script>
<script src="lib/underscore-1.4.4.min.js"></script>
<script src="lib/bootstrap.min.js"></script>
<script src="lib/angular/angular.js"></script>
<script src="lib/angular/angular-sanitize.js"></script>
<script src="js/app.js"></script>
<script src="js/controllers/PostMovieController.js"></script>
<script src="js/filters.js"></script>
</body>
</html>
```

As you can see in the snippet, I have mentioned **PostMovieController** as my controller. Next, I am going to create the same. Below is the snippet for the same.

```js
/**
 * Created by Rahul_Sahay on 7/10/2015.
 */

'use strict';

moviesApp.controller('PostMovieController',function($scope){

});
```

Currently, nothing is there. However, that is ok. With the above change in place, it will produce the below output.

Chapter 2: Controllers & markups

Getting Started with Angular JS

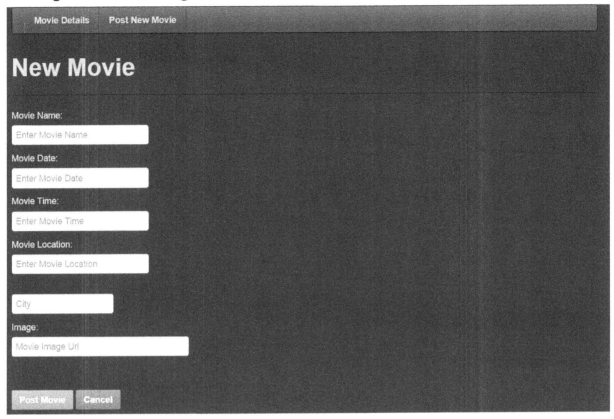

If you look at the markup snippet, I have bind the image URL in another img tag as well, just to show the output what is getting attached to the model inside the scope. As soon as I put this URL in the URL bar http://cnt.in.bookmyshow.com/Events/Mobile/ET00024245.jpg. This will produce me the below output.

Getting Started with Angular JS

In addition, as I change the same to some other URL say
http://cnt.in.bookmyshow.com/Events/Mobile/ET00024242.jpg, it automatically updates the
img tag as well. Therefore, this is how two way binding works.

Getting Started with Angular JS

VALIDATION:-

In this section, we are going to cover the basics of validation. Hence, let us first cover the required directive.

```
<fieldset>
    <label for="movieName">Movie Name:</label>
    <input id="movieName" type="text" required ng-
model="show.movieName" placeholder="Enter Movie Name"/>
    <label for="movieDate">Movie Date:</label>
    <input id="movieDate" type="text" required ng-
model="show.movieDate" placeholder="Enter Movie Date"/>
    <label for="movieTime">Movie Time:</label>
    <input id="movieTime" type="text" required ng-
model="show.movieTime" placeholder="Enter Movie Time"/>
    <label for="movieLocation">Movie Location:</label>
    <input id="movieLocation" type="text" required ng-
model="show.movieLocation" placeholder="Enter Movie Location"/>
    <br>
    <input id="showCity" type="text" required class="input-medium" ng-
model="show.showCity" placeholder="City"/>
    <label for="movieImageURL">Image:</label>
    <input id="movieImageURL" type="url" class="input-xlarge" ng-
model="show.movieImageURL" placeholder="Movie Image Url"/>
</fieldset>
```

With the above change in place, if I simply click on Post Movie button, it will pop up below shown error.

Chapter 2: Controllers & markups

Getting Started with Angular JS

Hence, what angular is doing here, it is parsing the HTML and as soon as it encounters required attribute there, it marks the form as invalid and hence flags the appropriate message. Now, let us look pattern validation. Pattern validation is nothing but, **regex** validation. However, in order to explain the pattern validation, let me do few more things. First thing, I am going to write button click event while posting movie as shown below in the snippet.

```javascript
/**
 * Created by Rahul_Sahay on 7/10/2015.
 */

'use strict';

moviesApp.controller('PostMovieController',function($scope){
    $scope.save= function(show,newMovieForm){
        if(newMovieForm.$valid){
            window.alert("Form is valid")
        }
        else{
            window.alert("Correct your input");
        }
    };
    $scope.cancel= function(){
        window.location="MovieDetails.html";
    }
});
```

As you can see in the above snippet, save function takes two parameter. First is the show variable, which is having all the model values and another one is form name. Therefore, when form is valid it will popup form is valid message otherwise, it will ask to correct the input. In addition, below is the markup change for the same.

```html
<form name="newMovieForm">
    <fieldset>
        <label for="movieName">Movie Name:</label>
        <input id="movieName" type="text" required ng-model="show.movieName" placeholder="Enter Movie Name"/>
        <label for="movieDate">Movie Date:</label>
        <input id="movieDate" type="text" required ng-pattern="/\d\d/\d\d/\d\d\d\d/" ng-model="show.movieDate" placeholder="Enter Movie Date"/>
        <label for="movieTime">Movie Time:</label>
        <input id="movieTime" type="text" required ng-model="show.movieTime" placeholder="Enter Movie Time"/>
        <label for="movieLocation">Movie Location:</label>
        <input id="movieLocation" type="text" required ng-model="show.movieLocation" placeholder="Enter Movie Location"/>
        <br><br>
        <input id="showCity" type="text" required class="input-medium" ng-model="show.showCity" placeholder="City"/>
```

Getting Started with Angular JS

```
        <label for="movieImageURL">Image:</label>
        <input id="movieImageURL" type="url" class="input-xlarge" ng-
model="show.movieImageURL" placeholder="Movie Image Url"/>
    </fieldset>
    <img ng-src="{{show.movieImageURL}}" />
    <br><br>
    <button type="submit" ng-click="save(show,newMovieForm)"
class="btn btn-success">Post Movie</button>
    <button type="button" ng-click="cancel()" class="btn btn-
danger">Cancel</button>
</form>
```

With the above change in place, it will show the below error message, when form is dirty.

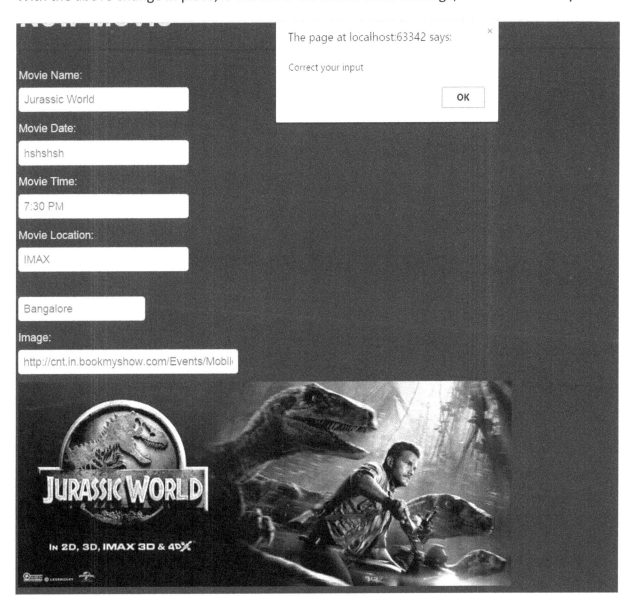

However, if I correct the date input, then it will give the following message.

Getting Started with Angular JS

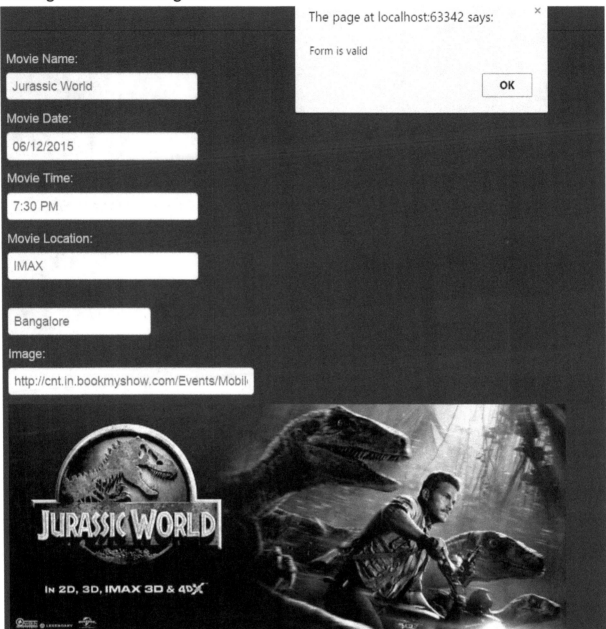

This is ok. However, let us improve the user experience by just disabling the submit button if form is invalid. With the below change in place,

```
<button type="submit" ng-disabled="newMovieForm.$invalid" ng-
click="save(show,newMovieForm)" class="btn btn-success">Post
Movie</button>
```

It will produce the below output.

Getting Started with Angular JS

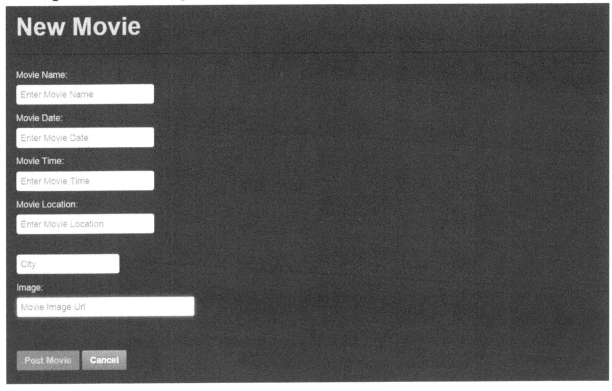

As you can see that, since nothing is there in the form, hence submit button is disabled. In addition to this, we can take advantage of many other things which angular form provides. Hence, let us log these details.

```
/**
 * Created by Rahul_Sahay on 7/10/2015.
 */

'use strict';

moviesApp.controller('PostMovieController',function($scope){
    $scope.save= function(show,newMovieForm){
        console.log(newMovieForm);
        if(newMovieForm.$valid){
            window.alert("Form is valid")
        }
        else{
            window.alert("Correct your input");
        }
    };
    $scope.cancel= function(){
        window.location="MovieDetails.html";
    }
});
```

Getting Started with Angular JS

With the above change in place, when I refresh the browser and see the console window, then it will produce the following event properties.

```
Q    🔲    Elements  Network  Sources  Timeline  Profiles  Resources  Audits | Console |
🚫  🔽   <top frame>  ▼  ☐ Preserve log

▼ Constructor {$error: Object, $name: "newMovieForm", $dirty: true, $pristine: false, $valid: true...}
  ▶ $addControl: function (control) {
    $dirty: true
  ▶ $error: Object
    $invalid: false
    $name: "newMovieForm"
    $pristine: false
  ▶ $removeControl: function (control) {
  ▶ $setDirty: function () {
  ▶ $setPristine: function () {
  ▶ $setValidity: function (validationToken, isValid, control) {
    $valid: true
  ▶ __proto__: FormController
>
```

There are few properties which you should note here, **$dirty** means form is changed. **$invalid** indicates form is invalid, **$pristine** is exact opposite of **$dirty** and **$valid** exact opposite of **$invalid**. Now, we can use these form states to do give some visual indication to user whether form is valid or not. Therefore, let us introduce custom style on our page as shown below.

```
<style>input.ng-invalid.ng-dirty {background-color: red}</style>
```

With the above change in place, when I refresh the page, then it will produce the below output.

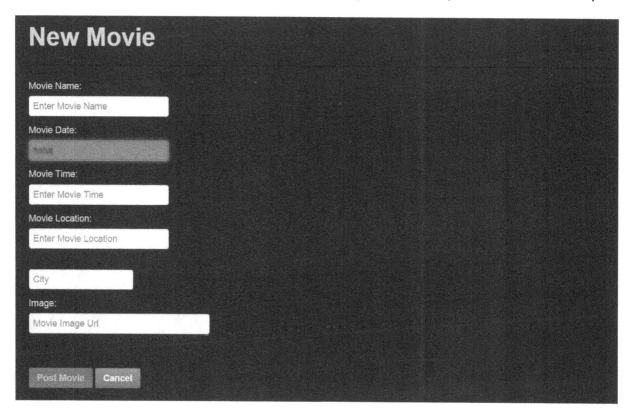

Getting Started with Angular JS

Here, background color of movie date turns red, once I entered invalid value. Hence, this visual indication is one of the key factors in improving the user experience.

SUMMARY:-

In this section, we get started with angular basics and discussed few basic points. First we created controllers then used the same in markup. We have also used scope to do the binding back and forth. We have also seen tons of directive in action. Then, we have covered some built-in filters and custom filters. Lastly, we have covered usage of two way binding with some basic validations.

WHAT DO you find in this CHAPTER?

- Introduction
- Creating Custom Service
- Creating User Page
- Built-in Services
- Using $http & $q Service
- Angular JS Graph
- Using $resource Service
- Using Cache Factory service
- Using Compile Service
- Using Parse Service
- Using Locale Service
- Exception Handler Service
- Filter Service
- Summary

INTRODUCTION:-

Hello and welcome again to this part of AngularJS. In this section, we will get started with angular services. We will first cover built in angular services; and how to use them then we see how to write custom services. So, what is a service? From angular definition, a service is just an object that performs some sort of business operations. However, services are often stateless. Angular ships with whole suite of built in services, which provide AJAX calls, navigations etc. However, Angular also makes it easy to create your own service. Now, next question comes, why you want to use services. Services help to encapsulate reusable business components. It also helps to break your application into small modules, which is easier to maintain. Services are designed keeping **Single Responsibility Principle** in mind. **SRP** is one of the **SOLID** principles. Another good reason to use services is you can inject the same in controllers whenever you need them. Finally, using services makes your code easy to test as you can isolate the code that you want to test. AngularJS is built in such a way that it should embrace full-fledged testing and

Getting Started with Angular JS

services makes it possible. AngularJS service is just a simple object. Only thing is, here you create the object and it is intended to use as a service. Only by creating the angular service it cannot be used until it is registered with angular.

CREATING CUSTOM SERVICE:-

In this section, we are going to feed the home page data via angular service rather keeping everything in controller code. Therefore, first we will create one service, inject the same in controller, and use it in controller. Below I have created new JavaScript file with the name **MovieDataService**.

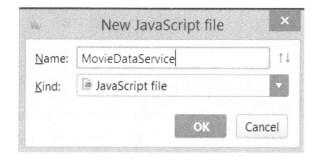

```javascript
/**
 * Created by Rahul_Sahay on 7/12/2015.
 */

'use strict';

moviesApp.factory('movieDataService', function () {
    return {
        show: {
            name: 'Jurassic World',
            date: new Date("June 12, 2015 07:30"),
            time: '07:30 pm',
            location: {
                address: 'IMAX',
                city: 'Bangalore',
                province: 'KA'
            },
            imageUrl: 'img/movie-background.jpg',
            movies: [
                {
                    name: 'Titanic',
                    directorName: 'James Cameron',
                    duration: '2 hr',
                    about: 'This movie was about great Titanic Ship',
                    price: 250,
                    voteCount: 10
                },
                {
```

Getting Started with Angular JS

```
                         name: 'Tomorrow Never Dies',
                         directorName: 'Roger Spottiswoode',
                         duration: '1 hr',
                         about: 'Crazy James Bond Movie',
                         price: 350,
                         voteCount: 11
                     },
                     {

                         name: 'Die Another Day',
                         directorName: 'Lee Tamahori',
                         duration: '3 hr',
                         about: 'Crazy James Bond Movie',
                         price: 150,
                         voteCount: 12
                     }

                 ]
             }
         }
});
```

As you can see the above snippet, I have created my custom service with the method factory.
Again, factory is used to create custom angular services and register the same with angular.
Here, I just moved the code from controller to service. Then, I have also modified my controller
code as shown below.

```
/**
 * Created by Rahul_Sahay on 7/5/2015.
 */

'use strict';

moviesApp.controller('MovieController',function
MovieController($scope,movieDataService){

    $scope.sortMovie = 'name';
    $scope.show = movieDataService.show;
    $scope.upVotemMovie=function(movie){
        movie.voteCount++;
    };
    $scope.downVotemMovie=function(movie){
        movie.voteCount--;
    };
});
```

Here in the controller code, I have injected the service and set the same against **$scope.show**.
One last change, I have done here is the inclusion of service file at the bottom of the html file.

```
<script src="lib/jquery.min.js"></script>
<script src="lib/underscore-1.4.4.min.js"></script>
```

Getting Started with Angular JS

```
<script src="lib/bootstrap.min.js"></script>
<script src="lib/angular/angular.js"></script>
<script src="lib/angular/angular-sanitize.js"></script>
<script src="js/app.js"></script>
<script src="js/controllers/MovieController.js"></script>
<script src="js/filters.js"></script>
<script src="js/services/MovieDataService.js"></script>
```

With the above change in place, it will produce me the same output. No visual difference. However, this time data is coming via service.

Getting Started with Angular JS

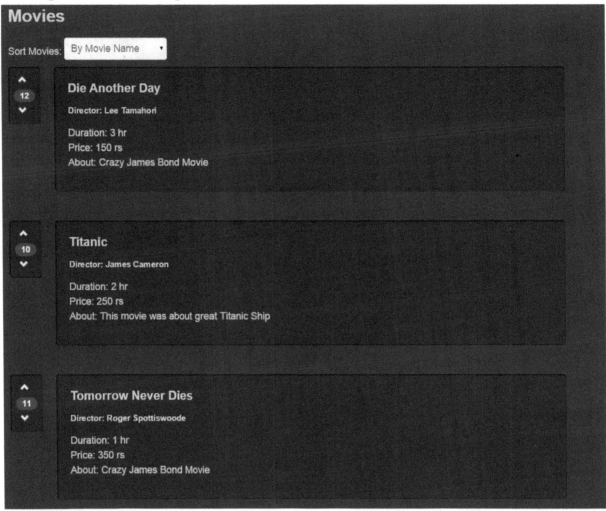

CREATING USER PAGE:-

In this section, I am going to create another service that will help user to edit their profile. Below I have created new page for editing user details as shown below.

```html
<html lang="en" ng-app="moviesApp">
<head>
    <meta charset="utf-8">
    <title>Movie Review</title>
    <link rel="stylesheet" href="css/bootstrap.min.css"/>
    <link rel="stylesheet" href="css/app.css"/>
</head>
<body>
<div class="container">
    <div class="navbar">
        <div class="navbar-inner">
            <ul class="nav">
                <li><a href="MovieDetails.html">Movie Details</a></li>
                <li><a href="NewMovie.html">Post New Movie</a></li>
```

Getting Started with Angular JS

```html
                    <li><a href="EditUser.html">Edit profile</a></li>
                </ul>
            </div>
        </div>
    </div>
</div>
<div class="container-fluid" ng-controller="EditUserController">
    <form name="profileForm">
        <div class="row-fluid">
            <div class="span3">
                <img src="img/user.png">
            </div>
            <div class="span3">
                <fieldset>
                    <label for="userName">User Name:</label>
                    <input focus id="userName" required ng-
pattern="/^[-A-Za-z0-9]{2,20}$/" type="text"
                            placeholder="Username" ng-
model="user.userName"/>
                    <label for="password">Password:</label>
                    <input id="password" required type="password"
placeholder="Password" ng-model="user.password"/>
                </fieldset>
                <div style="margin-top:15px">
                    <fieldset>
                        <label for="name">Name:</label>
                        <input id="name" type="text"
placeholder="Name" ng-model="user.name"/>
                        <label for="emailAddress">Email
Address:</label>
                        <input id="emailAddress" type="email"
placeholder="Email Address" ng-model="user.emailAddress"/>
                    </fieldset>
                </div>
            </div>
        </div>
        <div class="row-fluid">
            <div class="span6 offset3">
                <label for="bio">Bio:</label>
                <textarea id="bio" rows="6" style="width:97%;
color:#52575c" placeholder="Bio"
                        ng-model="user.bio"></textarea>
            </div>
        </div>
        <div class="row-fluid">
            <div class="span6 offset3">
                <div class="pull-left"><span class="btn btn-
danger">Cancel</span></div>
                <div class="pull-right">
                    <button type="submit" class="btn btn-
success">Save</button>
                </div>
```

Getting Started with Angular JS

```html
        </div>
      </div>
    </form>
</div>


<script src="lib/jquery.min.js"></script>
<script src="lib/underscore-1.4.4.min.js"></script>
<script src="lib/bootstrap.min.js"></script>
<script src="lib/angular/angular.js"></script>
<script src="lib/angular/angular-sanitize.js"></script>
<script src="js/app.js"></script>
<script src="js/controllers/MovieController.js"></script>
<script src="js/filters.js"></script>
<script src ="js/controllers/EditUserController.js"></script>


</body>
</html>
```

As you can see that this markup is dependent on **EditUserController**, which I have not created yet. Let me go ahead and create the same as well.

```javascript
/**
 * Created by Rahul_Sahay on 7/13/2015.
 */

moviesApp.controller('EditUserController', function($scope){
    $scope.user={};
});
```

With the above change in place, it will produce the following output.

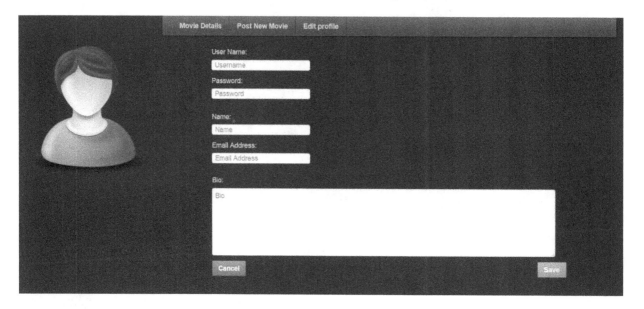

Getting Started with Angular JS

Currently, we have a blank image here. However, here I will be constructing gravatar URL based on email address. Below is the controller snippet for the same where in I am constructing the same based on valid mail id. If email id is not valid or not registered with gravatar site, I am returning this blank image.

```
/**
 * Created by Rahul_Sahay on 7/13/2015.
 */

moviesApp.controller('EditUserController', function ($scope) {
    $scope.user = {};

    $scope.getGravatarUrl= function (email) {
        var defaultGravatarUrl =
"http://www.gravatar.com/avatar/000?s=200";

        var regex =
/^((([^<>()[\]\\.,;:\s@\"]+(\.[^<>()[\]\\.,;:\s@\"]+)*)|(\".+\"))@((\[[
0-9]{1,3}\.[0-9]{1,3}\.[0-9]{1,3}\.[0-9]{1,3}\])|(([a-zA-Z\-0-
9]+\.)+[a-zA-Z]{2,})))$/;
        if (!regex.test(email))
            return "img/user.png";

        var MD5 = function (s) {
        function L(k, d) {
            return (k << d) | (k >>> (32 - d))
        }

        function K(G, k) {
            var I, d, F, H, x;
            F = (G & 2147483648);
            H = (k & 2147483648);
            I = (G & 1073741824);
            d = (k & 1073741824);
            x = (G & 1073741823) + (k & 1073741823);
            if (I & d) {
                return (x ^ 2147483648 ^ F ^ H)
            }
            if (I | d) {
                if (x & 1073741824) {
                    return (x ^ 3221225472 ^ F ^ H)
                } else {
                    return (x ^ 1073741824 ^ F ^ H)
                }
            } else {
                return (x ^ F ^ H)
            }
        }
```

Getting Started with Angular JS

```javascript
function r(d, F, k) {
    return (d & F) | ((~d) & k)
}

function q(d, F, k) {
    return (d & k) | (F & (~k))
}

function p(d, F, k) {
    return (d ^ F ^ k)
}

function n(d, F, k) {
    return (F ^ (d | (~k)))
}

function u(G, F, aa, Z, k, H, I) {
    G = K(G, K(K(r(F, aa, Z), k), I));
    return K(L(G, H), F)
}

function f(G, F, aa, Z, k, H, I) {
    G = K(G, K(K(q(F, aa, Z), k), I));
    return K(L(G, H), F)
}

function D(G, F, aa, Z, k, H, I) {
    G = K(G, K(K(p(F, aa, Z), k), I));
    return K(L(G, H), F)
}

function t(G, F, aa, Z, k, H, I) {
    G = K(G, K(K(n(F, aa, Z), k), I));
    return K(L(G, H), F)
}

function e(G) {
    var Z;
    var F = G.length;
    var x = F + 8;
    var k = (x - (x % 64)) / 64;
    var I = (k + 1) * 16;
    var aa = Array(I - 1);
    var d = 0;
    var H = 0;
    while (H < F) {
        Z = (H - (H % 4)) / 4;
        d = (H % 4) * 8;
        aa[Z] = (aa[Z] | (G.charCodeAt(H) << d));
        H++
    }
```

Getting Started with Angular JS

```javascript
        Z = (H - (H % 4)) / 4;
        d = (H % 4) * 8;
        aa[Z] = aa[Z] | (128 << d);
        aa[I - 2] = F << 3;
        aa[I - 1] = F >>> 29;
        return aa
    }

    function B(x) {
        var k = "", F = "", G, d;
        for (d = 0; d <= 3; d++) {
            G = (x >>> (d * 8)) & 255;
            F = "0" + G.toString(16);
            k = k + F.substr(F.length - 2, 2)
        }
        return k
    }

    function J(k) {
        k = k.replace(/rn/g, "n");
        var d = "";
        for (var F = 0; F < k.length; F++) {
            var x = k.charCodeAt(F);
            if (x < 128) {
                d += String.fromCharCode(x)
            } else {
                if ((x > 127) && (x < 2048)) {
                    d += String.fromCharCode((x >> 6) | 192);
                    d += String.fromCharCode((x & 63) | 128)
                } else {
                    d += String.fromCharCode((x >> 12) | 224);
                    d += String.fromCharCode(((x >> 6) & 63) |
128);

                    d += String.fromCharCode((x & 63) | 128)
                }
            }
        }
        return d
    }

    var C = Array();
    var P, h, E, v, g, Y, X, W, V;
    var S = 7, Q = 12, N = 17, M = 22;
    var A = 5, z = 9, y = 14, w = 20;
    var o = 4, m = 11, l = 16, j = 23;
    var U = 6, T = 10, R = 15, O = 21;
    s = J(s);
    C = e(s);
    Y = 1732584193;
    X = 4023233417;
    W = 2562383102;
```

Getting Started with Angular JS

```
V = 271733878;
for (P = 0; P < C.length; P += 16) {
h = Y;
E = X;
v = W;
g = V;
Y = u(Y, X, W, V, C[P + 0], S, 3614090360);
V = u(V, Y, X, W, C[P + 1], Q, 3905402710);
W = u(W, V, Y, X, C[P + 2], N, 606105819);
X = u(X, W, V, Y, C[P + 3], M, 3250441966);
Y = u(Y, X, W, V, C[P + 4], S, 4118548399);
V = u(V, Y, X, W, C[P + 5], Q, 1200080426);
W = u(W, V, Y, X, C[P + 6], N, 2821735955);
X = u(X, W, V, Y, C[P + 7], M, 4249261313);
Y = u(Y, X, W, V, C[P + 8], S, 1770035416);
V = u(V, Y, X, W, C[P + 9], Q, 2336552879);
W = u(W, V, Y, X, C[P + 10], N, 4294925233);
X = u(X, W, V, Y, C[P + 11], M, 2304563134);
Y = u(Y, X, W, V, C[P + 12], S, 1804603682);
V = u(V, Y, X, W, C[P + 13], Q, 4254626195);
W = u(W, V, Y, X, C[P + 14], N, 2792965006);
X = u(X, W, V, Y, C[P + 15], M, 1236535329);
Y = f(Y, X, W, V, C[P + 1], A, 4129170786);
V = f(V, Y, X, W, C[P + 6], z, 3225465664);
W = f(W, V, Y, X, C[P + 11], y, 643717713);
X = f(X, W, V, Y, C[P + 0], w, 3921069994);
Y = f(Y, X, W, V, C[P + 5], A, 3593408605);
V = f(V, Y, X, W, C[P + 10], z, 38016083);
W = f(W, V, Y, X, C[P + 15], y, 3634488961);
X = f(X, W, V, Y, C[P + 4], w, 3889429448);
Y = f(Y, X, W, V, C[P + 9], A, 568446438);
V = f(V, Y, X, W, C[P + 14], z, 3275163606);
W = f(W, V, Y, X, C[P + 3], y, 4107603335);
X = f(X, W, V, Y, C[P + 8], w, 1163531501);
Y = f(Y, X, W, V, C[P + 13], A, 2850285829);
V = f(V, Y, X, W, C[P + 2], z, 4243563512);
W = f(W, V, Y, X, C[P + 7], y, 1735328473);
X = f(X, W, V, Y, C[P + 12], w, 2368359562);
Y = D(Y, X, W, V, C[P + 5], o, 4294588738);
V = D(V, Y, X, W, C[P + 8], m, 2272392833);
W = D(W, V, Y, X, C[P + 11], l, 1839030562);
X = D(X, W, V, Y, C[P + 14], j, 4259657740);
Y = D(Y, X, W, V, C[P + 1], o, 2763975236);
V = D(V, Y, X, W, C[P + 4], m, 1272893353);
W = D(W, V, Y, X, C[P + 7], l, 4139469664);
X = D(X, W, V, Y, C[P + 10], j, 3200236656);
Y = D(Y, X, W, V, C[P + 13], o, 681279174);
V = D(V, Y, X, W, C[P + 0], m, 3936430074);
W = D(W, V, Y, X, C[P + 3], l, 3572445317);
X = D(X, W, V, Y, C[P + 6], j, 76029189);
Y = D(Y, X, W, V, C[P + 9], o, 3654602809);
```

Getting Started with Angular JS

```
            V = D(V, Y, X, W, C[P + 12], m, 3873151461);
            W = D(W, V, Y, X, C[P + 15], l, 530742520);
            X = D(X, W, V, Y, C[P + 2], j, 3299628645);
            Y = t(Y, X, W, V, C[P + 0], U, 4096336452);
            V = t(V, Y, X, W, C[P + 7], T, 1126891415);
            W = t(W, V, Y, X, C[P + 14], R, 2878612391);
            X = t(X, W, V, Y, C[P + 5], O, 4237533241);
            Y = t(Y, X, W, V, C[P + 12], U, 1700485571);
            V = t(V, Y, X, W, C[P + 3], T, 2399980690);
            W = t(W, V, Y, X, C[P + 10], R, 4293915773);
            X = t(X, W, V, Y, C[P + 1], O, 2240044497);
            Y = t(Y, X, W, V, C[P + 8], U, 1873313359);
            V = t(V, Y, X, W, C[P + 15], T, 4264355552);
            W = t(W, V, Y, X, C[P + 6], R, 2734768916);
            X = t(X, W, V, Y, C[P + 13], O, 1309151649);
            Y = t(Y, X, W, V, C[P + 4], U, 4149444226);
            V = t(V, Y, X, W, C[P + 11], T, 3174756917);
            W = t(W, V, Y, X, C[P + 2], R, 718787259);
            X = t(X, W, V, Y, C[P + 9], O, 3951481745);
            Y = K(Y, h);
            X = K(X, E);
            W = K(W, v);
            V = K(V, g)
        }
        var i = B(Y) + B(X) + B(W) + B(V);
        return i.toLowerCase()
    };

        return 'http://www.gravatar.com/avatar/' + MD5(email) +
".jpg?s=200&r=g";
    }
});
```

Here, no need to focus on gravatar URL construction code. Now, below is the markup change for the same.

```
<img ng-src="{{getGravatarUrl(user.emailAddress)}}"
title="{{user.name}}">
```

With the above change in place, it will produce the below output if I put my email id in there otherwise blank image.

Getting Started with Angular JS

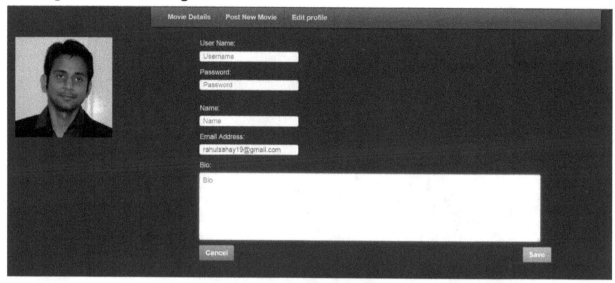

If the email id is not registered with gravatar, then it will produce the following output.

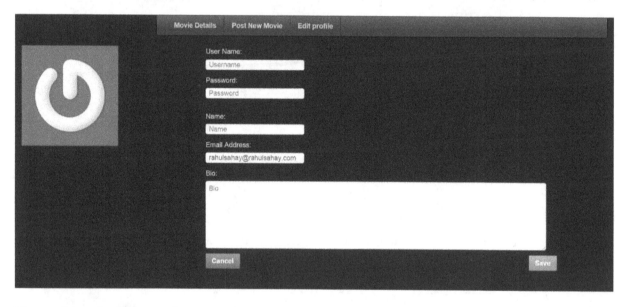

The problem is entire code currently in controller, which is making it bit messy. Therefore, let us move this logic out in one new service. Below is my new service snippet for the same.

```
/**
 * Created by Rahul_Sahay on 7/14/2015.
 */
'use strict';
moviesApp.factory('buildGravatarUrl',function(){
return{
    gravatarUrl: function (email) {
        var defaultGravatarUrl =
"http://www.gravatar.com/avatar/000?s=200";
```

Getting Started with Angular JS

```javascript
        var regex =
/^(([^<>()[\]\\.,;:\s@\"]+(\.[^<>()[\]\\.,;:\s@\"]+)*)|(\".+\"))@((\[[
0-9]{1,3}\.[0-9]{1,3}\.[0-9]{1,3}\.[0-9]{1,3}\])|(([a-zA-Z\-0-
9]+\.)+[a-zA-Z]{2,}))$/;
        if (!regex.test(email))
            return "img/user.png";

        var MD5 = function (s) {
            function L(k, d) {
                return (k << d) | (k >>> (32 - d))
            }

            function K(G, k) {
                var I, d, F, H, x;
                F = (G & 2147483648);
                H = (k & 2147483648);
                I = (G & 1073741824);
                d = (k & 1073741824);
                x = (G & 1073741823) + (k & 1073741823);
                if (I & d) {
                    return (x ^ 2147483648 ^ F ^ H)
                }
                if (I | d) {
                    if (x & 1073741824) {
                        return (x ^ 3221225472 ^ F ^ H)
                    } else {
                        return (x ^ 1073741824 ^ F ^ H)
                    }
                } else {
                    return (x ^ F ^ H)
                }
            }

            function r(d, F, k) {
                return (d & F) | ((~d) & k)
            }

            function q(d, F, k) {
                return (d & k) | (F & (~k))
            }

            function p(d, F, k) {
                return (d ^ F ^ k)
            }

            function n(d, F, k) {
                return (F ^ (d | (~k)))
            }

            function u(G, F, aa, Z, k, H, I) {
                G = K(G, K(K(r(F, aa, Z), k), I));
```

Getting Started with Angular JS

```javascript
        return K(L(G, H), F)
    }

    function f(G, F, aa, Z, k, H, I) {
        G = K(G, K(K(q(F, aa, Z), k), I));
        return K(L(G, H), F)
    }

    function D(G, F, aa, Z, k, H, I) {
        G = K(G, K(K(p(F, aa, Z), k), I));
        return K(L(G, H), F)
    }

    function t(G, F, aa, Z, k, H, I) {
        G = K(G, K(K(n(F, aa, Z), k), I));
        return K(L(G, H), F)
    }

    function e(G) {
        var Z;
        var F = G.length;
        var x = F + 8;
        var k = (x - (x % 64)) / 64;
        var I = (k + 1) * 16;
        var aa = Array(I - 1);
        var d = 0;
        var H = 0;
        while (H < F) {
            Z = (H - (H % 4)) / 4;
            d = (H % 4) * 8;
            aa[Z] = (aa[Z] | (G.charCodeAt(H) << d));
            H++
        }
        Z = (H - (H % 4)) / 4;
        d = (H % 4) * 8;
        aa[Z] = aa[Z] | (128 << d);
        aa[I - 2] = F << 3;
        aa[I - 1] = F >>> 29;
        return aa
    }

    function B(x) {
        var k = "", F = "", G, d;
        for (d = 0; d <= 3; d++) {
            G = (x >>> (d * 8)) & 255;
            F = "0" + G.toString(16);
            k = k + F.substr(F.length - 2, 2)
        }
        return k
    }
```

Chapter 3: Services

Getting Started with Angular JS

```javascript
function J(k) {
    k = k.replace(/rn/g, "n");
    var d = "";
    for (var F = 0; F < k.length; F++) {
        var x = k.charCodeAt(F);
        if (x < 128) {
            d += String.fromCharCode(x)
        } else {
            if ((x > 127) && (x < 2048)) {
                d += String.fromCharCode((x >> 6) | 192);
                d += String.fromCharCode((x & 63) | 128)
            } else {
                d += String.fromCharCode((x >> 12) | 224);
                d += String.fromCharCode(((x >> 6) & 63) |
128);
                d += String.fromCharCode((x & 63) | 128)
            }
        }
    }
    return d
}

var C = Array();
var P, h, E, v, g, Y, X, W, V;
var S = 7, Q = 12, N = 17, M = 22;
var A = 5, z = 9, y = 14, w = 20;
var o = 4, m = 11, l = 16, j = 23;
var U = 6, T = 10, R = 15, O = 21;
s = J(s);
C = e(s);
Y = 1732584193;
X = 4023233417;
W = 2562383102;
V = 271733878;
for (P = 0; P < C.length; P += 16) {
    h = Y;
    E = X;
    v = W;
    g = V;
    Y = u(Y, X, W, V, C[P + 0], S, 3614090360);
    V = u(V, Y, X, W, C[P + 1], Q, 3905402710);
    W = u(W, V, Y, X, C[P + 2], N, 606105819);
    X = u(X, W, V, Y, C[P + 3], M, 3250441966);
    Y = u(Y, X, W, V, C[P + 4], S, 4118548399);
    V = u(V, Y, X, W, C[P + 5], Q, 1200080426);
    W = u(W, V, Y, X, C[P + 6], N, 2821735955);
    X = u(X, W, V, Y, C[P + 7], M, 4249261313);
    Y = u(Y, X, W, V, C[P + 8], S, 1770035416);
    V = u(V, Y, X, W, C[P + 9], Q, 2336552879);
    W = u(W, V, Y, X, C[P + 10], N, 4294925233);
    X = u(X, W, V, Y, C[P + 11], M, 2304563134);
```

Getting Started with Angular JS

```
Y = u(Y, X, W, V, C[P + 12], S, 1804603682);
V = u(V, Y, X, W, C[P + 13], Q, 4254626195);
W = u(W, V, Y, X, C[P + 14], N, 2792965006);
X = u(X, W, V, Y, C[P + 15], M, 1236535329);
Y = f(Y, X, W, V, C[P + 1], A, 4129170786);
V = f(V, Y, X, W, C[P + 6], z, 3225465664);
W = f(W, V, Y, X, C[P + 11], y, 643717713);
X = f(X, W, V, Y, C[P + 0], w, 3921069994);
Y = f(Y, X, W, V, C[P + 5], A, 3593408605);
V = f(V, Y, X, W, C[P + 10], z, 38016083);
W = f(W, V, Y, X, C[P + 15], y, 3634488961);
X = f(X, W, V, Y, C[P + 4], w, 3889429448);
Y = f(Y, X, W, V, C[P + 9], A, 568446438);
V = f(V, Y, X, W, C[P + 14], z, 3275163606);
W = f(W, V, Y, X, C[P + 3], y, 4107603335);
X = f(X, W, V, Y, C[P + 8], w, 1163531501);
Y = f(Y, X, W, V, C[P + 13], A, 2850285829);
V = f(V, Y, X, W, C[P + 2], z, 4243563512);
W = f(W, V, Y, X, C[P + 7], y, 1735328473);
X = f(X, W, V, Y, C[P + 12], w, 2368359562);
Y = D(Y, X, W, V, C[P + 5], o, 4294588738);
V = D(V, Y, X, W, C[P + 8], m, 2272392833);
W = D(W, V, Y, X, C[P + 11], l, 1839030562);
X = D(X, W, V, Y, C[P + 14], j, 4259657740);
Y = D(Y, X, W, V, C[P + 1], o, 2763975236);
V = D(V, Y, X, W, C[P + 4], m, 1272893353);
W = D(W, V, Y, X, C[P + 7], l, 4139469664);
X = D(X, W, V, Y, C[P + 10], j, 3200236656);
Y = D(Y, X, W, V, C[P + 13], o, 681279174);
V = D(V, Y, X, W, C[P + 0], m, 3936430074);
W = D(W, V, Y, X, C[P + 3], l, 3572445317);
X = D(X, W, V, Y, C[P + 6], j, 76029189);
Y = D(Y, X, W, V, C[P + 9], o, 3654602809);
V = D(V, Y, X, W, C[P + 12], m, 3873151461);
W = D(W, V, Y, X, C[P + 15], l, 530742520);
X = D(X, W, V, Y, C[P + 2], j, 3299628645);
Y = t(Y, X, W, V, C[P + 0], U, 4096336452);
V = t(V, Y, X, W, C[P + 7], T, 1126891415);
W = t(W, V, Y, X, C[P + 14], R, 2878612391);
X = t(X, W, V, Y, C[P + 5], O, 4237533241);
Y = t(Y, X, W, V, C[P + 12], U, 1700485571);
V = t(V, Y, X, W, C[P + 3], T, 2399980690);
W = t(W, V, Y, X, C[P + 10], R, 4293915773);
X = t(X, W, V, Y, C[P + 1], O, 2240044497);
Y = t(Y, X, W, V, C[P + 8], U, 1873313359);
V = t(V, Y, X, W, C[P + 15], T, 4264355552);
W = t(W, V, Y, X, C[P + 6], R, 2734768916);
X = t(X, W, V, Y, C[P + 13], O, 1309151649);
Y = t(Y, X, W, V, C[P + 4], U, 4149444226);
V = t(V, Y, X, W, C[P + 11], T, 3174756917);
W = t(W, V, Y, X, C[P + 2], R, 718787259);
```

Chapter 3: Services

Getting Started with Angular JS

```
            X = t(X, W, V, Y, C[P + 9], O, 3951481745);
            Y = K(Y, h);
            X = K(X, E);
            W = K(W, v);
            V = K(V, g)
        }

        var i = B(Y) + B(X) + B(W) + B(V);
        return i.toLowerCase()
    };

        return 'http://www.gravatar.com/avatar/' + MD5(email) +
".jpg?s=200&r=g";
    }
}
});
```

Then my controller code will look cleaner as shown below

```
/**
 * Created by Rahul_Sahay on 7/13/2015.
 */

'use strict';
moviesApp.controller('EditUserController', function
($scope,buildGravatarUrl) {
    $scope.user = {};

    $scope.getGravatarUrl=function(email){
        return  buildGravatarUrl.gravatarUrl(email);
    }
});
```

Since, we have created new service; hence, we need to include the physical file as well in the view. Hence, below is the markup change.

```
<script src="lib/jquery.min.js"></script>
<script src="lib/underscore-1.4.4.min.js"></script>
<script src="lib/bootstrap.min.js"></script>
<script src="lib/angular/angular.js"></script>
<script src="lib/angular/angular-sanitize.js"></script>
<script src="js/app.js"></script>
<script src="js/controllers/MovieController.js"></script>
<script src="js/filters.js"></script>
<script src ="js/controllers/EditUserController.js"></script>
<script src ="js/services/BuildGravatarUrl.js"></script>
```

BUILT-IN SERVICES:-

In this section, we will discuss angular built in services. There are no of ng services, which I will be touching in detail. That are-

Getting Started with Angular JS

- $http
- $resource
- $q
- $cacheFactory
- $compile
- $parse
- $locale
- $exceptionHandler
- $filter
- $cookieStore

Hence, without wasting time, let us get started with different usages of services.

USING $HTTP & $Q SERVICE:-

In this section, we will look at how http service works. In the previous section, we have created movie controller that is calling **movieDataService**. Let us now retrieve the same values using AJAX call. Let us go ahead and do the same using http service as shown below in the snippet. Hence, in order to use this built in service first I need to inject the same.

```
/**
 * Created by Rahul_Sahay on 7/12/2015.
 */

'use strict';

moviesApp.factory('movieDataService', function ($http,$log) {
    return {
        getshows: function (succeeded) {
            $http({method:'GET',url:'/data/shows/1stMovie
'}).success(function(data,status,headers,config){
                succeeded(data);
            }).error(function(data,status,headers,config){
                $log.error(data,status,headers,config);
            });
        }
    };
});
```

Let me explain the snippet for a moment. Here, first I have registered the $http and $log service. Then I created one function **getshows()**, which makes an AJAX call to the JSON data URL and returns the same data but this time via AJAX call. Here, I have supplied success method. This section will get executed when AJAX call succeed. In case of error due to any reason, I have also supplied error method which is using angular **$log** directive just to log the error. This directive we usually use for debugging purpose. In addition, in the success method, I am passing

Getting Started with Angular JS

the data received from the server to the callback, which will be used in controller to assign the values to properties. Similarly, below is the corresponding change to controller code.

```
/**
 * Created by Rahul_Sahay on 7/5/2015.
 */

'use strict';

moviesApp.controller('MovieController',function MovieController($scope,movieDataService){

    $scope.sortMovie = 'name';
    movieDataService.getshows(function(show){
        $scope.show =show;
    });
    $scope.upVotemMovie=function(movie){
        movie.voteCount++;
    };
    $scope.downVotemMovie=function(movie){
        movie.voteCount--;
    };
});
```

As you can see here, it makes the function call and assign the data using callback back to the scope variable. Now, let us look at my json file for the same.

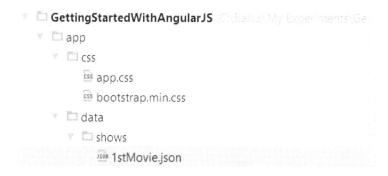

```
{"name": "Movies Review",
        "id": 1,
        "date": "1/1/2013",
        "time": "10:30 am",
        "location": {
            "address": "IMAX",
            "city": "Bangalore",
            "province": "KA"
        },
        "imageUrl": "img/movie-background.jpg",
        "movies": [
            {
            "id": 1,
                "name": "Godzilla",
                "directorName": "Gareth Edwards",
                "duration": 2,
                "about": "This movie is about Godzilla!",
                "voteCount": 0
            },
            {
```

Getting Started with Angular JS

```
        "id": 2,
            "name": "Avatar",
            "directorName": "James Cameron",
            "duration": 3,
            "about": "This is a science fiction movie with cool 3D and animations.",
            "voteCount": 0
        },
        {
        "id": 3,
            "name": "Titanic",
            "directorName": "James Cameron",
            "duration": 2,
            "about": "This movie is about great Titanic Ship.",
            "voteCount": 0
        }
    ]
}
```

With the above change in place, I have just started the server.bat file from webstorm terminal window as shown below in the screen shot.

Getting Started with Angular JS

Hence, with the above change in place, I need to use below mentioned URL as shown http://localhost:8000/MovieDetails.html.

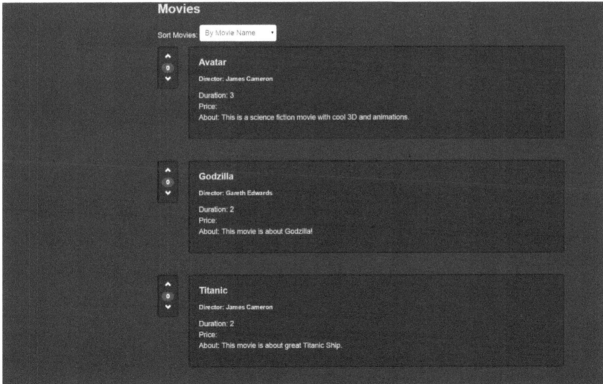

Let us go ahead and log the info, which is being returned from the server just for understanding.

```
/**
 * Created by Rahul_Sahay on 7/12/2015.
```

Getting Started with Angular JS

```javascript
*/
'use strict';

moviesApp.factory('movieDataService', function ($http,$log) {
    return {
        getshows: function (succeeded) {

$http({method:'GET',url:'/data/shows/1stMovie'}).success(function(data,status,headers,config){
                $log.info(data,status,headers,config);
                succeeded(data);
            }).error(function(data,status,headers,config){
                $log.error(data,status,headers,config);
            });
        }
    };
});
```

With the log in place, when I refresh the page and see the console, then it will produce the following output.

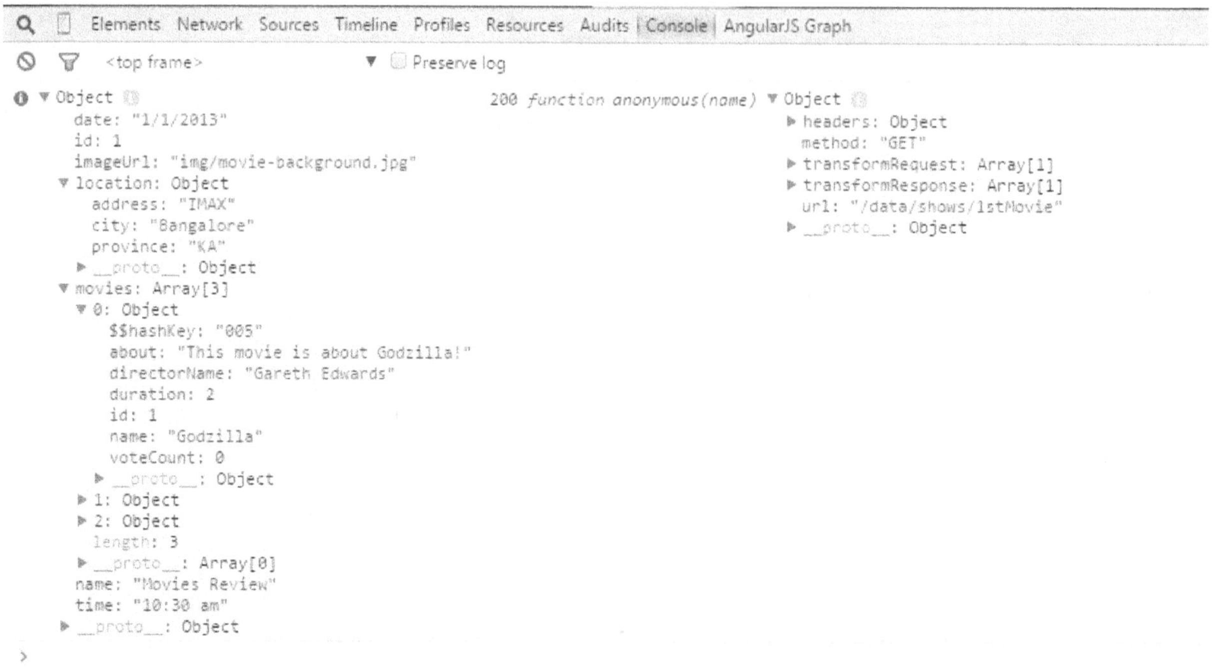

```
Q  []   Elements  Network  Sources  Timeline  Profiles  Resources  Audits  Console  AngularJS Graph

⊘  ▽   <top frame>                      ▼  ☐ Preserve log

ⓘ ▼ Object                   200 function anonymous(name) ▼ Object
     date: "1/1/2013"                                ▶ headers: Object
     id: 1                                             method: "GET"
     imageUrl: "img/movie-background.jpg"            ▶ transformRequest: Array[1]
   ▼ location: Object                                ▶ transformResponse: Array[1]
        address: "IMAX"                                url: "/data/shows/1stMovie"
        city: "Bangalore"                            ▶ __proto__: Object
        province: "KA"
      ▶ __proto__: Object
   ▼ movies: Array[3]
     ▼ 0: Object
          $$hashKey: "005"
          about: "This movie is about Godzilla!"
          directorName: "Gareth Edwards"
          duration: 2
          id: 1
          name: "Godzilla"
          voteCount: 0
        ▶ __proto__: Object
     ▶ 1: Object
     ▶ 2: Object
       length: 3
     ▶ __proto__: Array[0]
     name: "Movies Review"
     time: "10:30 am"
   ▶ __proto__: Object

 >
```

Therefore, this kind of info is quite descriptive from debugging point of view. Now, let us look at the **$q** promise library which comes with angular. Let us go to the movie data service and in there we will create the promise as shown below in the snippet.

```javascript
/**
 * Created by Rahul_Sahay on 7/12/2015.
 */

'use strict';
```

Getting Started with Angular JS

```
moviesApp.factory('movieDataService', function ($http,$log,$q) {
    return {
        getshows: function () {
            var deferred=$q.defer();

$http({method:'GET',url:'/data/shows/1stMovie'}).success(function(data,status,headers,config){
                deferred.resolve(data);
            }).error(function(data,status,headers,config){
                deferred.reject(status);
                $log.error(data,status,headers,config);
            });
            return deferred.promise;
        }
    };
});
```

Here, first I have created promise object with the name **deferred** with the help of $q library. You may also notice that in order to use the same I have injected $q service for the same. Promise is a way to avoid the callback. With the above change in place, I also need to make small change in controller as shown below.

```
/**
 * Created by Rahul_Sahay on 7/5/2015.
 */

'use strict';

moviesApp.controller('MovieController', function MovieController($scope, movieDataService,
$log) {

  $scope.sortMovie = 'name';
  movieDataService.getshows().then(function (show) {
    $scope.show = show;
  }, function (reason) {
    $log.error(reason);
  });
  $scope.upVotemMovie = function (movie) {
    movie.voteCount++;
  };
  $scope.downVotemMovie = function (movie) {
    movie.voteCount--;
  };
});
```

With the above change in place, it will produce me the same result, but this time it is coming with promises. I have also changed the theme for look and feel to avoid the monotonic look. Hence, with the new change it will look like

Getting Started with Angular JS

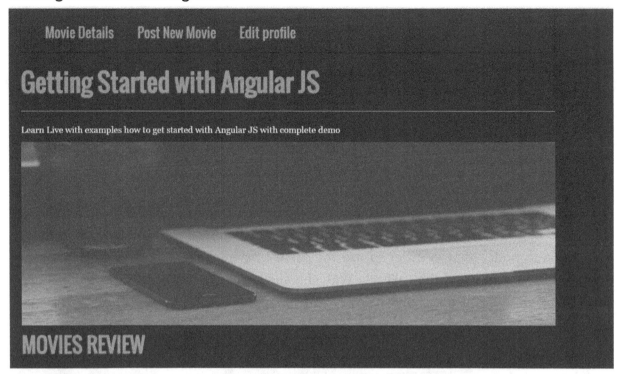

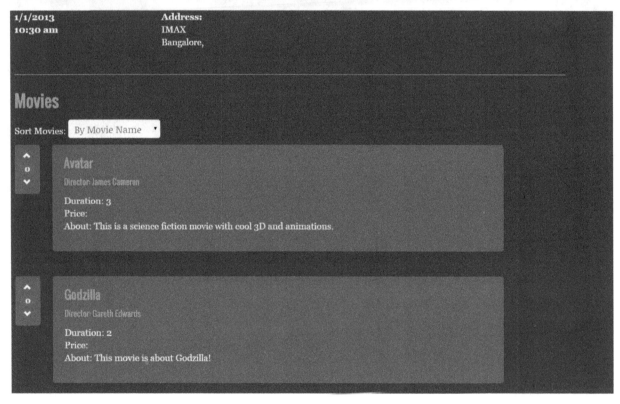

Getting Started with Angular JS

ANGULAR JS GRAPH:-

I have also installed one chrome extension for visualizing the ng components used in the application. This is nice extension to give you snapshot of all ng components, which you are using in the application.

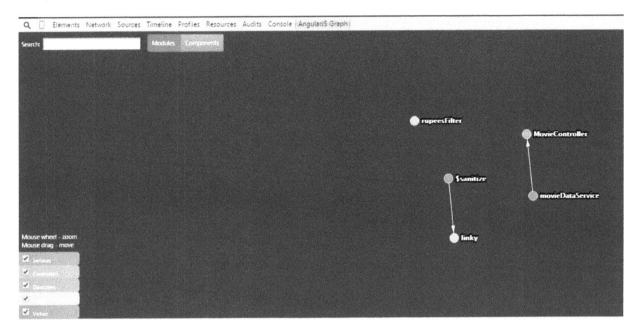

Similarly, on the right hand side panel you can see tabular format for the same selected values.

Getting Started with Angular JS

```
moviesApp
Dependencies (1):
ngSanitize,
Required by (0):
none
Services (1):
movieDataService,
Controllers (1):
MovieController,
Directives (0):
none
Filters (0):

Options
  Sticky nodes
Show modules
Ignore:  ngLocale, ui.*, template*
Filter:
```

USING $RESOURCE SERVICE:-

All right, now let us look how to use **$resource** service. Functionality is pretty much used for same sort of things like making AJAX calls. Only difference here is it is based on RESTFUL architecture. Below is the snippet for the same.

```
/**
 * Created by Rahul_Sahay on 7/12/2015.
 */

'use strict';

moviesApp.factory('movieDataService', function ($resource) {
    return {
        getshows: function () {
            return $resource('/data/shows/:id',{id:'@id'}).get({id:'1stMovie'});
        }
    };
});
```

Then corresponding controller change for the same is

```
/**
 * Created by Rahul_Sahay on 7/5/2015.
 */

'use strict';
```

Chapter 3: Services

Getting Started with Angular JS

```
moviesApp.controller('MovieController', function MovieController($scope, movieDataService) {

  $scope.sortMovie = 'name';
   $scope.show = movieDataService.getshows();

  $scope.upVotemMovie = function (movie) {
    movie.voteCount++;
  };
  $scope.downVotemMovie = function (movie) {
    movie.voteCount--;
  };
});
```

With the above change in place, when I refresh the page, it will produce the below error.

This happened because resource itself in different module. For this reason, we need to inject the resource module as shown below.

```
'use strict';

var moviesApp = angular.module('moviesApp', ['ngResource']);
```

Even after that it produced the below error

To fix the same, we need to include the physical file in the markup as shown below

```
<script src="lib/jquery.min.js"></script>
<script src="lib/underscore-1.4.4.min.js"></script>
<script src="lib/bootstrap.min.js"></script>
```

Chapter 3: Services

Getting Started with Angular JS

```html
<script src="lib/angular/angular.js"></script>
<script src="lib/angular/angular-sanitize.js"></script>
<script src="lib/angular/angular-resource.min.js"></script>
<script src="js/app.js"></script>
<script src="js/controllers/MovieController.js"></script>
<script src="js/filters.js"></script>
<script src="js/services/MovieDataService.js"></script>
```

With the above change in place, it will produce the same output, but this time via resource module. Now, let me explain the resource service here, resource service is taking couple of parameters here. First thing is the URL, second parameter is the default value and then we are calling get on that resource by providing the JSON file name there. Then, on the controller side, it will take time for the request to get fulfilled, and once request is fulfilled scope variable will be assigned with the same values.

Nevertheless, the current resource usage is not really a promise. However, the object returned from the resource call does have a promise at your service. Promise is useful when you want to inspect the data and take certain action on returned data. Moreover, if you just want to bind the data, then current RESTFUL call is ok. Let us look now how to use the same with promise.

```javascript
/**
 * Created by Rahul_Sahay on 7/5/2015.
 */

'use strict';

moviesApp.controller('MovieController', function MovieController($scope, movieDataService, $log) {

  $scope.sortMovie = 'name';
  //Success Call
  movieDataService.getshows().$promise.then(function (show) {
    $scope.show = show;
    $log.info(show);
  }, //Error Case
    function (status) {
    $log.error(status);
  });

  $scope.upVotemMovie = function (movie) {
    movie.voteCount++;
  };
  $scope.downVotemMovie = function (movie) {
    movie.voteCount--;
  };
});
```

With the above change in place, it has produced the same output, but if we inspect the output in console, it has printed the complete set fetched.

Getting Started with Angular JS

And in case of error case, means while retrieving the value from the server, if it fails for any reason, then it will look something like below. Now, let us try to retrieve wrong URL.

As you can see, it returned **status 404**. Resource can also be used for saving data. Below is the snippet for the same.

```
/**
 * Created by Rahul_Sahay on 7/12/2015.
 */

'use strict';

moviesApp.factory('movieDataService', function ($resource) {
  var res = $resource('/data/shows/:id',{id:'@id'});
    return {
        getshows: function () {
            return res.get({id:'1stMovie'});
```

Getting Started with Angular JS

```
    },
    save:function(show){
        //Temporary way
        //You can have one function which will return highest id from the disk
        //But, for demo this is ok.
        show.id=2;
        return res.save(show);
    }
};
});
```

In order to use the same save function, we need to modify the controller code as well. Let us modify Post New Movie controller. Below is the snippet for the same.

```
/**
 * Created by Rahul_Sahay on 7/10/2015.
 */

'use strict';

moviesApp.controller('PostMovieController', function ($scope, movieDataService) {
    $scope.save = function (show, newMovieForm) {
        if (newMovieForm.$valid) {
            movieDataService.save(show)
                .$promise.then(function(status){
                    console.log("New Value Saved! " + status);
                },function(status){
                    console.log("Error Occured! " + status);
                });

        }
        else {
            window.alert("Correct your input");
        }
    };
    $scope.cancel = function () {
        window.location = "MovieDetails.html";
    }
});
```

With the above change in place, when I post the below form, then it will save the in file system.

Getting Started with Angular JS

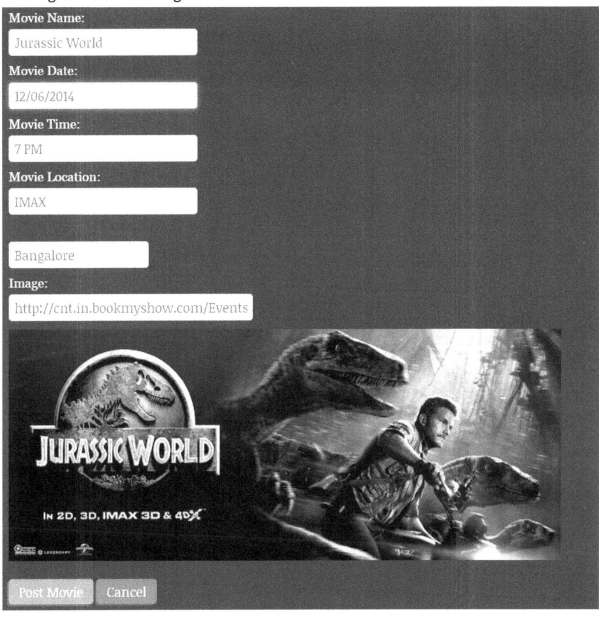

New value saved. Ignore this object here; this is nothing but the response received from the server. However, when you check the data folder as shown below, it saved the new JSON file in file system.

Getting Started with Angular JS

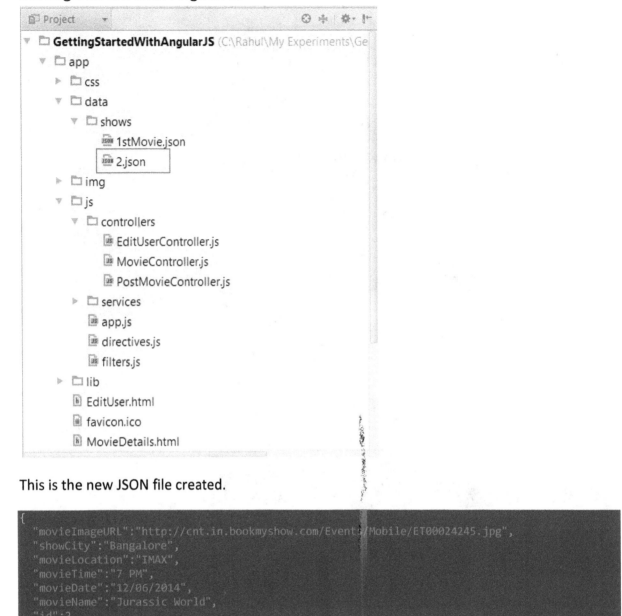

This is the new JSON file created.

```
{
  "movieImageURL":"http://cnt.in.bookmyshow.com/Events/Mobile/ET00024245.jpg",
  "showCity":"Bangalore",
  "movieLocation":"IMAX",
  "movieTime":"7 PM",
  "movieDate":"12/06/2014",
  "movieName":"Jurassic World",
  "id":2
}
```

USING CACHE FACTORY SERVICE:-

In this section, we will see how to work with cache factory service. For this, I will first create the service and then demonstrate the same using controller on one page. Below is the snippet for the same.

```
/**
 * Created by Rahul_Sahay on 7/21/2015.
 */
```

Getting Started with Angular JS

```
'use strict';

moviesApp.factory('cacheFactory',function($cacheFactory){
  return $cacheFactory('cacheFactory',{capacity:5})
});
```

Here, I have given my service name as **cacheFactory**. I have created this service like any other service. Only thing here I have taken **$cacheFactory** as an input to create the cacheFactory. I have also specified cache size 5 which it can keep five elements in the cache. If I store more than five elements in the cache, first element will get popped out of cache. However, we can create cache service without any capacity as well. I have also created new controller for the same. Below is the snippet.

```
/**
 * Created by Rahul_Sahay on 7/21/2015.
 */

'use strict';

moviesApp.controller('cacheController',function cacheController($scope,cacheFactory){

  //Add to Cache
  $scope.putInCache = function(key,value){
    cacheFactory.put(key,value);
  };
  //Read from Cache
  $scope.readFromCache= function (key) {
    return cacheFactory.get(key);
  }

  //Cache Capacity

  $scope.currentCapacity=function(){
    return cacheFactory.info();
  }

  //Delete from Cache based on key
  $scope.deleteFromCache= function (key) {
    cacheFactory.remove(key);
  }

  //Delete from Cache based on key
  $scope.flushCache= function () {
    cacheFactory.removeAll();
  }
});
```

Let me explain the code briefly, as you can see that this controller relies on the new custom service that we have written. I have also created bunch of methods to explain the functioning of cache. You can get complete understanding of this at http://bit.ly/ng-cachefactory. I have also used the same thing to give the demo. Here, I have used put, get, remove, removeAll to explain the API. Apart from this, I have also created one new screen to explain the same.

```
<html lang="en" ng-app="moviesApp">
<head>
```

Getting Started with Angular JS

```html
  <meta charset="utf-8">
  <title>Movie Review</title>
  <link rel="stylesheet" href="css/bootstrap.superhero.min.css"/>
  <link rel="stylesheet" href="css/app.css"/>


</head>
<body>
<div class="container">
  <div class="navbar">
    <div class="navbar-inner">
      <ul class="nav">
        <li><a href="MovieDetails.html">Movie Details</a></li>
        <li><a href="NewMovie.html">Post New Movie</a></li>
        <li><a href="EditUser.html">Edit profile</a></li>
        <li><a href="cachePage.html">Cache Demo</a></li>
      </ul>
    </div>
  </div>
</div>
<div class="container-fluid" style="align-items: center;padding-left: 300px;" ng-
controller="cacheController">
  <h1>Cache Demo</h1>
  <hr/>
  <div class="container-fluid" style="padding: 20px;">
    <table class="table-bordered">
      <tr>
        <td>
          Key: <input type="text" ng-model="key"/> <br/>
        </td>
        <td>
          value: <input type="text" ng-model="value"/> <br/>
        </td>
        <td>
          <button type="button" class="btn btn-success" ng-click="putInCache(key,value)">Add
To Cache</button>
        </td>
      </tr>
      <tr>
        <td>
          Key: <input type="text" ng-model="keyToRead"/><br/>
        </td>
        <td>
          <h3>Value From Cache: {{readFromCache(keyToRead)}}</h3>
        </td>
      </tr>
      <tr>
        <td> Key: <input type="text" ng-model="key"/>
        </td>
        <td>
          <button type="button" class="btn btn-danger" ng-click="deleteFromCache(key)">Delete
From Cache</button>
        </td>
      </tr>
      <tr>
        <td>
        <button type="button" class="btn btn-danger" ng-click="flushCache()">Flush
Cache</button>
        </td>
```

Chapter 3: Services

Getting Started with Angular JS

```
      </tr>
      <tr>
        <td><h3>Cache Size: {{currentCapacity()}}</h3></td>
      </tr>
    </table>
  </div>
</div>

<div class="container">
  <div class="navbar">
    <div class="navbar-inner">
      <ul class="nav">
        <li><span class="pull-right text-info credit">Movie Review - &copy; <a
href="http://rahulsahay.com"

target="_blank">Rahul Sahay</a></span>
        </li>
      </ul>
    </div>
  </div>
</div>

<script src="lib/jquery.min.js"></script>
<script src="lib/underscore-1.4.4.min.js"></script>
<script src="lib/bootstrap.min.js"></script>
<script src="lib/angular/angular.js"></script>
<script src="lib/angular/angular-sanitize.js"></script>
<script src="lib/angular/angular-resource.min.js"></script>
<script src="js/app.js"></script>
<script src="js/services/cacheFactoryService.js"></script>
<script src="js/controllers/cacheController.js"></script>


</body>
</html>
```

With the above change in place, when I refresh the browser, then it will produce the below result.

Getting Started with Angular JS

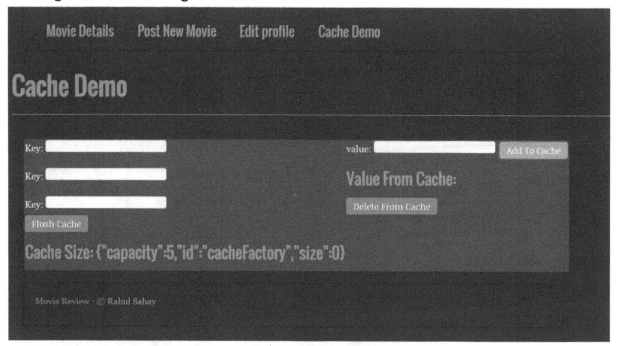

Therefore, here I can insert key-values like shown below. Once, I insert, cache size will also increment as shown below.

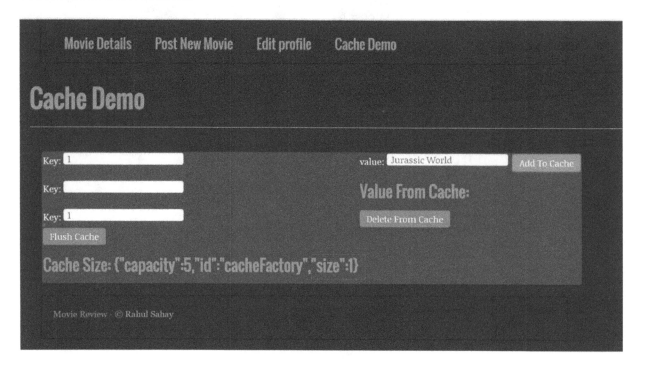

In addition, if you notice last key also get populated with the same value because this text box is also using the same data binding field. Similarly, if I put the same key in second field, then value from cache will get populated.

Chapter 3: Services

Getting Started with Angular JS

However, if I delete click on delete from cache by giving the key in the corresponding value, then value from cache will get deleted. Moreover, size will set back to 0.

Flush Cache also works the same way, only thing is that irrespective of key, it flushes all the values from cache.

USING COMPILE SERVICE:-

In this section, we are going to talk about compile service. Compile service is used heavily internally by angular. Whenever any page gets loaded, compile service look through the page

Chapter 3: Services

Getting Started with Angular JS

for the directives to process them. In order to explain the same, I have created new page and
controller for the same.

```
/**
 * Created by Rahul_Sahay on 7/25/2015.
 */

'use strict';

moviesApp.controller('compileSample',function compileSample($scope, $compile){
  $scope.attachDiv = function (element) {
    return $compile(element)($scope).appendTo(angular.element("#attachHere"));
  };
});
```

As you can see in the above snippet, it is using angular compile service and here one method is
created with the name **attachDiv**, which simply takes the HTML element passed from the page
and append the same in the div with id **attachHere**. Below, is the corresponding page for the
same.

```
<html lang="en" ng-app="moviesApp">
<head>
  <meta charset="utf-8">
  <title>Movie Review</title>
  <link rel="stylesheet" href="css/bootstrap.superhero.min.css"/>
  <link rel="stylesheet" href="css/app.css"/>


</head>
<body>
<div class="container">
  <div class="navbar">
    <div class="navbar-inner">
      <ul class="nav">
        <li><a href="MovieDetails.html">Movie Details</a></li>
        <li><a href="NewMovie.html">Post New Movie</a></li>
        <li><a href="EditUser.html">Edit profile</a></li>
        <li><a href="cachePage.html">Cache Demo</a></li>
        <li><a href="compileSample.html">Compile Sample</a></li>
      </ul>
    </div>
  </div>
</div>

<div class="container-fluid" ng-controller="compileSample" style="align-items: center;padding-
left: 300px;">
  <h1>Compile Service</h1>
  <hr/>
  <div class="container-fluid" style="padding: 20px;">
    <table class="table-bordered">
      <tr>
        <td>
          <div id="attachHere"></div>
        </td>
      </tr>
      <tr>
        <td>
```

Getting Started with Angular JS

```html
        Your Wish: <input type="text" ng-model="name"/>
      </td>
    </tr>
    <tr>
      <td>
        My Command: <input type="text" ng-model="element"/> <br/>
      </td>
    </tr>
    <tr>
      <td>
        <button class="btn btn-success" ng-click="attachDiv(element)">Attach</button>
      </td>
    </tr>
  </table>
 </div>
</div>
<div class="container">
  <div class="navbar">
    <div class="navbar-inner">
      <ul class="nav">
        <li><span class="pull-right text-info credit">Movie Review - &copy; <a
href="http://rahulsahay.com"

target="_blank">Rahul Sahay</a></span>
      </li>
    </ul>
  </div>
 </div>
</div>

<script src="lib/jquery.min.js"></script>
<script src3="lib/underscore-1.4.4.min.js"></script>
<script src="lib/bootstrap.min.js"></script>
<script src="lib/angular/angular.js"></script>
<script src="lib/angular/angular-sanitize.js"></script>
<script src="lib/angular/angular-resource.min.js"></script>
<script src="js/app.js"></script>
<script src="js/services/cacheFactoryService.js"></script>
<script src="js/controllers/cacheController.js"></script>
<script src="js/controllers/compileSample.js"></script>

</body>
</html>
```

With the above change in place, if I simply go and refresh the browser, then it will produce the below page.

Getting Started with Angular JS

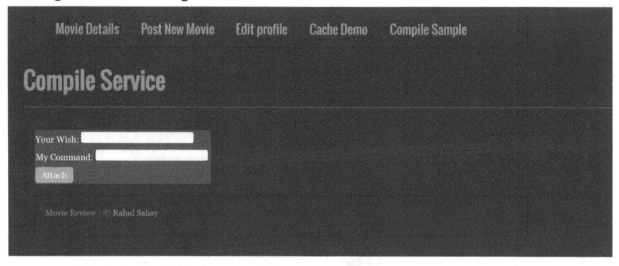

Let us suppose your wish here is to produce the Jurassic world poster here. Therefore, for that, you will give URL http://cnt.in.bookmyshow.com/Events/Mobile/ET00024245.jpg in the first text box, and then, corresponding HTML element tag like this **<img ng-src={{name}}></img>** you will again put in second textbox. Therefore, this will produce the img tag and attach the same to div element like shown below.

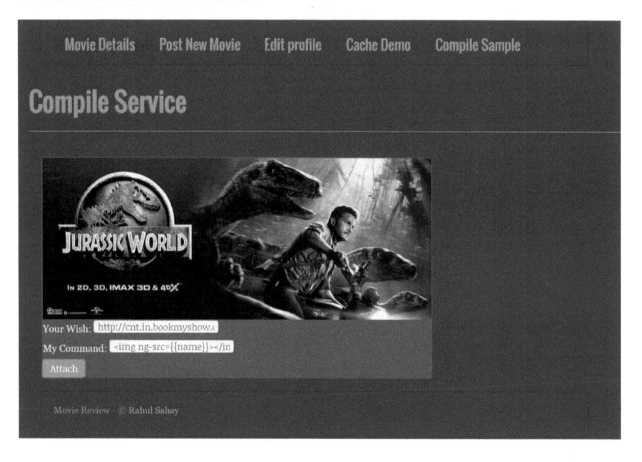

Getting Started with Angular JS

However, previous example was sophisticated one. Let us see some simple examples. Like producing movie-name "**Jurassic World**" as bootstrap button "<button class="**btn btn-info**">{{name}}</button>". With the above change in place, it will produce the below output.

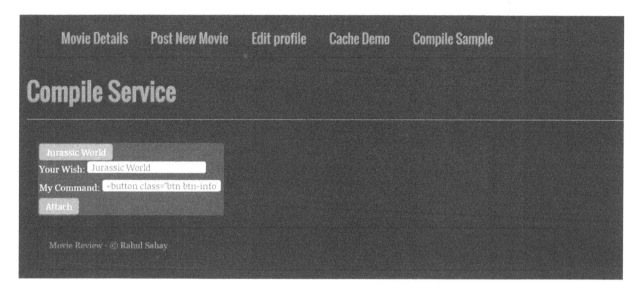

USING PARSE SERVICE:-

Parse service is also similar to compile service. Parse service is used to evaluate an expression and turned expression into function. Below is the simple example for the same. I have used the same controller. Only thing, I have used additional angular parse service to parse the expression and produce the same as function.

```
/**
 * Created by Rahul_Sahay on 7/25/2015.
 */

'use strict';

moviesApp.controller('compileSample',function compileSample($scope, $compile,$parse){
    var sample1 = {
        show:{
            movieName:'Jurassic World',
            location:'IMAX',
            time:'7PM'
        }
    };

    var readMovieName =$parse('show.movieName');
    var readMovieLocation =$parse('show.location');
    var readMovieTime =$parse('show.time');

    console.log("Movie Name:- "+readMovieName(sample1));
    console.log("Movie Location:- "+readMovieLocation(sample1));
    console.log("Movie Time:- "+readMovieTime(sample1));

    //you can also do any other operation like
    var add= $parse('1+1');
```

Getting Started with Angular JS

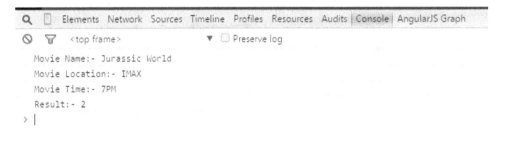

```
console.log("Result:- "+add());
$scope.attachDiv = function (element) {
  return $compile(element)($scope).appendTo(angular.element("#attachHere"));
};
});
```

With the above change in place, when I refresh the page and open the console window, then it will produce the following output.

```
Q  🔲  Elements  Network  Sources  Timeline  Profiles  Resources  Audits | Console | AngularJS Graph

⊘  ▽  <top frame>              ▼  ☐ Preserve log

  Movie Name:- Jurassic World
  Movie Location:- IMAX
  Movie Time:- 7PM
  Result:- 2

>  |
```

USING LOCALE SERVICE:-

Locale service is fairly simple and straightforward. This service is used for localization purpose like for printing currency, date-time or language in its own format. Now, if you see my solution, I have already imported all the required files in here.

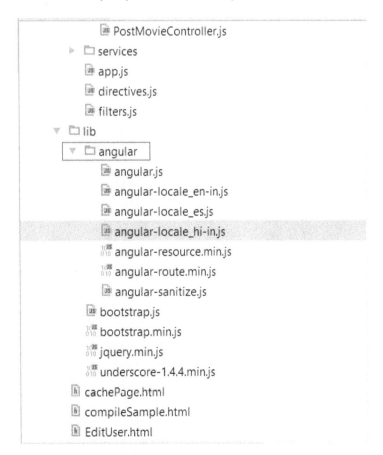

```
              PostMovieController.js
    ▶  ☐ services
          app.js
          directives.js
          filters.js
    ▼  ☐ lib
        ▼  ☐ angular
              angular.js
              angular-locale_en-in.js
              angular-locale_es.js
              angular-locale_hi-in.js
              angular-resource.min.js
              angular-route.min.js
              angular-sanitize.js
          bootstrap.js
          bootstrap.min.js
          jquery.min.js
          underscore-1.4.4.min.js
      cachePage.html
      compileSample.html
      EditUser.html
```

Chapter 3: Services

Getting Started with Angular JS

Now, let us use the same in the same compile page. Let me rename this page as activities page. You can get entire list of locales from GIT. http://bit.ly/ng-locale.

I have modified both my controller and markup code as shown below.

```
/**
 * Created by Rahul_Sahay on 7/25/2015.
 */

'use strict';

moviesApp.controller('localeController',function localeController($scope,$locale){
  $scope.price= 20;
  $scope.date= new Date();
});
```

In the above snippet, I have created new controller for locale demo. As you can see, here I am just demonstrating price and date.

```
<html lang="en" ng-app="moviesApp">
<head>
  <meta charset="utf-8">
  <title>Movie Review</title>
  <link rel="stylesheet" href="css/bootstrap.superhero.min.css"/>
  <link rel="stylesheet" href="css/app.css"/>


</head>
<body>
<div class="container">
  <div class="navbar">
    <div class="navbar-inner">
      <ul class="nav">
        <li><a href="MovieDetails.html">Movie Details</a></li>
        <li><a href="NewMovie.html">Post New Movie</a></li>
        <li><a href="EditUser.html">Edit profile</a></li>
        <li><a href="cachePage.html">Cache Demo</a></li>
        <li><a href="compileSample.html">Activities</a></li>
      </ul>
    </div>
  </div>
</div>

<div class="container-fluid" ng-controller="compileSample" style="align-items: center;padding-
left: 300px;">
  <h1>Compile Service</h1>
  <hr/>
  <div class="container-fluid" style="padding: 20px;">
    <table class="table-bordered">
      <tr>
        <td>
          <div id="attachHere"></div>
        </td>
      </tr>
      <tr>
        <td>
          Your Wish:       <input type="text" ng-model="name"/>
        </td>
```

Getting Started with Angular JS

```html
        </tr>
        <tr>
          <td>
            My Command: <input type="text" ng-model="element"/> <br/>
          </td>
        </tr>
        <tr>
          <td>
            <button class="btn btn-success" ng-click="attachDiv(element)">Attach</button>
          </td>
        </tr>
      </table>
    </div>
</div>

<div class="container-fluid" ng-controller="localeController" style="align-items:
center;padding-left: 300px;">
  <h1>Locale Demo</h1>
  <hr/>
  Price:- {{price | currency}}
  Time:- {{date | date:'fullDate' }}
  <div class="container-fluid" style="padding: 20px;">
    <table class="table-bordered">

    </table>
  </div>
</div>
<div class="container">
  <div class="navbar">
    <div class="navbar-inner">
      <ul class="nav">
        <li><span class="pull-right text-info credit">Movie Review - &copy; <a
href="http://rahulsahay.com"

target="_blank">Rahul Sahay</a></span>
        </li>
      </ul>
    </div>
  </div>
</div>

<script src="lib/jquery.min.js"></script>
<script src3="lib/underscore-1.4.4.min.js"></script>
<script src="lib/bootstrap.min.js"></script>
<script src="lib/angular/angular.js"></script>
<script src="lib/angular/angular-sanitize.js"></script>
<script src="lib/angular/angular-resource.min.js"></script>
<script src="js/app.js"></script>
<script src="js/services/cacheFactoryService.js"></script>
<script src="js/controllers/cacheController.js"></script>
<script src="js/controllers/compileSample.js"></script>
<script src="js/controllers/localeController.js"></script>
<script src="lib/angular/angular-locale_hi-in.js"></script>
</body>
</html>
```

Moreover, in the above markup code, I have simply created another div element where in I have introduced locale controller and included two physical files one for controller and another

Getting Started with Angular JS

one for locale. With the above change in place, when I refresh the page, then it will produce the following output.

However, if I simply comment out the locale file from markup, then it will switch to default locale, which is nothing but US and then it will produce the following output.

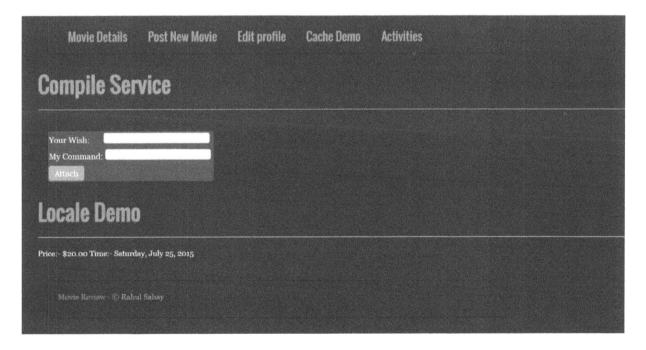

EXCEPTION HANDLER SERVICE:-

In this section, we will discuss about exception handler service. This service is useful in scenarios when you want to override the default behaviors of angular exceptions and want to

Getting Started with Angular JS

handle the same yourself. Hence, let us go ahead and create one service for the same. Below is the snippet for the same.

```
/**
 * Created by Rahul_Sahay on 7/25/2015.
 */

'use strict';

moviesApp.factory('$exceptionHandler',function($log){
  return function(exception){
    $log.error("Exception Occured:- "+exception.exceptionMessage);
  }
})
```

You might notice that I have used $ sign before **exceptionHandler**. This is just a way to override any default functionality and implement yours. Now, below is the corresponding controller change for the same.

```
/**
 * Created by Rahul_Sahay on 7/25/2015.
 */

'use strict';

moviesApp.controller('localeController', function localeController($scope, $locale) {
  $scope.price = 20;
  $scope.date = new Date();

  throw {exceptionMessage:'Purposely Thrown!'};
});
```

Here, I have simply thrown the exception. I have also done one small change in the physical file that is nothing but the inclusion of new service file in the markup as shown below.

```
<script src="lib/jquery.min.js"></script>
<script src3="lib/underscore-1.4.4.min.js"></script>
<script src="lib/bootstrap.min.js"></script>
<script src="lib/angular/angular.js"></script>
<script src="lib/angular/angular-sanitize.js"></script>
<script src="lib/angular/angular-resource.min.js"></script>
<script src="js/app.js"></script>
<script src="js/services/cacheFactoryService.js"></script>
<script src="js/controllers/cacheController.js"></script>
<script src="js/controllers/compileSample.js"></script>
<script src="js/controllers/localeController.js"></script>
<!--<script src="lib/angular/angular-locale_hi-in.js"></script>-->
<script src="js/services/exceptionHandlerService.js"></script>
```

With the above change in place, when I go ahead and refresh the page, then it will produce the following output.

Getting Started with Angular JS

Q ☐ Elements Network Sources Timeline Profiles Resources Audits | Console | AngularJS Graph

⊘ ▽ <top frame>   ▼ ☐ Preserve log

    Movie Name:- Jurassic World
    Movie Location:- IMAX
    Movie Time:- 7PM
    Result:- 2
⊕ ▶ Exception Occured:- Purposely Thrown!
    >

FILTER SERVICE:-

In this section, we are going to look at the filter service. Filter service allows you to access the filters, which you have created, or filters which is built in angular. In order to demonstrate the same, I will create another div section on my activities page. However, before that let us go ahead and create the controller for the same.

```
/**
 * Created by Rahul_Sahay on 7/25/2015.
 */

'use strict';

moviesApp.controller('filterController', function filterController($scope, $filter) {
  $scope.show = {};

  var grabFilterData = $filter('rupeesFilter');
  $scope.show.first = grabFilterData(150);
  $scope.show.seconnd = grabFilterData(250);
  $scope.show.third = grabFilterData(350);
})
```

Let me explain the code briefly. As you can see here I have injected **$filter** service to gain access of the rupeesFilter, which I have created initially. **$filter** then gets the same in local scoped variable and then by simply passing the input type to filter, it will produce the filter output. Below is the markup change for the same.

```
<html lang="en" ng-app="moviesApp">
<head>
  <meta charset="utf-8">
  <title>Movie Review</title>
  <link rel="stylesheet" href="css/bootstrap.superhero.min.css"/>
  <link rel="stylesheet" href="css/app.css"/>


</head>
<body>
<div class="container">
  <div class="navbar">
    <div class="navbar-inner">
      <ul class="nav">
        <li><a href="MovieDetails.html">Movie Details</a></li>
        <li><a href="NewMovie.html">Post New Movie</a></li>
        <li><a href="EditUser.html">Edit profile</a></li>
```

Getting Started with Angular JS

```
          <li><a href="cachePage.html">Cache Demo</a></li>
          <li><a href="compileSample.html">Activities</a></li>
        </ul>
      </div>
    </div>
</div>

<div class="container-fluid" ng-controller="compileSample" style="align-items: center;padding-
left: 300px;">
  <h1>Compile Service</h1>
  <hr/>
  <div class="container-fluid" style="padding: 20px;">
    <table class="table-bordered">
      <tr>
        <td>
          <div id="attachHere"></div>
        </td>
      </tr>
      <tr>
        <td>
          Your Wish:       <input type="text" ng-model="name"/>
        </td>
      </tr>
      <tr>
        <td>
          My Command: <input type="text" ng-model="element"/> <br/>
        </td>
      </tr>
      <tr>
        <td>
          <button class="btn btn-success" ng-click="attachDiv(element)">Attach</button>
        </td>
      </tr>
    </table>
  </div>
</div>

<div class="container-fluid" ng-controller="localeController" style="align-items:
center;padding-left: 300px;">
  <h1>Locale Demo</h1>
  <hr/>
  Price:- {{price | currency}}
  Time:- {{date | date:'fullDate' }}
  <div class="container-fluid" style="padding: 20px;">
    <table class="table-bordered">

    </table>
  </div>
</div>

<div class="container-fluid" ng-controller="filterController" style="align-items:
center;padding-left: 300px;">
  <h1>Filter Demo</h1>
  <hr/>
  <ul>
    <li>{{show.first}}</li>
    <li>{{show.second}}</li>
    <li>{{show.third}}</li>
  </ul>
</div>
```

Chapter 3: Services

Getting Started with Angular JS

```html
</div>
<div class="container">
  <div class="navbar">
    <div class="navbar-inner">
      <ul class="nav">
        <li><span class="pull-right text-info credit">Movie Review - &copy; <a
href="http://rahulsahay.com"

target="_blank">Rahul Sahay</a></span>
        </li>
      </ul>
    </div>
  </div>
</div>

<script src="lib/jquery.min.js"></script>
<script src3="lib/underscore-1.4.4.min.js"></script>
<script src="lib/bootstrap.min.js"></script>
<script src="lib/angular/angular.js"></script>
<script src="lib/angular/angular-sanitize.js"></script>
<script src="lib/angular/angular-resource.min.js"></script>
<script src="js/app.js"></script>
<script src="js/services/cacheFactoryService.js"></script>
<script src="js/controllers/cacheController.js"></script>
<script src="js/controllers/compileSample.js"></script>
<script src="js/controllers/localeController.js"></script>
<!--<script src="lib/angular/angular-locale_hi-in.js"></script>-->
<!--<script src="js/services/exceptionHandlerService.js"></script>-->
<script src="js/filters.js"></script>
<script src="js/controllers/filterController.js"></script>
</body>
</html>
```

With the above change in place, it will produce the following output as shown below.

CREATING AUTH SERVICE:-

In this section, we are going to introduce a new service, which will help user to register on the site, hence allows user to login and logout. However, this functionality uses bunch of techniques as if I am storing user credentials currently in the browser. However, I really do not like this approach, as I believe storing the credentials on the server side and retrieving the same from there. However, for demo I think this is ok. In addition, this section may appear little advanced for starters, but that is ok. Atleast, it will give you a glimpse of real world app. First thing I have done here is, I have created login controller and register controller as shown below.

Getting Started with Angular JS

```
/**
 * Created by Rahul_Sahay on 8/14/2015.
 */

'use strict';

  moviesApp.controller('LoginController', LoginController);

    function LoginController($location, AuthenticationService, $log,$rootScope) {
    var vm = this;

    var path =$location.path();
    console.log("Path:-" +path);
    console.log("Rootscope:-" +$rootScope.isAuthenticated);

    if(path=="/login" &&($rootScope.isAuthenticated==true)){
      $rootScope.isAuthenticated = false;
      $('#nav-login').text('Login');
    }


    vm.login = login;

    (function initController() {
      // reset login status
      AuthenticationService.ClearCredentials();
    })();

    function login() {
      vm.dataLoading = true;
      AuthenticationService.Login(vm.username, vm.password, function (response) {
        if (response.success) {
          AuthenticationService.SetCredentials(vm.username, vm.password);
          loggedin=true;
          toastr.success("Logged in successfully!")

          $location.path('/');
        } else {
          toastr.error("Error in Logging:- "+ response.message);
          vm.dataLoading = false;
        }
      });
    };
  }

/**
 * Created by Rahul_Sahay on 8/14/2015.
 */


  'use strict';



  moviesApp.controller('RegisterController', RegisterController);

    function RegisterController(UserService) {
    var vm = this;

    vm.register = register;
```

Getting Started with Angular JS

```
function register() {
  vm.dataLoading = true;
  UserService.Create(vm.user)
    .then(function (response) {
      if (response.success) {
        toastr.success('Registration Successful!!!');
      }
      else {
        toastr.error('Error in Registration! ' +response.message)
        vm.dataLoading = false;
      }
    });
  }
}
```

Then corresponding views for the same.

```
<div class="col-md-6 col-md-offset-3">
  <h2>Login</h2>
  <div ng-show="vm.error" class="alert alert-danger">{{vm.error}}</div>
  <form name="form" ng-submit="vm.login()" role="form">
    <div class="form-group" ng-class="{ 'has-error': form.username.$dirty &&
form.username.$error.required }">
      <label for="username">Username</label>
      <input type="text" name="username" id="username" class="form-control" ng-
model="vm.username" required />
      <span ng-show="form.username.$dirty && form.username.$error.required" class="help-
block">Username is required</span>
    </div>
    <div class="form-group" ng-class="{ 'has-error': form.password.$dirty &&
form.password.$error.required }">
      <label for="password">Password</label>
      <input type="password" name="password" id="password" class="form-control" ng-
model="vm.password" required />
      <span ng-show="form.password.$dirty && form.password.$error.required" class="help-
block">Password is required</span>
    </div>
    <div class="form-actions">
      <button type="submit" ng-disabled="form.$invalid || vm.dataLoading" class="btn btn-
primary">Login</button>
      <img ng-if="vm.dataLoading" src="../img/ajax-loader.gif" />
      <a href="#/register" class="btn btn-link">Register</a>
    </div>
  </form>
</div>
<div class="col-md-6 col-md-offset-3">
  <h2>Register</h2>
  <div ng-show="vm.error" class="alert alert-danger">{{vm.error}}</div>
  <form name="form" ng-submit="vm.register()" role="form">
    <div class="form-group" ng-class="{ 'has-error': form.firstName.$dirty &&
form.firstName.$error.required }">
      <label for="username">First name</label>
      <input type="text" name="firstName" id="firstName" class="form-control" ng-
model="vm.user.firstName" required />
      <span ng-show="form.firstName.$dirty && form.firstName.$error.required" class="help-
block">First name is required</span>
    </div>
    <div class="form-group" ng-class="{ 'has-error': form.lastName.$dirty &&
```

Getting Started with Angular JS

```
form.lastName.$error.required }">
    <label for="username">Last name</label>
    <input type="text" name="lastName" id="Text1" class="form-control" ng-
model="vm.user.lastName" required />
    <span ng-show="form.lastName.$dirty && form.lastName.$error.required" class="help-
block">Last name is required</span>
  </div>
  <div class="form-group" ng-class="{ 'has-error': form.username.$dirty &&
form.username.$error.required }">
    <label for="username">Username</label>
    <input type="text" name="username" id="username" class="form-control" ng-
model="vm.user.username" required />
    <span ng-show="form.username.$dirty && form.username.$error.required" class="help-
block">Username is required</span>
  </div>
  <div class="form-group" ng-class="{ 'has-error': form.password.$dirty &&
form.password.$error.required }">
    <label for="password">Password</label>
    <input type="password" name="password" id="password" class="form-control" ng-
model="vm.user.password" required />
    <span ng-show="form.password.$dirty && form.password.$error.required" class="help-
block">Password is required</span>
  </div>
  <div class="form-actions">
    <button type="submit" ng-disabled="form.$invalid || vm.dataLoading" class="btn btn-
primary">Register</button>
    <img ng-if="vm.dataLoading" src="../img/ajax-loader.gif" />
    <a href="#/" class="btn btn-link">Cancel</a>
  </div>
 </form>
</div>
```

I have also created menus for the same. Hence, with the above change in place, it will look like as shown below

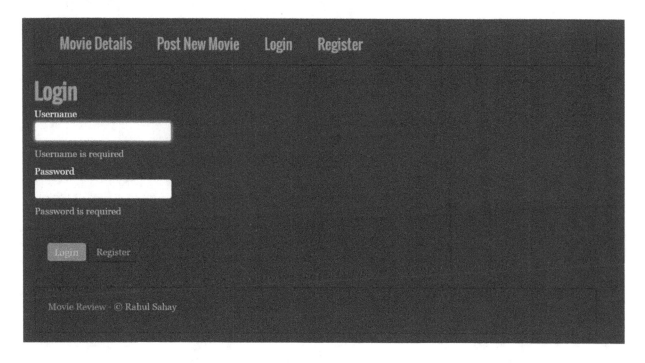

Getting Started with Angular JS

However, my login and register controller are dependent on authentication and local storage service. Their snippet are as shown below.

```
/**
 * Created by Rahul_Sahay on 8/14/2015.
 */

'use strict';

moviesApp.factory('AuthenticationService', AuthenticationService);

function AuthenticationService($http, $cookieStore, $rootScope, $timeout, UserService) {
    var service = {};

    service.Login = Login;
    service.SetCredentials = SetCredentials;
    service.ClearCredentials = ClearCredentials;

    return service;

    function Login(username, password, callback) {

        /* Sample authentication */
        $timeout(function () {
            var response;
            UserService.GetByUsername(username)
```

Getting Started with Angular JS

```javascript
        .then(function (user) {
          if (user !== null && user.password === password) {
            response = { success: true };
            $rootScope.isAuthenticated=true;
          } else {
            response = { success: false, message: 'Username or password is incorrect' };
            $rootScope.isAuthenticated=false;

          }
          callback(response);
        });
      }, 1000);



  }

  function SetCredentials(username, password) {
    var authdata = Base64.encode(username + ':' + password);

    $rootScope.globals = {
      currentUser: {
        username: username,
        authdata: authdata
      }
    };

    $http.defaults.headers.common['Authorization'] = 'Basic ' + authdata;
    $cookieStore.put('globals', $rootScope.globals);
  }

  function ClearCredentials() {
    $rootScope.globals = {};
    $cookieStore.remove('globals');
    $http.defaults.headers.common.Authorization = 'Basic ';
  }
}

// Base64 encoding service used by AuthenticationService
var Base64 = {

  keyStr: 'ABCDEFGHIJKLMNOPQRSTUVWXYZabcdefghijklmnopqrstuvwxyz0123456789+/=',

  encode: function (input) {
    var output = "";
    var chr1, chr2, chr3 = "";
    var enc1, enc2, enc3, enc4 = "";
    var i = 0;

    do {
      chr1 = input.charCodeAt(i++);
      chr2 = input.charCodeAt(i++);
      chr3 = input.charCodeAt(i++);

      enc1 = chr1 >> 2;
      enc2 = ((chr1 & 3) << 4) | (chr2 >> 4);
      enc3 = ((chr2 & 15) << 2) | (chr3 >> 6);
      enc4 = chr3 & 63;

      if (isNaN(chr2)) {
        enc3 = enc4 = 64;
      } else if (isNaN(chr3)) {
```

Getting Started with Angular JS

```javascript
          enc4 = 64;
        }

      output = output +
        this.keyStr.charAt(enc1) +
        this.keyStr.charAt(enc2) +
        this.keyStr.charAt(enc3) +
        this.keyStr.charAt(enc4);
      chr1 = chr2 = chr3 = "";
      enc1 = enc2 = enc3 = enc4 = "";
    } while (i < input.length);

    return output;
  },

  decode: function (input) {
    var output = "";
    var chr1, chr2, chr3 = "";
    var enc1, enc2, enc3, enc4 = "";
    var i = 0;

    // remove all characters that are not A-Z, a-z, 0-9, +, /, or =
    var base64test = /[^A-Za-z0-9\+\/\=]/g;
    if (base64test.exec(input)) {
      window.alert("There were invalid base64 characters in the input text.\n" +
        "Valid base64 characters are A-Z, a-z, 0-9, '+', '/',and '='\n" +
        "Expect errors in decoding.");
    }
    input = input.replace(/[^A-Za-z0-9\+\/\=]/g, "");

    do {
      enc1 = this.keyStr.indexOf(input.charAt(i++));
      enc2 = this.keyStr.indexOf(input.charAt(i++));
      enc3 = this.keyStr.indexOf(input.charAt(i++));
      enc4 = this.keyStr.indexOf(input.charAt(i++));

      chr1 = (enc1 << 2) | (enc2 >> 4);
      chr2 = ((enc2 & 15) << 4) | (enc3 >> 2);
      chr3 = ((enc3 & 3) << 6) | enc4;

      output = output + String.fromCharCode(chr1);

      if (enc3 != 64) {
        output = output + String.fromCharCode(chr2);
      }
      if (enc4 != 64) {
        output = output + String.fromCharCode(chr3);
      }

      chr1 = chr2 = chr3 = "";
      enc1 = enc2 = enc3 = enc4 = "";

    } while (i < input.length);

    return output;
  }
};
```

Let me explain the snippet here, authentication service contains the method for authenticating a user.

Getting Started with Angular JS

```javascript
/**
 * Created by Rahul_Sahay on 8/14/2015.
 */

'use strict';

//Local Storage API

moviesApp.factory('UserService', UserService);

  UserService.$inject = ['$timeout', '$filter', '$q'];
  function UserService($timeout, $filter, $q) {

    var service = {};

    service.GetById = GetById;
    service.GetByUsername = GetByUsername;
    service.Create = Create;

    return service;

    function GetById(id) {
      var deferred = $q.defer();
      var filtered = $filter('filter')(getUsers(), { id: id });
      var user = filtered.length ? filtered[0] : null;
      deferred.resolve(user);
      return deferred.promise;
    }

    function GetByUsername(username) {
      var deferred = $q.defer();
      var filtered = $filter('filter')(getUsers(), { username: username });
      var user = filtered.length ? filtered[0] : null;
      deferred.resolve(user);
      return deferred.promise;
    }

    function Create(user) {
      var deferred = $q.defer();

      // simulate api call with $timeout
      $timeout(function () {
        GetByUsername(user.username)
          .then(function (duplicateUser) {
            if (duplicateUser !== null) {
              deferred.resolve({ success: false, message: 'Username "' + user.username + '" is
already taken' });
            } else {
              var users = getUsers();

              // assign id
              var lastUser = users[users.length - 1] || { id: 0 };
              user.id = lastUser.id + 1;

              // save to local storage
              users.push(user);
              setUsers(users);

              deferred.resolve({ success: true });
            }
```

Getting Started with Angular JS

```javascript
      });
    }, 1000);

    return deferred.promise;
  }

  // private functions

  function getUsers() {
    if(!localStorage.users){
      localStorage.users = JSON.stringify([]);
    }

    return JSON.parse(localStorage.users);
  }

  function setUsers(users) {
    localStorage.users = JSON.stringify(users);
  }
}
```

Above snippet is for interacting with a web service in restful manner. Here, it stores the credential in HTML 5 Local storage. Apart from these changes, I have also done changes in app.js file.

```javascript
'use strict';

var loggedin=false;

var moviesApp = angular.module('moviesApp', ['ngResource', 'ngRoute','ngCookies'])
  .config(function ($routeProvider) {
    $routeProvider.when('/', {
      templateUrl: 'templates/MovieDetails.html',
      controller: 'MovieController'
    });
    $routeProvider.when('/NewMovie', {
      templateUrl: 'templates/NewMovie.html',
      controller: 'PostMovieController'
    });
    $routeProvider.when('/MovieDetails', {
      templateUrl: 'templates/MovieDetails.html',
      controller: 'MovieController'
    });
    $routeProvider.when('/EditUser', {
      templateUrl: 'templates/EditUser.html',
      controller: 'EditUserController'
    });
    $routeProvider.when('/cachePage', {
      templateUrl: 'templates/cachePage.html',
      controller: 'cacheController'
    });
    /*$routeProvider.when('/compileSample',{
    templateUrl:'templates/compileSample.html',
    controller: 'compileSample'
    });*/
    $routeProvider.when('/show/:id', {
      templateUrl: 'templates/MovieDetail.html',
      controller: 'MovieDetailController'
    });
```

Getting Started with Angular JS

```
    $routeProvider.when('/customPage', {
      templateUrl: 'templates/customPage.html',
      controller: 'customDirectiveController'
    });
    $routeProvider.when('/calcTime', {
      templateUrl: 'templates/directiveController.html'
    });
    $routeProvider.when('/helloAngular', {
      templateUrl: 'templates/helloAngular.html'
    });
    $routeProvider.when('/login', {
      controller: 'LoginController',
      templateUrl: 'templates/login.html',
      controllerAs: 'vm'
    });

    $routeProvider.when('/register', {
      controller: 'RegisterController',
      templateUrl: 'templates/register.html',
      controllerAs: 'vm'
    });

    $routeProvider.otherwise({templateUrl: 'templates/errorPage.html'});
  });


run.$inject = ['$rootScope', '$location', '$cookieStore', '$http'];
function run($rootScope, $location, $cookieStore, $http) {
  // keep user logged in after page refresh
  $rootScope.globals = $cookieStore.get('globals') || {};
  if ($rootScope.globals.currentUser) {
    $http.defaults.headers.common['Authorization'] = 'Basic ' +
$rootScope.globals.currentUser.authdata; // jshint ignore:line
  }
}
```

Here, part of authentication lies in this file. When, the app starts, it checks whether a cookie is there which contains user credentials. These were the changes around Register/Login functionality. Apart from the above changes, same physical files need to be referred in index page. Now, with the above change in place, when I go ahead run the app, it will appear like

Getting Started with Angular JS

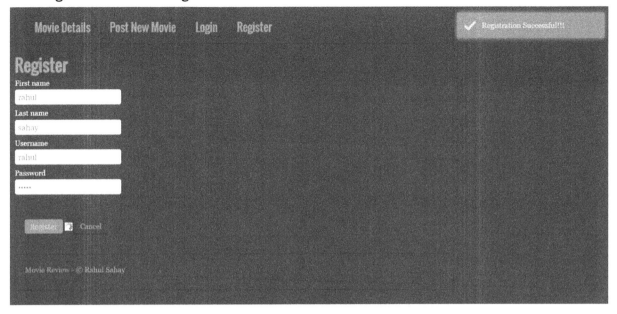

Then, it will take you to the login page as shown below.

Once, you provide the credentials and click on Login, it will take you to the home page as shown below.

Getting Started with Angular JS

SUMMARY:-

In this section, we have seen bunch of useful angular services and their usages. One point to note here, that I have covered those services, which you will need on day-to-day basis for writing any kind of web app. However, for complete list of angular services and its usage, you can always refer https://angularjs.org/ site. This site is always getting updated with the new angular features.

Getting Started with Angular JS

WHAT DO you find in this CHAPTER?

- Introduction
- Adding First Route
- Adding More Routes
- Parameterized Routes
- Default Route
- Using Location Service
- Summary

INTRODUCTION:-

In this section, we will see how to get started with routing. Until this point, we have seen various parts of angular. However, for every example, we have used different HTML page. In real world Single Page App, only one main page will be there and their views getting injected based on the route request. Routing is the big part of AngularJS. It actually helps making any app Single Page app. AngularJS provides us with an optional module **ngRoute**, which is used to do routing in AngularJS Application.

ADDING FIRST ROUTE:-

The first thing which we need to do here for adding first route is to add one single page for our application where in different views will be injected. Below is the markup for the same.

```
<!doctype html>
<html lang="en" ng-app="moviesApp">
<head>
  <meta charset="utf-8">
  <title>Movie Review</title>
  <link rel="stylesheet" href="css/bootstrap.superhero.min.css"/>
  <link rel="stylesheet" href="css/app.css"/>
</head>
<body>
<div class="container">
  <div class="navbar">
    <div class="navbar-inner">
      <ul class="nav">
        <li><a href="#/MovieDetails">Movie Details</a></li>
        <li><a href="#/NewMovie">Post New Movie</a></li>
```

Getting Started with Angular JS

```
      <li><a href="#/EditUser">Edit profile</a></li>
      <li><a href="#/cachePage">Cache Demo</a></li>
      <li><a href="#/compileSample">Activities</a></li>
    </ul>
  </div>
</div>

<ng-view></ng-view>
</div>
<div class="container">
  <div class="navbar">
    <div class="navbar-inner">
      <ul class="nav">
        <li><span class="pull-right text-info credit">Movie Review - &copy; <a
href="http://rahulsahay.com" target="_blank">Rahul Sahay</a></span></li>
      </ul>
    </div>
  </div>
</div>
</div>

<script src="lib/jquery.min.js"></script>
<script src="lib/underscore-1.4.4.min.js"></script>
<script src="lib/bootstrap.min.js"></script>
<script src="lib/angular/angular.js"></script>
<script src="lib/angular/angular-sanitize.js"></script>
<script src="lib/angular/angular-resource.min.js"></script>
<script src="js/app.js"></script>
<script src="js/controllers/MovieController.js"></script>
<script src="js/filters.js"></script>
<script src="js/services/MovieDataService.js"></script>
</body>
</html>
```

Let me explain the code a bit. As you can see, there is a tag with the name **<ng-view>**. Inside this tag, templates or views will get produced interchangeably whenever you request for any different route. Now, this page will be served as our layout page and inside the **ng-view** tag, different HTML templates will get replaced.

Chapter 4: Routing

Getting Started with Angular JS

As you can see in the above screen shot, I have created new **templates** folder where in I have moved all the HTML files. Now, a template will look like

```html
<style>input.ng-invalid.ng-dirty {
    background-color: red
}</style>


<div>
  <div class="container">
    <h1>New Movie</h1>
    <hr/>
    <form name="newMovieForm">
      <fieldset>
        <label for="movieName">Movie Name:</label>
        <input id="movieName" type="text" required ng-model="show.movieName"
placeholder="Enter Movie Name"/>
        <label for="movieDate">Movie Date:</label>
        <input id="movieDate" type="text" required ng-pattern="/\d\d/\d\d/\d\d\d\d/" ng-
model="show.movieDate"
              placeholder="Enter Movie Date"/>
        <label for="movieTime">Movie Time:</label>
        <input id="movieTime" type="text" required ng-model="show.movieTime"
placeholder="Enter Movie Time"/>
        <label for="movieLocation">Movie Location:</label>
```

Getting Started with Angular JS

```html
        <input id="movieLocation" type="text" required ng-model="show.movieLocation"
            placeholder="Enter Movie Location"/>
        <br><br>
        <input id="showCity" type="text" required class="input-medium" ng-
model="show.showCity" placeholder="City"/>
        <label for="movieImageURL">Image:</label>
        <input id="movieImageURL" type="url" class="input-xlarge" ng-
model="show.movieImageURL"
            placeholder="Movie Image Url"/>
    </fieldset>
    <img ng-src="{{show.movieImageURL}}"/>
    <br><br>
    <button type="submit" ng-disabled="newMovieForm.$invalid" ng-
click="save(show,newMovieForm)"
            class="btn btn-success">Post Movie
    </button>
    <button type="button" ng-click="cancel()" class="btn btn-danger">Cancel</button>
    </form>
  </div>
 </div>
</div>
```

Therefore, now with the usage of route, template will get injected in the **ng-view** tag. Now, I need to setup the route. Below is the snippet for the same.

```javascript
'use strict';

var moviesApp = angular.module('moviesApp', ['ngResource','ngRoute'])
  .config(function ($routeProvider) {
    $routeProvider.when('/NewMovie',{
      templateUrl:'templates/NewMovie.html',
      controller: 'PostMovieController'
    })
  });
```

Now, let me explain the code briefly. Here, I have used config block in the module. Moreover, this config block runs when the application first bootstrapped. Config block takes **$routeProvider**, here routeProvider matches the route and outputs the template accordingly. In addition, on the index page, in the navigation bar section, I have mentioned the route with the # sign. This is angular convention. # is used for linking the page. One last thing, which is pending, is introducing the route file on the page.

```html
<script src="lib/jquery.min.js"></script>
<script src="lib/underscore-1.4.4.min.js"></script>
<script src="lib/bootstrap.min.js"></script>
<script src="lib/angular/angular.js"></script>
<script src="lib/angular/angular-route.min.js"></script>
<script src="lib/angular/angular-sanitize.js"></script>
<script src="lib/angular/angular-resource.min.js"></script>
<script src="js/app.js"></script>
<script src="js/controllers/MovieController.js"></script>
<script src="js/controllers/PostMovieController.js"></script>
<script src="js/filters.js"></script>
<script src="js/services/MovieDataService.js"></script>
```

Getting Started with Angular JS

With the above change in place, when I navigate the URL http://localhost:8000/#/NewMovie or click on **Post New Movie**, then it will produce the below result, but with routing.

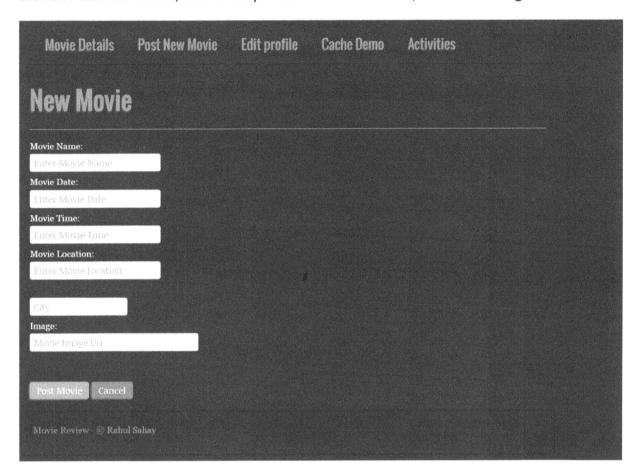

Now, let us open debugger tool in chrome and switch to network tab as shown below. Therefore, when I requested http://localhost:8000/, it loaded entire asset and all the required stuffs in the initial call.

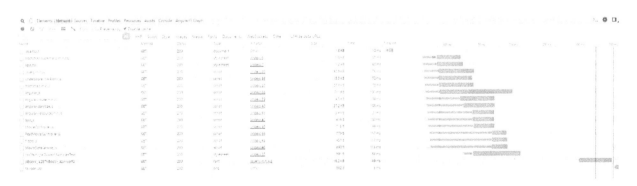

However, when I clicked on **Post New Movie** link, then in the network tab only one request is there.

Getting Started with Angular JS

Moreover, this is nothing but the new template that we created. This is the beauty of angular; it smartly replaced the template there without any round trip to the server. This is why angular apps are very fast in nature. When, I clicked on template link, it actually produced the exact template, which we wrote.

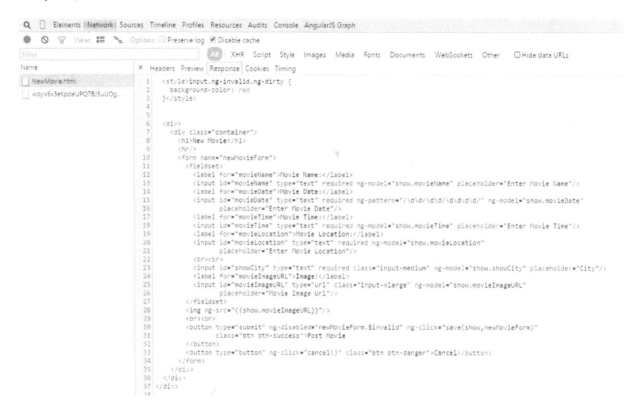

ADDING MORE ROUTES:-

In this section, I am going to add few more routes. As you can see below snippet, here I have created two routes for the same page. First, is the default route and last one is explicit route for the particular page.

```
'use strict';

var moviesApp = angular.module('moviesApp', ['ngResource','ngRoute'])
    .config(function ($routeProvider) {
        $routeProvider.when('/',{
            templateUrl:'templates/MovieDetails.html',
            controller: 'MovieController'
        });
```

Getting Started with Angular JS

```
    $routeProvider.when('/NewMovie',{
        templateUrl:'templates/NewMovie.html',
        controller: 'PostMovieController'
    });
    $routeProvider.when('/MovieDetails',{
        templateUrl:'templates/MovieDetails.html',
        controller: 'MovieController'
    });
});
```

In addition, below is the markup change for the same.

```
<div>
    <header>
        <div class="header-content">
            <div class="header-content-inner">

                <h1>Getting Started with Angular JS</h1>
                <hr>
                <p>Learn Live with examples how to get started with Angular JS with
complete demo</p>
                <img ng-src="{{show.imageUrl}}" alt="{{show.name}}"
style="width:1000px;height: 300px;"/>
            </div>
        </div>
    </header>


    <div class="row">

        <div class="span11">
            <h2 > {{show.name | uppercase}}</h2>
        </div>

    </div>
     <br/>


    <div class="row">
        <div class="span3">
            <div><strong>{{show.date | date:'short'}}</strong></div>
            <div><strong>{{show.time}}</strong></div>
        </div>
        <div class="span4">
            <address>
                <strong>Address:</strong><br/>
                {{show.location.address}}<br/>
                {{show.location.city}},{{event.location.province}}
            </address>
        </div>
    </div>
    <hr/>
    <h3>Movies</h3>
    Sort Movies:
    <select ng-model="sortMovie" class="input-medium">
        <option selected value="name">By Movie Name</option>
        <option value="-voteCount">By Vote</option>
    </select>
    <ul class="thumbnails">
```

Getting Started with Angular JS

```html
<li ng-repeat="movie in show.movies | orderBy:sortMovie">
    <div class="row show">
        <div class="span0 well votingWidget">
            <div class="votingButton" ng-click="upVotemMovie(movie)">
                <i class="icon-chevron-up icon-white"></i>
            </div>
            <div class="badge badge-inverse">
                <div>{{movie.voteCount}}</div>
            </div>
            <div class="votingButton" ng-click="downVotemMovie(movie)">
                <i class="icon-chevron-down icon-white"></i>
            </div>
        </div>
        <div class="well span9">
            <h4 class="show-title">{{movie.name}}</h4>
            <h6 style="margin-top: -10ox;">Director: {{movie.directorName}}</h6>
            <span>Duration: {{movie.duration}} </span><br />
            <span>Price: {{movie.price | rupeesFilter }} </span>
            <p>About: {{movie.about}}</p>
        </div>

    </div>
</li>
</ul>
</div>
</div>
```

With the above change in place, when I hit http://localhost:8000/ or
http://localhost:8000/#/MovieDetails or click on Movie Details link, it produced the below
output.

Getting Started with Angular JS

Now the app started getting maturity as far as Single Page App (SPA) is concerned.

PARAMETERIZED ROUTES:-

In this section, I am going to access another page by clicking on individual movie shown on the home page. Here based on movie ID, new page will get rendered with complete details. Below is the snippet of modified Movie Details page.

```html
<div>
  <header>
    <div class="header-content">
      <div class="header-content-inner">

        <h1>Getting Started with Angular JS</h1>
        <hr>
        <p>Learn Live with examples how to get started with Angular JS with complete demo</p>
        <img ng-src="{{show.imageUrl}}" alt="{{show.name}}" style="width:1000px;height:
300px;"/>
      </div>
    </div>
  </header>


  <div class="row">

    <div class="span11">
      <h2> {{show.name | uppercase}}</h2>
    </div>

  </div>
  <br/>


  <div class="row">
    <div class="span3">
      <div><strong>{{show.date | date:'short'}}</strong></div>
      <div><strong>{{show.time}}</strong></div>
    </div>
    <div class="span4">
      <address>
        <strong>Address:</strong><br/>
        {{show.location.address}}<br/>
        {{show.location.city}},{{event.location.province}}
      </address>
    </div>
  </div>
  <hr/>
  <h3>Movies</h3>
  Sort Movies:
  <select ng-model="sortMovie" class="input-medium">
    <option selected value="name">By Movie Name</option>
    <option value="-voteCount">By Vote</option>
  </select>
  <ul class="thumbnails">
    <li ng-repeat="movie in show.movies | orderBy:sortMovie">
      <a href="#/show/{{movie.id}}">
```

Getting Started with Angular JS

```html
<div class="row show">
  <div class="span0 well votingWidget">
    <div class="votingButton" ng-click="upVotemMovie(movie)">
      <i class="icon-chevron-up icon-white"></i>
    </div>
    <div class="badge badge-inverse">
      <div>{{movie.voteCount}}</div>
    </div>
    <div class="votingButton" ng-click="downVotemMovie(movie)">
      <i class="icon-chevron-down icon-white"></i>
    </div>
  </div>
  <div class="well span9">
    <h4 class="show-title">{{movie.name}}</h4>
    <h6 style="margin-top: -10ox;">Director: {{movie.directorName}}</h6>
    <span>Duration: {{movie.duration}} </span><br/>
    <span>Price: {{movie.price | rupeesFilter }} </span>

    <p>About: {{movie.about}}</p>
  </div>
</div>
      </a>
    </li>
  </ul>
</div>
</div>
```

Here, I added one anchor tag with id passed as parameter. Now, when you hover, on any of the movies, it will produce the following address at the bottom of the page as shown below.

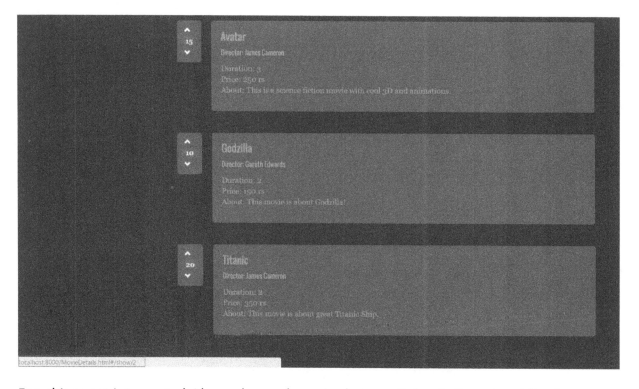

For, this to get intercepted, I have also made route changes. Below is the snippet for the same.

Getting Started with Angular JS

```javascript
'use strict';

var moviesApp = angular.module('moviesApp', ['ngResource','ngRoute'])
  .config(function ($routeProvider) {
    $routeProvider.when('/',{
      templateUrl:'templates/MovieDetails.html',
      controller: 'MovieController'
    });
    $routeProvider.when('/NewMovie',{
      templateUrl:'templates/NewMovie.html',
      controller: 'PostMovieController'
    });
    $routeProvider.when('/MovieDetails',{
      templateUrl:'templates/MovieDetails.html',
      controller: 'MovieController'
    });
    $routeProvider.when('/show/:id',{
      templateUrl:'templates/MovieDetail.html',
      controller: 'MovieDetailController'
    });
  });
```

As you can see in the above snippet, this route expects new page, **MovieDetail** and new
controller. I have also created both the required stuffs and added the reference in index.html.
Below is the snippet for the same.

```html
<div>
  <header>
    <div class="header-content">
      <div class="header-content-inner">

        <h1>Getting Started with Angular JS</h1>
        <hr>
        <p>Learn Live with examples how to get started with Angular JS with complete demo</p>
        <img ng-src="{{show.imageUrl}}" alt="{{show.name}}" style="width:1000px;height:
300px;"/>
      </div>
    </div>
  </header>


  <div class="row">

    <div class="span11">
      <h2> {{show.name | uppercase}}</h2>
    </div>

  </div>
  <hr/>

  <div class="row">
    <div class="span3">
      <div><strong>Date:- {{show.date | date:'short'}}</strong></div>
      <div><strong>Time:- {{show.time}}</strong></div>
    </div>
    <div class="span4">
      <address>
        <strong>Address:</strong><br/>
```

Getting Started with Angular JS

```
      {{show.location.address}}<br/>
      {{show.location.city}},{{event.location.province}}
    </address>
  </div>
</div>
<hr/>
  <div class="row">
  <div class="span3">
    <div><strong>Director:- {{show.directorName }}</strong></div>
    <div><strong>Release Year:- {{show.releaseYear }}</strong></div>
  </div>
  <div class="span4">
    <div><strong>Rating:- {{show.rating }}</strong></div>
    <div><strong>Reviews:- {{show.reviews }}</strong></div>
  </div>
  </div>


</div>
</div>
<br />
```

In addition, controller code.

```
/**
 * Created by Rahul_Sahay on 7/26/2015.
 */

'use strict';

moviesApp.controller('MovieDetailController',function
MovieDetailController($scope,movieDataService,$routeParams){
  $scope.show = movieDataService.getshow($routeParams.id);
});
```

Very straight forward. Here, controller makes a call to service that takes id as parameter and to access the route values, we have angular routeParams. I have also introduced one new service method, which takes parameterized input as shown below in the snippet.

```
/**
 * Created by Rahul_Sahay on 7/12/2015.
 */

'use strict';

moviesApp.factory('movieDataService', function ($resource) {
  var res = $resource('/data/shows/:id',{id:'@id'});
    return {
        getshows: function () {
            return res.get({id:'1stMovie'});
        },
      save:function(show){
        //Temporary way
        //You can have one function which will return highest id from the disk
        //But, for demo this is ok.
        show.id=2;
        return res.save(show);
      },
      getshow:function(id){
```

Getting Started with Angular JS

```
        return res.get({id:id});
    }
  };
});
```

Last, but not the least, I have constructed few straightforward JSONs to get returned based on this call. Below is the sample snippet for the same.

```
GettingStartedWithAngularJS (C:\Rahul\My Experiments\Ge
  app
    css
    data
      shows
        JSON  1.json
        JSON  1stMovie.json
        JSON  2.json
        JSON  3.json
        JSON  99.json
```

```
{
  "name": "Movie Review",
  "id": 1,
  "date": "1/6/2014",
  "time": "10:30 am",
  "location": {
    "address": "IMAX",
    "city": "Bangalore",
    "province": "KA"
  },
  "imageUrl": "img/Godzilla.jpg",
  "directorName": "Gareth Edwards",
  "releaseYear": "2014",
  "rating":"5",
  "reviews":"100"
}
```

With the above change in place, when I click on any individual list item as shown below, it will produce the following output.

Chapter 4: Routing

Getting Started with Angular JS

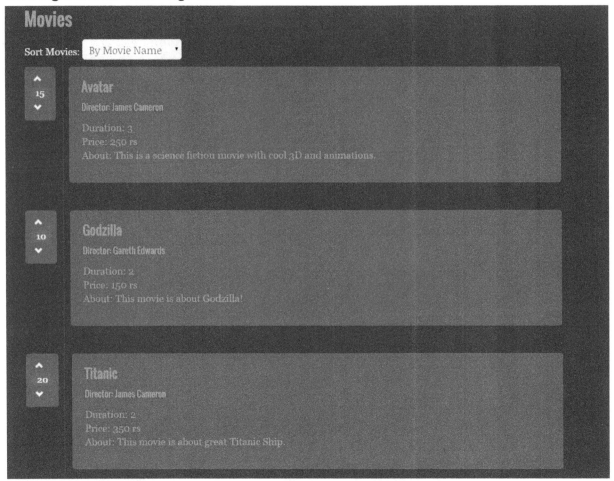

Clicking on first one, will take you on the below detail page with URL

http://localhost:8000/MovieDetails.html#/show/2

Getting Started with Angular JS

Similarly, clicking on other links will take you on the same page but with different data.

Getting Started with Angular JS

Getting Started with Angular JS

DEFAULT ROUTE:-

In this section, I am going to create one default route. Default route will come into picture, when something wrong was typed in the URL. Then at this instant, it will land you on the default page. In the below snippet, I have used **$routeProvider.otherwise** mechanism to redirect to existing route.

```
'use strict';

var moviesApp = angular.module('moviesApp', ['ngResource','ngRoute'])
  .config(function ($routeProvider) {
    $routeProvider.when('/',{
      templateUrl:'templates/MovieDetails.html',
      controller: 'MovieController'
    });
    $routeProvider.when('/NewMovie',{
      templateUrl:'templates/NewMovie.html',
      controller: 'PostMovieController'
    });
    $routeProvider.when('/MovieDetails',{
      templateUrl:'templates/MovieDetails.html',
      controller: 'MovieController'
    });
```

Getting Started with Angular JS

```
$routeProvider.when('/show/:id',{
    templateUrl:'templates/MovieDetail.html',
    controller: 'MovieDetailController'
});
$routeProvider.otherwise({redirectTo:'/MovieDetails'});
});
```

With the above change in place, if I type any garbage like http://localhost:8000/234; I will get redirected to MovieDetails page as shown below in the screen shot.

USING LOCATION SERVICE-

In this section, we will see how to make use of location service. Location service used to provide bunch of information like what protocol you are using, what port you are on, what URL and many other things. Let us demonstrate the same with simple example.

```
/**
 * Created by Rahul_Sahay on 7/5/2015.
 */
```

Getting Started with Angular JS

```javascript
'use strict';

moviesApp.controller('MovieController', function MovieController($scope, movieDataService,
$log,$location) {

  $scope.sortMovie = 'name';
  //location service in action
  $log.info('protocol:- '+$location.protocol());
  $log.info('port:- '+$location.port());
  $log.info('host:- '+$location.host());
  $log.info('path:- '+$location.path());
  $log.info('url:- '+$location.url());

  //Success Call
  movieDataService.getshows().$promise.then(function (show) {
    $scope.show = show;
    $log.info(show);
  }, //Error Case
    function (status) {
    $log.error(status);
  });

  $scope.upVotemMovie = function (movie) {
    movie.voteCount++;
  };
  $scope.downVotemMovie = function (movie) {
    movie.voteCount--;
  };
});
```

With the above change in place, you will get the below information's. This is very useful in many scenarios when you want to inspect any particular use case.

```
Q    Elements  Network  Sources  Timeline  Profiles  Resources  Audits  Console  AngularJS Graph

     <top frame>              ▼  Preserve log
 ⓘ protocol:- http
 ⓘ port:- 8000
 ⓘ host:- localhost
 ⓘ path:- /MovieDetails
 ⓘ url:- /MovieDetails
```

One more thing I would like to fix here is the default route. Actually, rather navigating to home page even in case of error, let us show an error page rather. Below is the code change for the same.

```javascript
$routeProvider.otherwise({templateUrl: 'templates/errorPage.html'});
```

In addition, below is the markup code.

```html
<div class="container-fluid">
  <h1>Error Occurred!</h1>
  <hr/>
  <div class="container-fluid" style="padding: 20px;">
    <img img src='img/github-404.png' style="width:1000px;height: 300px;"/>
```

Getting Started with Angular JS

```
</div>
</div>
```

With the above change in place, when I type something useless like http://localhost:8000/#/234, then it will produce the following output.

Now, this looks more meaningful and relevant to user.

SUMMARY:-

In this section, we have seen routing concepts in detail. With the help of routing, we actually gave SPA shape to our application. We also saw how to add bunch of routes using route provider. Then, we saw how to setup default route. We also worked with route params to grab the route data and utilize the same. In the end, we have also seen how to make use of location service.

Getting Started with Angular JS

WHAT DO you find in this CHAPTER?

- Introduction
- Creating First Directive
- Encapsulating Elements
- Isolating Directive Scope
- Handling Events
- Using Controllers
- Using Require
- Directive Priority
- Nested Directives
- Summary

INTRODUCTION:-

In this section, we will be looking at how to use directives for custom elements and events in angular. Hence, in this section we will be creating elements with custom embedded functionality in it. Therefore, once you get habituated with these components, you will use these as reusable components across different pages in your application. Directives are AngularJS way of dealing with DOM and rendering the components on the page. In this chapter, we will start with very basic use cases of directive and then we will explore some common options like template, templateUrl, link and scope. Apart from these we will also do deep dive in directives with few complex use cases.

CREATING FIRST DIRECTIVE:-

In this case, I will be creating my first directive, which will simply link html element to the html page. Off course before attaching the HTML element, it has to be compiled as well. Below, in the snippet, I have created my controller and template.

```
/**
 * Created by Rahul_Sahay on 7/30/2015.
 */
'use strict';
```

Getting Started with Angular JS

```
moviesApp.controller('customDirectiveController',function customDirectiveController($scope){

});
```

```
<div custom-directive></div>
```

Then, I have also configured the route for the same in app.js file as shown below.

```
$routeProvider.when('/customPage',{
  templateUrl:'templates/customPage.html',
  controller: 'customDirectiveController'
});
```

These are straightforward changes. Now, let me show the snippet for directive.

```
'use strict';

moviesApp.directive('customDirective', function ($compile) {
  //It Returns directive defintion object
  //Refer more on this here https://docs.angularjs.org/api/ng/directive
  return {
    link: function (scope, elem) {
      var htmlElement = "<input type='text' ng-model='customData' /> Output:- {{customData}}
<br>";
      angular.element(elem).html($compile(htmlElement)(scope));
    }
  };
})
```

Let me explain this snippet a bit. As you can see that, directive definition is having link method on it that takes two parameters as **scope** and **elem**. Here, for first example, I have simply created one markup that will allow you to input the value and the same get produced as output field. Last piece, is to output the markup on the page. For this piece, I have used **angular.element**. You may also notice that I have used compile service to compile the markup and then passed the same to scope. Currently, it is set to parent scope, which means scope for custom directive template.

Later in the chapter, we will also see how to make use of isolated scope as well. Another very important thing to note here is directive name. "**customDirective**" is the name of the directive which is again camel case. In order to emit the same directive on the page, there is a rule like shown below.

```
<div custom-directive></div>
```

It has to be used this way. Hence, "**custom-directive**" will get translated to "**customDirective**". Apart from these changes, off course, I need to reference the same on the index page as shown below.

```
<script src="js/directives.js"></script>
<script src="js/controllers/customDirectiveController.js"></script>
```

Chapter 5: Creating Custom Directives

Getting Started with Angular JS

With the above change in place, when I go ahead and run the app, it will produce the below output.

When I click on Custom Directive link highlighted above, it will take me to the following page.

Moreover, when I type anything, it will output the same as shown below.

Here, in this example, we have used a div with attribute. However, we can also use directly same as an element as shown below in the example.

```
<custom-directive/>
```

Chapter 5: Creating Custom Directives

Getting Started with Angular JS

In order to use the same as element, I need to make small change in directive's code as shown below.

```
'use strict';

moviesApp.directive('customDirective', function ($compile) {
  //It Returns directive definition object
  //Refer more on this here https://docs.angularjs.org/api/ng/directive
  return {
    restrict:'E',
    link: function (scope, elem, attr, controller) {
      var htmlElement = "<input type='text' ng-model='customData' /> Output:- {{customData}}
<br>";
      angular.element(elem).html($compile(htmlElement)(scope));
    }
  };
})
```

Here, I have used restrict property to "**E**" to use the same as element. With the above change in place, I will get the same behavior but getting as element. Default behavior is attribute type which is of type "**A**". Now, when I inspect the element in chrome, it will produce the below result.

```
<!DOCTYPE html>
▼<html lang="en" ng-app="moviesApp" class="ng-scope">
 ▶<head>...</head>
 ▼<body>
   ▼<div class="container">
      ::before
    ▶<div class="navbar">...</div>
      <!-- ngView: undefined -->
    ▼<ng-view class="ng-scope">
      ▼<custom-directive class="ng-scope">
          <input type="text" ng-model="customData" class="ng-scope ng-valid ng-dirty">
          <span class="ng-scope ng-binding"> Output:- Jurassic World </span>
          <br class="ng-scope">
        </custom-directive>
      </ng-view>
```

Earlier, the same was

```
<!DOCTYPE html>
▼<html lang="en" ng-app="moviesApp" class="ng-scope">
 ▶<head>...</head>
 ▼<body>
   ▼<div class="container">
      ::before
    ▶<div class="navbar">...</div>
      <!-- ngView: undefined -->
    ▼<ng-view class="ng-scope">
      ▼<div custom-directive class="ng-scope">
          <input type="text" ng-model="customData" class="ng-scope ng-valid ng-dirty">
          <span class="ng-scope ng-binding"> Output:- Jurassic World </span>
          <br class="ng-scope">
        </div>
      </ng-view>
      ::after
   </div>
```

However, we really do not need this kind of complex logic to emit just a template. Rather than that, we can make use of template property and wrap the same inside that like shown below.

Getting Started with Angular JS

```
'use strict';

moviesApp.directive('customDirective', function () {
  //It Returns directive definition  object
  //Refer more on this here https://docs.angularjs.org/api/ng/directive
  return {
      restrict:'E',
      template:"<input type='text' ng-model='customData' /> Output:- {{customData}} <br>"
  };
})
```

This approach looks pretty nice and clean. With the above change, result will remain same. Only thing is you do not need to compile explicitly. Templates are pre-compiled by angular. I can make use of one more attribute and that is class or "**C**". Below, is the modified code for the same.

```
'use strict';

moviesApp.directive('customDirective', function () {
  //It Returns directive definition  object
  //Refer more on this here https://docs.angularjs.org/api/ng/directive
  return {
      restrict:'C',
      template:"<input type='text' ng-model='customData' /> Output:- {{customData}} <br>"
  };
})
```

Moreover, here is the corresponding markup change.

```
<div class="custom-directive"></div>
```

Again, with the above change, result will remain the same. However, added advantage with this is you can make use styles to style your custom directive on the top of embedded functionality what you already have. Another, restrict option you can make use of "**M**" which is for comment. However, this is not often used.

ENCAPSULATING ELEMENTS:-

In this section, I am going to encapsulate the directives into a specific requirement. In addition, this is the best thing about writing custom components; you can encapsulate the entire set under one directory. This directory could be some specific functionality for the main site. This way, you can isolate different functionalities with different components.

Getting Started with Angular JS

In the above screen shot, I have moved my directive code in newly created directives folder. I have also changed the reference in the index page as shown below.

```
<script src="js/directives/customDirective.js"></script>
```

With the above change in place, when I refresh the page, then it will not break rather it will produce me the same output. Similarly, we can encapsulate whatever we need. For instance, let us wrap the below section

Getting Started with Angular JS

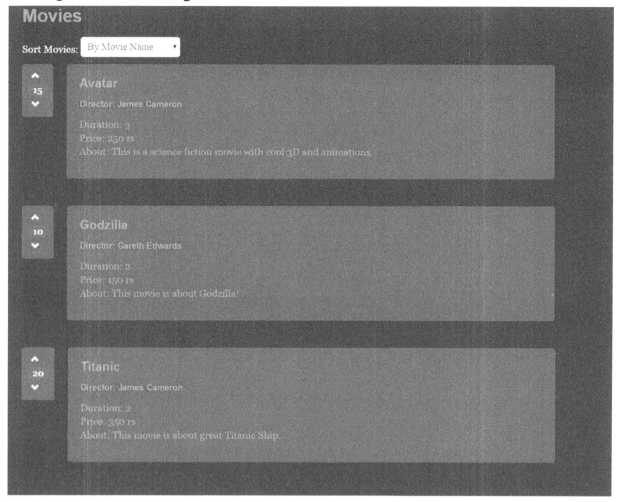

In one custom component and produce, the same result from there. In the below screen shot, I have created individual folders and corresponding items there.

Getting Started with Angular JS

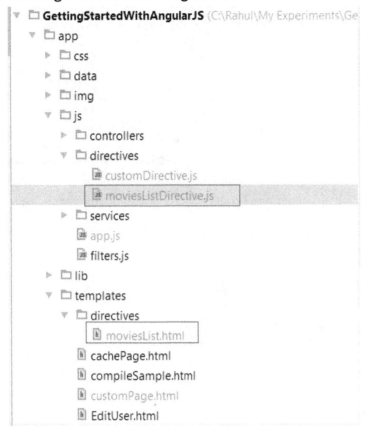

Hence, if you look at the below snippet, you find that, this is very clean.

```
/**
 * Created by Rahul_Sahay on 7/31/2015.
 */

'use strict';

moviesApp.directive('moviesListDirective',function(){
  return{
    restrict:'E',
    templateUrl:'/templates/directives/moviesList.html'
  }
});
```

Here, rather than putting whole bunch of HTML as inline code, I have referenced the same with template URL. And, below is the template snippet which it is referring.

```
<a href="#/show/{{movie.id}}">

  <div class="row show">
    <div class="span0 well votingWidget">
      <div class="votingButton" ng-click="upVotemMovie(movie)">
        <i class="icon-chevron-up icon-white"></i>
      </div>
      <div class="badge badge-inverse">
        <div>{{movie.voteCount}}</div>
      </div>
```

Chapter 5: Creating Custom Directives

Getting Started with Angular JS

```
        <div class="votingButton" ng-click="downVotemMovie(movie)">
          <i class="icon-chevron-down icon-white"></i>
        </div>
      </div>
      <div class="well span9">
        <h4 class="show-title">{{movie.name}}</h4>
        <h6 style="margin-top: -10ox;">Director: {{movie.directorName}}</h6>
        <span>Duration: {{movie.duration}} </span><br/>
        <span>Price: {{movie.price | rupeesFilter }} </span>

        <p>About: {{movie.about}}</p>
      </div>
    </div>
</a>
```

Moreover, this template I have referred as shown below in the snippet.

```
<div>
  <header>
    <div class="header-content">
      <div class="header-content-inner">

        <h1>Getting Started with Angular JS</h1>
        <hr>
        <p>Learn Live with examples how to get started with Angular JS with complete demo</p>
        <img ng-src="{{show.imageUrl}}" alt="{{show.name}}" style="width:1000px;height:
300px;"/>
      </div>
    </div>
  </header>


  <div class="row">

    <div class="span11">
      <h2> {{show.name | uppercase}}</h2>
    </div>

  </div>
  <br/>


  <div class="row">
    <div class="span3">
      <div><strong>{{show.date | date:'short'}}</strong></div>
      <div><strong>{{show.time}}</strong></div>
    </div>
    <div class="span4">
      <address>
        <strong>Address:</strong><br/>
        {{show.location.address}}<br/>
        {{show.location.city}},{{event.location.province}}
      </address>
    </div>
  </div>
</div>
<hr/>
<h3>Movies</h3>
Sort Movies:
<select ng-model="sortMovie" class="input-medium">
  <option selected value="name">By Movie Name</option>
```

Getting Started with Angular JS

```
    <option value="-voteCount">By Vote</option>
  </select>
  <ul class="thumbnails">
    <li ng-repeat="movie in show.movies | orderBy:sortMovie">
      <movies-list-directive/>
    </li>
  </ul>
</div>
</div>
```

Hence, below line is having all functionality embedded in it.

```
<movies-list-directive/>
```

Last change that I need to do here is referring the script on the index page as shown below.

```
<script src="js/directives/moviesListDirective.js"></script>
```

With the above change in place, when I refresh the page, it will produce me the same output, but this time via custom component as shown below in the screen shot.

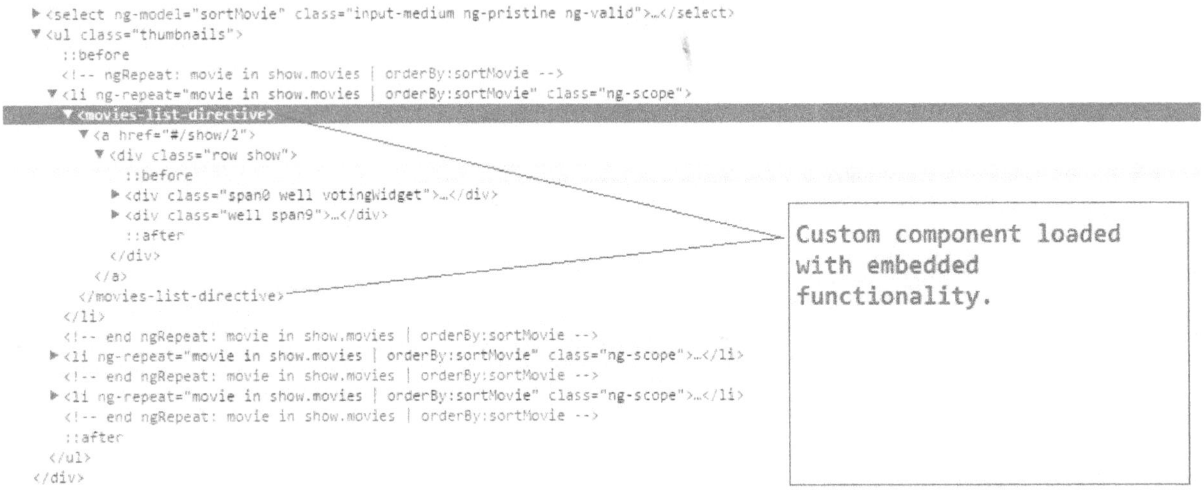

```
▶ <select ng-model="sortMovie" class="input-medium ng-pristine ng-valid">…</select>
▼ <ul class="thumbnails">
    ::before
    <!-- ngRepeat: movie in show.movies | orderBy:sortMovie -->
  ▼ <li ng-repeat="movie in show.movies | orderBy:sortMovie" class="ng-scope">
    ▼ <movies-list-directive>
      ▼ <a href="#/show/2">
        ▼ <div class="row show">
            ::before
          ▶ <div class="span0 well votingWidget">…</div>
          ▶ <div class="well span9">…</div>
            ::after
          </div>
        </a>
      </movies-list-directive>
    </li>
    <!-- end ngRepeat: movie in show.movies | orderBy:sortMovie -->
  ▶ <li ng-repeat="movie in show.movies | orderBy:sortMovie" class="ng-scope">…</li>
    <!-- end ngRepeat: movie in show.movies | orderBy:sortMovie -->
  ▶ <li ng-repeat="movie in show.movies | orderBy:sortMovie" class="ng-scope">…</li>
    <!-- end ngRepeat: movie in show.movies | orderBy:sortMovie -->
    ::after
  </ul>
</div>
```

Custom component loaded with embedded functionality.

ISOLATING DIRECTIVE SCOPE:-

In this section, we are going to discuss how to isolate the directive scope. Let us consider the below scenario.

```
<div class="custom-directive"></div>
<div class="custom-directive"></div>
<div class="custom-directive"></div>
<div class="custom-directive"></div>
<div class="custom-directive"></div>
```

Instead of one element, I just reused the same five times. Now, when I refresh the page, and look the output, it will produce the following output.

Getting Started with Angular JS

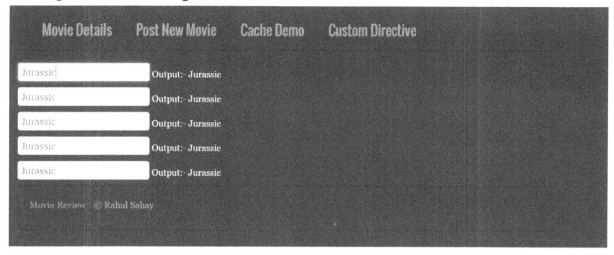

Here, I am typing in first text box, but it is getting cascaded everywhere, but this was not the intended thing. The problem here is everything is tied up with parent scope. We can fix this problem by isolating the scope as shown below in the snippet.

```
/**
 * Created by Rahul_Sahay on 7/31/2015.
 */

'use strict';

moviesApp.directive('customDirective', function () {
  //It Returns directive definition  object
  //Refer more on this here https://docs.angularjs.org/api/ng/directive
  return {
    restrict:'C',
    template:"<input type='text' ng-model='customData' /> Output:- {{customData}} <br>",
    scope:{

    }
  };
})
```

Here, in the above snippet I have just created an isolated scope with empty container. Here, I can provide additional properties on top of it. Nevertheless, in this case it is not needed. With the above change in place, when I refresh the page, then it will produce the actual intended output as shown below in the screen shot.

Getting Started with Angular JS

However, if I try the same approach with our movies list as shown below, then this will break the page.

```
/**
 * Created by Rahul_Sahay on 7/31/2015.
 */

'use strict';

moviesApp.directive('moviesListDirective',function(){
  return{
    restrict:'E',
    templateUrl:'/templates/directives/moviesList.html',
    scope:{

    }
  }
});
```

Getting Started with Angular JS

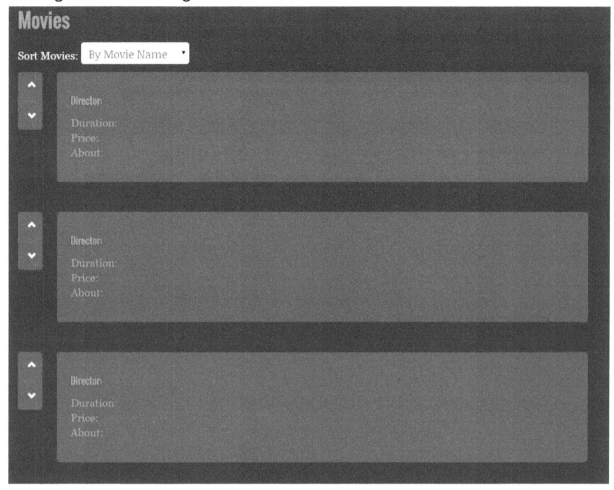

Nevertheless, when you inspect the problem, you will find that value is not getting passed here.

```
▶ <select ng-model="sortMovie" class="input-medium ng-pristine ng-valid">…</select>
▼ <ul class="thumbnails">
    ::before
    <!-- ngRepeat: movie in show.movies | orderBy:sortMovie -->
  ▼ <li ng-repeat="movie in show.movies | orderBy:sortMovie" class="ng-scope">
      ▼ <movies-list-directive class="ng-isolate-scope">
          ▼ <a href="#/show/">
              ▼ <div class="row show">
                  ::before
                ▶ <div class="span0 well votingWidget">…</div>
                ▼ <div class="well span9">
                    <h4 class="show-title ng-binding"></h4>
                    <h6 style="margin-top: -10ox;" class="ng-binding">Director: </h6>
                    <span class="ng-binding">Duration:  </span>
                    <br>
                    <span class="ng-binding">Price:  </span>
                    <p class="ng-binding">About: </p>
                  </div>
                  ::after
              </div>
          </a>
      </movies-list-directive>
  </li>
```

```
Value is not getting
passed here.
```

Getting Started with Angular JS

In order to fix the same, I need to do following changes, as shown below. First, I need to pass the movie explicitly as shown below.

```
<ul class="thumbnails">
  <li ng-repeat="movie in show.movies | orderBy:sortMovie">
    <movies-list-directive movie="movie"/>
  </li>
</ul>
```

This is because, below in my template, it expects movie to get passed in

```
<a href="#/show/{{movie.id}}">

  <div class="row show">
    <div class="span0 well votingWidget">
      <div class="votingButton" ng-click="upVotemMovie(movie)">
        <i class="icon-chevron-up icon-white"></i>
      </div>
      <div class="badge badge-inverse">
        <div>{{movie.voteCount}}</div>
      </div>
      <div class="votingButton" ng-click="downVotemMovie(movie)">
        <i class="icon-chevron-down icon-white"></i>
      </div>
    </div>
    <div class="well span9">
      <h4 class="show-title">{{movie.name}}</h4>
      <h6 style="margin-top: -10ox;">Director: {{movie.directorName}}</h6>
      <span>Duration: {{movie.duration}} </span><br/>
      <span>Price: {{movie.price | rupeesFilter }} </span>

      <p>About: {{movie.about}}</p>
    </div>
  </div>
</a>
```

Now, in the directive scope I need to pass the following.

```
/**
 * Created by Rahul_Sahay on 7/31/2015.
 */

'use strict';

moviesApp.directive('moviesListDirective',function(){
  return{
    restrict:'E',
    templateUrl:'/templates/directives/moviesList.html',
    scope:{
      movie:"="
    }
  }
});
```

Here, **movie:"="** means **movie:"=movie"**. This is just shortcut. This is valid because both the name matches. If I would be having some different name as variable, then in that case I would

Getting Started with Angular JS

have specified the complete signature. With the above change in place, when I refresh the page, then it will produce me the below output.

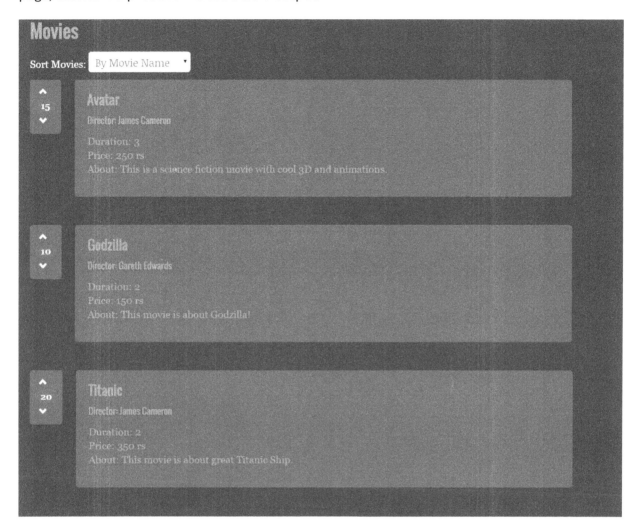

Now, if I inspect the element, then it will look like as shown below.

Getting Started with Angular JS

```
 Elements  Network  Sources  Timeline  Profiles  Resources  Audits  Console  AngularJS Graph
  ▶ <select ng-model="sortMovie" class="input-medium ng-pristine ng-valid">…</select>
  ▼ <ul class="thumbnails">
      ::before
      <!-- ngRepeat: movie in show.movies | orderBy:sortMovie -->
    ▼ <li ng-repeat="movie in show.movies | orderBy:sortMovie" class="ng-scope">
      ▼ <movies-list-directive movie="movie" class="ng-isolate-scope">
        ▼ <a href="#/show/2">
          ▼ <div class="row show">
              ::before
            ▶ <div class="span0 well votingWidget">…</div>
            ▼ <div class="well span9">
                <h4 class="show-title ng-binding">Avatar</h4>
                <h6 style="margin-top: -10ox;" class="ng-binding">Director: James Cameron</h6>
                <span class="ng-binding">Duration: 3 </span>
                <br>
                <span class="ng-binding">Price: 250 rs </span>
                <p class="ng-binding">About: This is a science fiction movie with cool 3D and animations.</p>
              </div>
              ::after
            </div>
          </a>
        </movies-list-directive>
      </li>
```

Let us suppose, that variable name would have been something like shown below.

```
<movies-list-directive mymovie="movie"/>
```

Then, in that case, my scope signature would have been,

```
/**
 * Created by Rahul_Sahay on 7/31/2015.
 */

'use strict';

moviesApp.directive('moviesListDirective',function(){
  return{
    restrict:'E',
    templateUrl:'/templates/directives/moviesList.html',
    scope:{
      movie:"=mymovie"
    }
  }
});
```

Moreover, this works fine. It entirely depends on you how do you like to keep it.

Getting Started with Angular JS

HANDLING EVENTS:-

In this section, we are going to learn how to handle events using directives. For instance, it would be good idea if we can prevent user from typing invalid value in the required field.

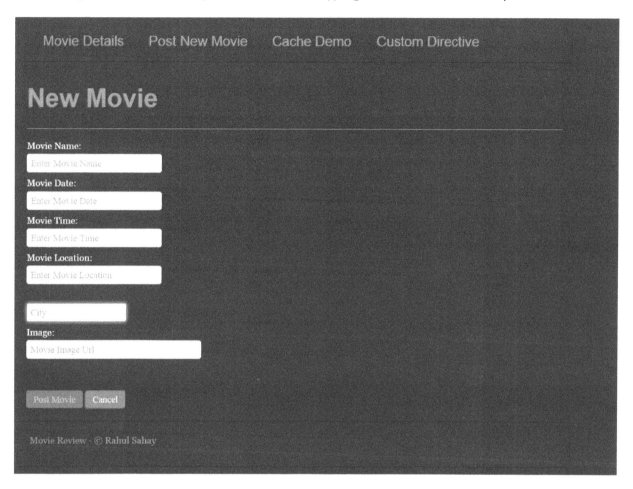

In the above shown screen shot, I would like to restrict user from typing numeric value. Below, in the snippet I have created a simple directive to restrict numeric values.

```
/**
 * Created by Rahul_Sahay on 8/1/2015.
 */

moviesApp.directive('restrictNumbersDirective',function(){
  return{
    restrict:'A',
    link:function(scope,elem){
      elem.on('keydown',function(key){
        if(isNumber(key.keyCode)){
          return false;
        }
        return true;
      })
    }
  }
}
```

Chapter 5: Creating Custom Directives

Getting Started with Angular JS

```
});

//Function to check if numbers
function isNumber(keyCode) {
    return (event.keyCode >= 48 && event.keyCode <= 57)
       || (event.keyCode >= 96 && event.keyCode <= 105);
}
```

As you can see that, very first thing I have done. I have created directive with an attribute type. Then, link method is checking for key code pressed whether it is in numeric range. If yes, then I am returning false else true. Then, I have included the same as attribute.

```
<input id="showCity" type="text" required class="input-medium" ng-model="show.showCity"
restrict-numbers-directive placeholder="City"/>
```

Last change is to include the same on index page.

```
<script src="js/directives/restrictNumbersDirective.js"></script>
```

With the above change in place, I cannot type any number in this field as shown below.

USING CONTROLLERS:-

In this section, I am going to use controller but from the directive. Below in the snippet, I have created simple directive for the same.

```
/**
 * Created by Rahul_Sahay on 8/1/2015.
 */

'use strict';
```

Getting Started with Angular JS

```
moviesApp.directive('calcTime',function(){
  return{
    restrict:'E',
    template:"<button class='btn btn-success' ng-click='returnTime()'>Current Time</button>"

  }
})
```

I have also created template for producing the same.

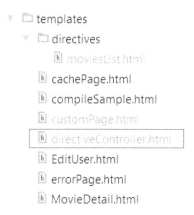

In addition, the markup for the same is fairly simple.

```
<calc-time/>
```

I have also modified the route JS to produce the same as template.

```
$routeProvider.when('/calcTime', {
  templateUrl: 'templates/directiveController.html'
});
```

Apart from this change, I have also included the directive reference on the index page and created one menu item for the same. With these changes in place, when I go ahead and refresh the page, then it will look like

Getting Started with Angular JS

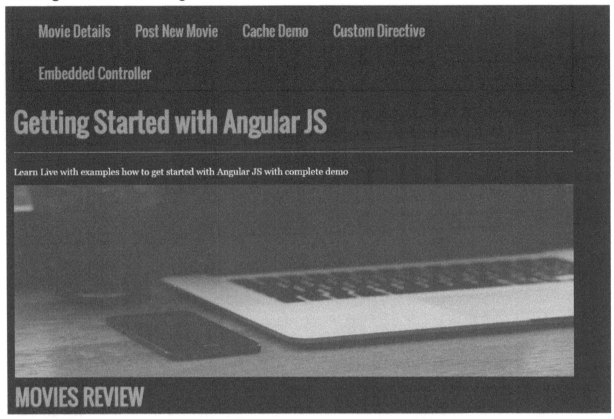

Not very impressive. Nevertheless, good enough to explain the logic here. Now, when I press the last link, it will produce the below page, **page of the millennium**, jokes apart.

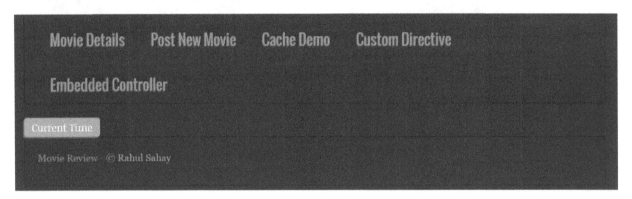

However, when I press the above shown button, currently it will not do anything. However, after adding controller logic as shown below, it will produce the expected output.

```
/**
 * Created by Rahul_Sahay on 8/1/2015.
 */

'use strict';

moviesApp.directive('calcTime',function(){
    return{
```

Chapter 5: Creating Custom Directives

Getting Started with Angular JS

```
    restrict:'E',
    template:"<button class='btn btn-success' ng-click='returnTime()'>Current Time</button>",
    controller:function($scope){
      $scope.returnTime = function () {
        var date = new Date();
        var time = date.toLocaleTimeString();
        return window.alert("Current Time:- "+time);
      }
    }
  }
})
```

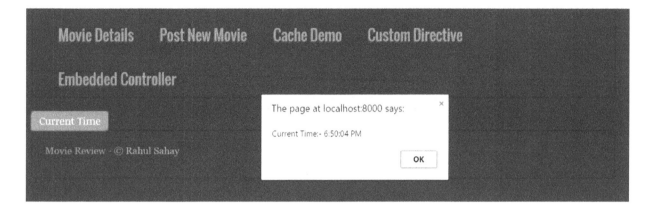

As you can see in the above snippet, in the controller section, I have created the method, which is getting returned on the ng-click event. Moreover, this event is doing nothing but returning the current system time. This way we can encapsulate controller's logic inside the directive and use accordingly.

USING REQUIRE-

In this section, we are going to discuss the when and how we should use require. There can be situation where in we are having multiple directives communicating with single controller. For this kind of scenario, we are going to need **require** property, which is nothing but an indication of dependency. In order to explain the same, I have created another directive as shown below in the snippet.

```
/**
 * Created by Rahul_Sahay on 8/1/2015.
 */

moviesApp.directive('helloAngular',function(){
  return{
    restrict:'E',
    template:"<button class='btn btn-success' ng-click='helloAngular()'>Hello
Angular</button>",
    controller:function($scope){
      var ngHello = ['Hello Angular'];
      $scope.helloAngular = function(){
```

Getting Started with Angular JS

```
        window.alert(ngHello);
        }
        this.addVersions = function (versions) {
        ngHello.push(versions);
        }
    }
  }
})

.directive('spanishVersion',function(){
    return{
        restrict:'A',
        require: 'helloAngular',
        link:function(scope,elem,attr,controller){
            controller.addVersions('hola Angular');
        }
    }
})

.directive('frenchVersion',function(){
    return{
        restrict:'A',
        require: 'helloAngular',
        link:function(scope,elem,attr,controller){
            controller.addVersions('bonjour angulaire');
        }
    }
});
```

As you can see in the above snippet, here I am using three directives and base directive **helloAngular** is using two another directives with the name **spanishVersion** and **frenchVersion.** Spanish and French version is just going to alert the message in respective language. In addition, first directive is used as element and other two directives used as attribute. Moreover, other two directives are also using require property which is just a way to indicate that this particular directive is dependent on the other directive. Then, link function is just calling the function **addVersions** with string in it. I have also done routing change what I done initially and respective menu and file reference on the index page. Below is the simple snippet for the element.

```
<hello-angular />
```

With the above change in place, when I refresh the page then it will look like as shown below.

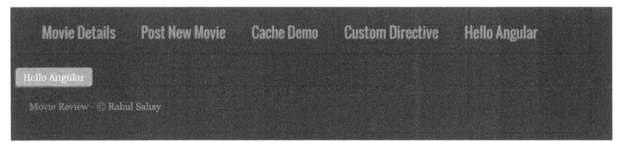

Now, when I click on Hello Angular button, then it will produce the below output.

Getting Started with Angular JS

Similarly, when I add attributes to the element,

```
<hello-angular french-version spanish-version />
```

Then, this will produce the below output.

This is how require property works.

DIRECTIVE PRIORITY:-

In this section, we are going to look at order of execution of these directives. If you notice from the below snippet,

```
<hello-angular french-version spanish-version />
```

French version should have come after English version and then the Spanish version. However, here it did not appear that way. In order to fix this, we need to specify Directive priority. Nevertheless, with the below change in place, it will print the message accordingly.

```
/**
 * Created by Rahul_Sahay on 8/1/2015.
 */

moviesApp.directive('helloAngular',function(){
  return{
    restrict:'E',
    priority:1,
    template:"<button class='btn btn-success' ng-click='helloAngular()'>Hello
Angular</button>",
    controller:function($scope){
      var ngHello = ['Hello Angular'];
      $scope.helloAngular = function(){
```

Getting Started with Angular JS

```
      window.alert(ngHello);
    }
    this.addVersions = function (versions) {
      ngHello.push(versions);
    }
  }
 }
})

.directive('spanishVersion',function(){
    return{
      restrict:'A',
      require: 'helloAngular',
      priority:2,
      link:function(scope,elem,attr,controller){
        controller.addVersions('hola Angular');
      }
    }
  })
.directive('frenchVersion',function(){
    return{
      restrict:'A',
      require: 'helloAngular',
      priority:1,
      link:function(scope,elem,attr,controller){
        controller.addVersions('bonjour angulaire');
      }
    }
  });
```

Here, I have done nothing but set the priority. With the above change in place, it will produce the below result.

NESTED DIRECTIVES:-

Consider, a situation, where in we want to use other directives as part of nested directive under the hood of parent directive.

```
<hello-angular>
  <div french-version spanish-version></div>
</hello-angular>
```

However, with above change in place, it is not producing me the expected output. Rather, it is producing me the below output.

Getting Started with Angular JS

In addition, the reason for the same is very simple. Here, the other directives are not able to traverse upwards in DOM Tree. Moreover, fix for the same is very simple. Here, I just need to add caret (**^**) symbol before directive name as shown below in the snippet and include **ng-Transclude** directive.

```
/**
 * Created by Rahul_Sahay on 8/1/2015.
 */
moviesApp.directive('helloAngular',function(){
  return{
    restrict:'E',
    priority:1,
    transclude:true,
    template:"<div><button class='btn btn-success' ng-click='helloAngular()'>Hello
Angular</button><div ng-transclude></div></div>",
    controller:function($scope){
      var ngHello = ['Hello Angular'];
      $scope.helloAngular = function(){
        window.alert(ngHello);
      }
      this.addVersions = function (versions) {
        ngHello.push(versions);
      }
    }
  }
})

.directive('spanishVersion',function(){
  return{
    restrict:'A',
    require: '^helloAngular',
    priority:2,
    link:function(scope,elem,attr,controller){
      controller.addVersions('hola Angular');
    }
  }
})

.directive('frenchVersion',function(){
  return{
    restrict:'A',
    require: '^helloAngular',
    priority:1,
    link:function(scope,elem,attr,controller){
      controller.addVersions('bonjour angulaire');
    }
```

Getting Started with Angular JS

```
    }
});
```

With the above change in place, it will output the value in the same fashion.

Here, I have also used transclusion. Transclusion typically means taking a portion of document and embedding the same in another document. You can more about transclusion @ https://docs.angularjs.org/api/ng/directive/ngTransclude.

SUMMARY:-

In this section, we have covered in and out of custom directives. We have started this chapter with simple creation rules of directive and then started delving inside it. We have also seen how to make use different properties associated with directives. We have also seen how to embed controller code inside directive itself. Then, we have covered how to handle dependencies using require property. Last but not the least we have also seen how to handle the order of execution by setting directive properties and then Nested directives.

Getting Started with Angular JS

CHAPTER 6: TESTING ANGULAR

WHAT DO you find in this CHAPTER?

- Introduction
- Installing Karma
- WebStorm Settings
- Testing Controllers
- Testing Service
- Writing AJAX Test
- Writing Filter Tests
- Writing End To End Tests
- Debugging Tips
- Yeoman
- Summary

INTRODUCTION:-

In this section, we are going to test the stuffs whatever we developed so far. Off-course for this we are going to use KARMA. Karma is one of the utilities built by google that you definitely want to take advantage. In order to learn more about Karma, you can refer this URL (http://karma-runner.github.io/0.13/index.html). Angular team uses Jasmine-Testing framework to test angular code. In this chapter, we will be testing controllers, services, filters and directives.

INSTALLING KARMA:-

In this section, we will get started with Karma Installation. Karma is a testing automation tool built by google. Karma is completely independent of angular; hence, you can use karma to test other types of JavaScript. Karma is again extremely fast, especially when you are running against chrome.

Getting Started with Angular JS

```
Terminal
+
X   C:\Rahul\My Experiments\GettingStartedWithAngularJS>npm install karma
```

One point to note here, whatever command I am typing here in the webstorm terminal you can do the same in windows command prompt. It entirely depends on you. Here, node package manager will go ahead and install karma test runner for me in this project. Then I installed two more packages, which I am going to need. They are karma chrome launcher with command "**npm install karma-chrome-launcher**" and karma jasmine with "**npm install karma-jasmine**". I have installed these modules locally.

However, I need to have few modules installed globally; karma command line interface needs to be installed globally. For this I need to issue the command as "**npm install karma-cli -g**". Now, I need to configure the karma. However, the skeleton project that you have downloaded already contains these things. Nevertheless, let me show you how to configure the same. I will type the following command "**karma init**" as shown below in the screen shot. Moreover, this will ask me series of questions. However, whatever setup process I am telling, you can understand the same in more detail on Karma website.

```
Terminal
+   Microsoft Windows [Version 6.3.9600]
X   (c) 2013 Microsoft Corporation. All rights reserved.

    C:\Rahul\My Experiments\GettingStartedWithAngularJS>karma init
```

Upon clicking, enter, it will ask another question.

```
Terminal
+   Microsoft Windows [Version 6.3.9600]
X   (c) 2013 Microsoft Corporation. All rights reserved.

    C:\Rahul\My Experiments\GettingStartedWithAngularJS>karma init

    Which testing framework do you want to use ?
    Press tab to list possible options. Enter to move to the next question.
    > jasmine
```

If you do not want to select jasmine, you can select another option by clicking tab there. However, I am good with this choice; hence will click enter here.

Getting Started with Angular JS

```
Terminal

C:\Rahul\My Experiments\GettingStartedWithAngularJS>karma init

Which testing framework do you want to use ?
Press tab to list possible options. Enter to move to the next question.
> jasmine

Do you want to use Require.js ?
This will add Require.js plugin.
Press tab to list possible options. Enter to move to the next question.
> no
```

Again, I will enter.

```
Terminal

Press tab to list possible options. Enter to move to the next question.
> jasmine

Do you want to use Require.js ?
This will add Require.js plugin.
Press tab to list possible options. Enter to move to the next question.
> no

Do you want to capture any browsers automatically ?
Press tab to list possible options. Enter empty string to move to the next quest
> Chrome
```

Then,

```
Terminal

Do you want to capture any browsers automatically ?
Press tab to list possible options. Enter empty string to move to the next quest
> Chrome
> Firefox
> ""

What is the location of your source and test files ?
You can use glob patterns, eg. "js/*.js" or "test/**/*Spec.js".
Enter empty string to move to the next question.
> **/*.js
```

Last but not the least,

Getting Started with Angular JS

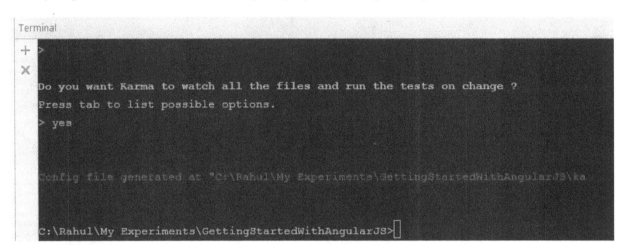

Finally, it gave the confirmation message saying that config file is generated.

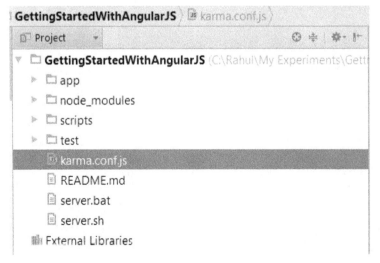

However, I will go ahead and delete this file. Instead of that, I will flip over my test folder and open the conf file here. Below, is the snippet for the same.

Getting Started with Angular JS

```javascript
module.exports = function(config){
  config.set({

    basePath : '../',

    files : [
      'app/lib/angular/angular.js',
      'app/lib/angular/angular-*.js',
      'test/lib/angular-mocks.js',
      'test/lib/sinon-1.10.2.js',
      'app/js/**/*.js',
      'test/unit/**/*.js'
    ],

    autoWatch : true,

    frameworks: ['jasmine'],

    browsers : ['Chrome'],

    plugins : [
            'karma-chrome-launcher',
            'karma-jasmine'
            ],

    junitReporter : {
      outputFile: 'test_out/unit.xml',
      suite: 'unit'
    }

  });
};
```

basepath, is the path which is relative to configs files is the root for all the other parts inside the file. Next, we have collection of files that is nothing but array of strings. This is very important to mention the files in correct order. Next setting, **autoWatch**, tells the karma, we want to watch the files that are getting changed and rerun the test on the same. Next is testing framework which is nothing but jasmine here, then we have supported browser chrome. After that, we have plugins for supporting chrome and then some output file settings.

Now, let me go ahead and show how to launch Karma test runner. Moreover, I will show the same from windows command prompt rather than webstorm terminal. Below in the screen shot I have typed **karma start** location of karma conf file.

Administrator: Command Prompt

```
C:\>cd C:\Rahul\My Experiments\GettingStartedWithAngularJS

C:\Rahul\My Experiments\GettingStartedWithAngularJS>karma start test/karma.conf.js
```

Getting Started with Angular JS

This launched the browser and also gave output in the cmd prompt.

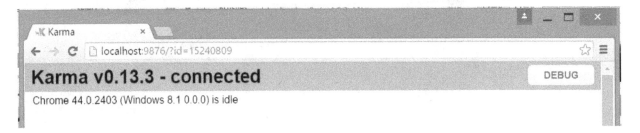

Since, I am not running any tests now, hence the window is blank now.

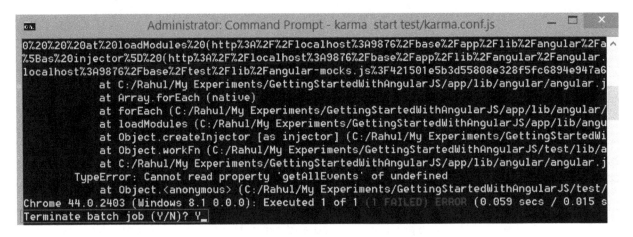

In order to stop the same, we need to type CTRL + C in terminal window or command window.

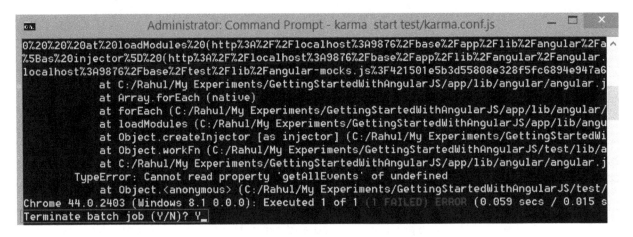

Typing Y will take you out of test runner.

WEBSTORM SETTINGS:-

In this section, we are going to set test settings for Karma in web storm. This is very easy and useful as well.

Getting Started with Angular JS

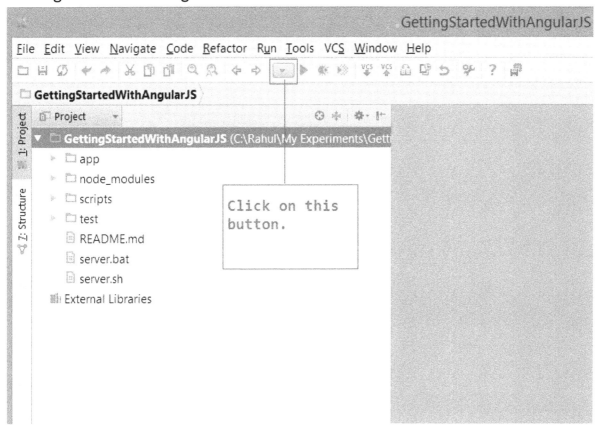

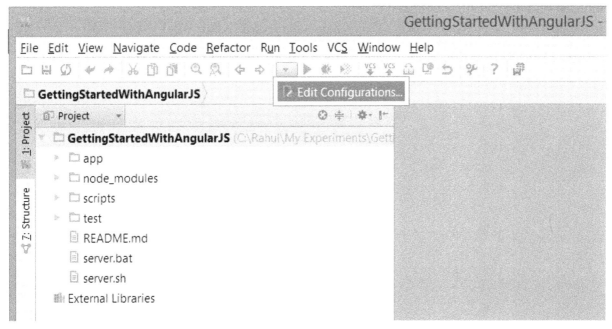

Then, click on Edit Configurations. This will open new suite as shown below.

Getting Started with Angular JS

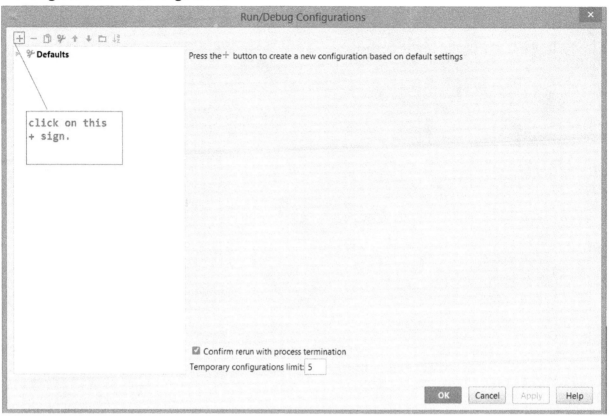

Then. Select Karma from the option shown.

Getting Started with Angular JS

This will open below settings window.

Getting Started with Angular JS

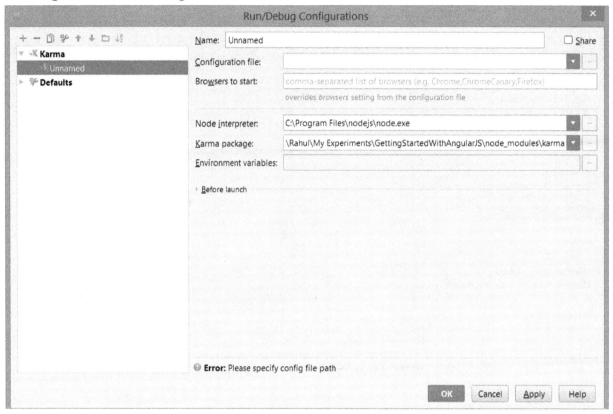

Then, give the proper name whatever you like and point to the karma configuration file section.

Getting Started with Angular JS

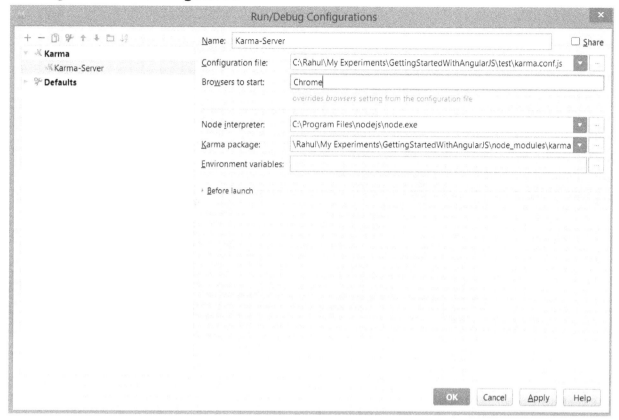

Now, click apply and then ok. With this parent editor window will get enabled as shown below in the screen shot.

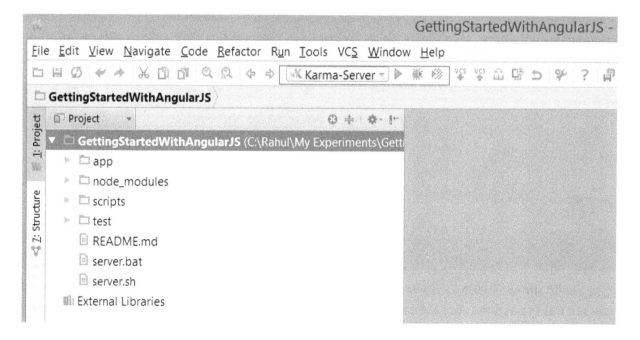

Getting Started with Angular JS

TESTING CONTROLLERS:-

In this section, I am going to first test controller. Now, let us look at the movies controller code.

```
/**
 * Created by Rahul_Sahay on 7/5/2015.
 */

'use strict';

moviesApp.controller('MovieController', function MovieController($scope, movieDataService) {

    $scope.sortMovie = 'name';

    $scope.show=movieDataService.getshows();

    $scope.upVotemMovie = function (movie) {
        movie.voteCount++;
    };
    $scope.downVotemMovie = function (movie) {
        movie.voteCount--;
    };
});
```

First thing this controller does is sets up the show object by calling method in service **getshows()**. Hence, this could be the first thing, which we can test. Let us go ahead and write the test for the same. Below, in the snippet, I have created empty jasmine file structure.

```
'use strict';

describe('MovieController', function() {

})
```

One point to note here, if you have never written any jasmine test first, please refer to jasmine tutorial first on its website http://jasmine.github.io/2.2/introduction.html.

```
'use strict';

describe('MovieController', function() {

    //Setting the rule here
    it('should set the scope.show', function () {
        //fake movies object
        var mockMovies={};

        //setting expectation here
        expect(scope.show).toBe(mockMovies);
    })
})
```

Here, in the above snippet, I have just declared mock value, which needs to be returned and then set the expectation for the same. With the above change in place, when I go ahead and run the same by clicking the below highlighted button.

Getting Started with Angular JS

It will produce the following error.

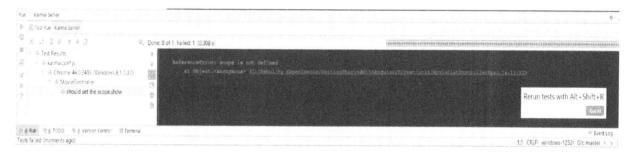

It is saying scope is not defined, which is correct. A shortcut for rerunning the tests is **ALT+ Shift + R**. Hence, let us go ahead and create the scope variable. Below is the modified snippet with other corresponding changes.

```
'use strict';

describe('MovieController', function() {
  var scope,$controllerConstructor;

  //Inject the controller dependency here
  beforeEach(inject(function($controller,){

    $controllerConstructor=$controller;

}));
  //Setting the rule here
  it('should set the scope.show', function () {
    //fake movies object
    var mockMovies={};

    var ctrl = $controllerConstructor("MovieController",{$scope:{},movieDataService:{}});
    //setting expectation here
    expect(scope.show).toBe(mockMovies);
  })
})
```

Chapter 6: Testing Angular

Getting Started with Angular JS

Here, after defining the scope variable created, I have also created the controller constructor for injecting the controller. Then, I have used controller constructor to create the movie controller object for me with dependencies as second parameter. Now, when I run the test, it will again fail.

```
Done: 0 of 1  Failed: 1  (0.233 s)

    Error: [ng:areq] Argument 'MovieController' is not a function, got undefined
    http://errors.angularjs.org/1.2.10/ng/areq?p0=MovieController&p1=not%20a%20function%2C%20got%20undefined
        at C:/Rahul/My Experiments/GettingStartedWithAngularJS/app/lib/angular/angular.js:78:12
        at assertArg (C:/Rahul/My Experiments/GettingStartedWithAngularJS/app/lib/angular/angular.js:1363:11)
        at assertArgFn (C:/Rahul/My Experiments/GettingStartedWithAngularJS/app/lib/angular/angular.js:1373:3)
        at C:/Rahul/My Experiments/GettingStartedWithAngularJS/app/lib/angular/angular.js:6767:9
        at Object.<anonymous> (C:/Rahul/My Experiments/GettingStartedWithAngularJS/test/unit/MovieListControllerSpec.js:18:16)
```

However, one point to note that I forgot to set the scope object. Here, I need to ask angular to give me scope object. Hence, I will go in the **beforeEach** function and use second parameter as $rootScope. Hence, with **$rootScope,** I can create scope object out of that.

```javascript
'use strict';

describe('MovieController', function() {
  var scope,$controllerConstructor;

  //Inject the controller dependency here
  beforeEach(inject(function($controller,$rootScope){
    scope=$rootScope.$new();

    $controllerConstructor=$controller;

  }));
  //Setting the rule here
  it('should set the scope.show', function () {
    //fake movies object
    var mockMovies={};

    var ctrl = $controllerConstructor("MovieController",{$scope:scope,movieDataService:{}});
    //setting expectation here
    expect(scope.show).toBe(mockMovies);
  })
})
```

With the above change in place, it is again producing the same error. Reason, for this is my module has not defined yet. In order to define the module, I need to make use one more before each function that will load the module as shown below.

```javascript
'use strict';

describe('MovieController', function() {
  var scope,$controllerConstructor;
```

Getting Started with Angular JS

```javascript
    //Inject the module
    beforeEach(module("moviesApp"));
    //Inject the controller dependency here
    beforeEach(inject(function($controller,$rootScope){
        scope=$rootScope.$new();

        $controllerConstructor=$controller;

    }));
    //Setting the rule here
    it('should set the scope.show', function () {
        //fake movies object
        var mockMovies={};

        var ctrl = $controllerConstructor("MovieController",{$scope:scope,movieDataService:{}});
        //setting expectation here
        expect(scope.show).toBe(mockMovies);
    })
})
```

Now, I will get different error.

```
TypeError: movieDataService.getshows is not a function
    at new MovieController (C:/Rahul/My Experiments/GettingStartedWithAngularJS/app/js/controllers/MovieController.js:11:32)
    at invoke (C:/Rahul/My Experiments/GettingStartedWithAngularJS/app/lib/angular/angular.js:3708:17)
    at Object.instantiate (C:/Rahul/My Experiments/GettingStartedWithAngularJS/app/lib/angular/angular.js:3719:23)
    at C:/Rahul/My Experiments/GettingStartedWithAngularJS/app/lib/angular/angular.js:6770:28
    at Object.<anonymous> (C:/Rahul/My Experiments/GettingStartedWithAngularJS/test/unit/MovieListControllerSpec.js:20:16)
```

It started giving service error. And, the reason for the same is **movieDataService**, which we are passing is just an empty object and there is no getshows function on it. Hence, in order to fix the same, we need to mock it.

```javascript
'use strict';

describe('MovieController', function() {
  var scope,$controllerConstructor,mockMoviesData;

    //Inject the module
    beforeEach(module("moviesApp"));
    //Inject the controller dependency here
    beforeEach(inject(function($controller,$rootScope){
        scope=$rootScope.$new();
        mockMoviesData=sinon.stub({getshows:function(){}});
        $controllerConstructor=$controller;

    }));
    //Setting the rule here
    it('should set the scope.show', function () {
        //fake movies object
        var mockMovies={};

        var ctrl =
$controllerConstructor("MovieController",{$scope:scope,movieDataService:mockMoviesData});
        //setting expectation here
        expect(scope.show).toBe(mockMovies);
```

Getting Started with Angular JS

```
    })
})
```

In the above snippet, I have mocked the required dependency and passed the same in controller constructor. With the above change in place, when I run the same, it will again produce me error.

```
Expected undefined to be Object({  }).
    at Object.<anonymous> (C:/Rahul/My Experiments/GettingStartedWithAngularJS/test/unit/MovieListControllerSpec.js:22:24)
```

In addition, the reason for this is it is returning undefined object and I want this to return mock object, which I have created.

```javascript
'use strict';

describe('MovieController', function() {
  var scope,$controllerConstructor,mockMoviesData;

  //Inject the module
  beforeEach(module("moviesApp"));
  //Inject the controller dependency here
  beforeEach(inject(function($controller,$rootScope){
    scope=$rootScope.$new();
    mockMoviesData=sinon.stub({getshows:function(){}});
    $controllerConstructor=$controller;

  }));
  //Setting the rule here
  it('should set the scope.show', function () {
    //fake movies object
    var mockMovies={};

    mockMoviesData.getshows.returns(mockMovies);
    var ctrl =
$controllerConstructor("MovieController",{$scope:scope,movieDataService:mockMoviesData});
    //setting expectation here
    expect(scope.show).toBe(mockMovies);
  })
})
```

With the above-required change in place, it will pass the test as shown below.

Getting Started with Angular JS

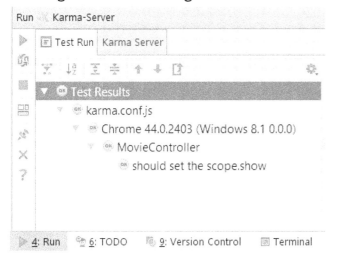

TESTING SERVICE:-

In this section, I am going to test Cache Factory Service. This is fairly simple test. Here, I have tested two methods of cache factory; one is for put and another one is for remove. Below is the snippet for the same.

```
/**
 * Created by Rahul_Sahay on 8/2/2015.
 */

'use strict';

describe('cacheFactoryServiceTest', function () {

  beforeEach(module('moviesApp'));

  it('Should put value in cache factory', inject(function (cacheFactory) {
    expect(cacheFactory.put('1', 'Jurassic World')).toBe('Jurassic World');
  }));

  it('Should remove value from cache factory', inject(function (cacheFactory) {
    expect(cacheFactory.remove('1'));
  }));
});
```

With the above change in place, it will produce me the below output.

Getting Started with Angular JS

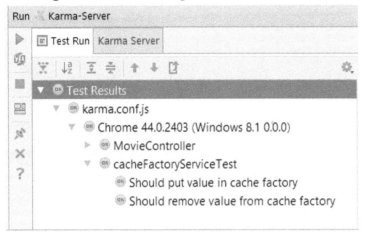

WRITING AJAX TEST:-

In this section, we are going to write test for AJAX call. If you remember from **movieDataService**, here, I have used **$resource** to make the HTTP call. **$resource** is a wrapper around HTTP object and gives easy access to restful services.

```
/**
 * Created by Rahul_Sahay on 8/3/2015.
 */

'use strict';

describe('Making AJAX call',function(){

  beforeEach(module('moviesApp'));

  describe('get call',function(){

    it('should return a GET request for /data/shows/1stMovie
',inject(function(movieDataService,$httpBackend){
      $httpBackend.when('GET','/data/shows/1stMovie').respond({name:'Jurassic World'});

      var movie = movieDataService.getshows();

      $httpBackend.flush();

      expect(movie.name).toBe('Jurassic World');

    }))

  });
});
```

Let me explain the code a bit. Here, in the snippet, I am testing Get call. Again, this is having dependency on my module. Hence, in before each function, I have injected that module here. Also, in the inject function, I have added the service as dependency as first parameter and

Getting Started with Angular JS

second parameter **$httpBackend**, for mocking AJAX call. This is the special service which angular mocks library provide which mocks the **XHR** object.

Hence, this object will intercept any call to **XHR** object and let me inspect this call and determine that my mock response based on the call returned correctly. Therefore, by calling **When**, function; I respond with my mock data. First parameter, **When** takes is the **GET** verb and second parameter is the **URL**.

Then, I made the service call in the next line. Last but not the least; I need to simulate the **async** nature of **XHR** request, I can do the same by calling flush method on the **$httpBackend** object. Hence, at this point it will respond to that request. In the end, I can set the expectation. With the above changes in place, when I go ahead and run the test, then it will pass and produce the below result.

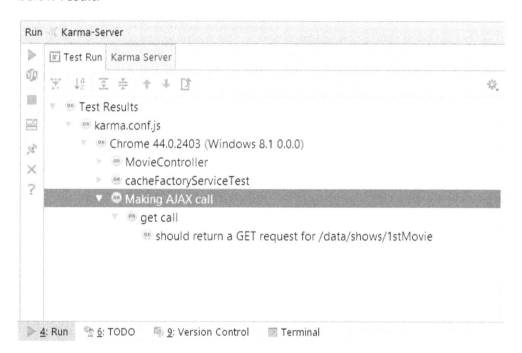

Apart from this, if you want to debug the test from karma server, then that is also very easy.

Getting Started with Angular JS

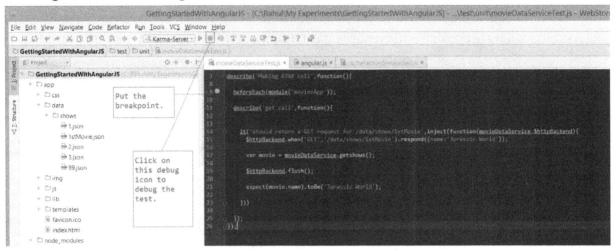

This will launch the debugger window as shown below

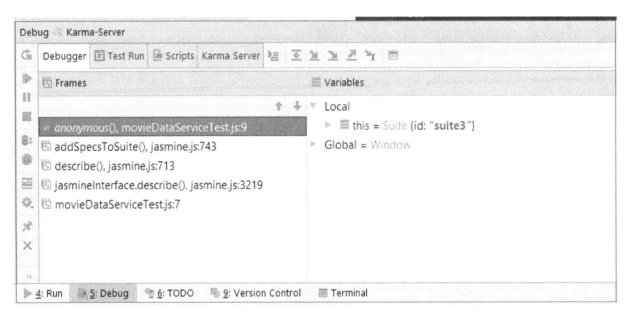

Moreover, from here you can step through, watch the variables, and inspect them as well.

Getting Started with Angular JS

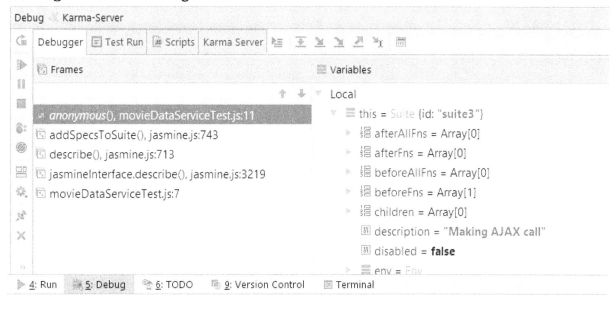

In this section, we are going to test filters. Filters are very easy and straightforward to test. In this case, we are going to test rupees filter. Rupees filter takes different input values and return output accordingly as shown below in the snippet.

```
'use strict';

moviesApp.filter('rupeesFilter',function(){
    return function(rupees){
        switch (rupees){
            case 150:
                return "150 rs";
            case 250:
                return "250 rs";
            case 350:
                return "350 rs";
        }
    }
});
```

Below, I have pasted the snippet in finished form.

```
/**
 * Created by Rahul_Sahay on 8/5/2015.
 */

'use strict';

describe('Rupees Filter Tests',function(){

    beforeEach(module('moviesApp'));

    // Filter name should be suffixed, when ever writing test for filters
    it('Should return 150 rs when 150 passed',inject(function(rupeesFilterFilter){
```

Chapter 6: Testing Angular

Getting Started with Angular JS

```
    expect(rupeesFilterFilter(150)).toEqual('150 rs');
  }));

  it('Should return 250 rs when 250 passed',inject(function(rupeesFilterFilter){
    expect(rupeesFilterFilter(250)).toEqual('250 rs');
  }));

  it('Should return 350 rs when 350 passed',inject(function(rupeesFilterFilter){
    expect(rupeesFilterFilter(350)).toEqual('350 rs');
  }));
});
```

Let me explain the code a bit. Here, only one thing needs to be kept in mind that whenever, you are writing filter test, test has to be suffixed with **Filter**. Hence, my filter name here is **rupeesFilterFilter**. With the above change in place, when I run the test, it will produce the below result.

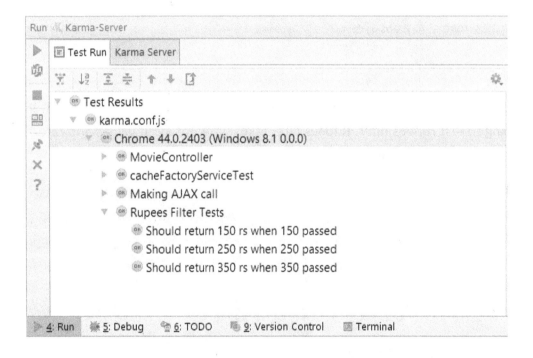

WRITING END-TO-END TESTS:-

In this section, I am going to write end-to-end test for my home page. End-To-End testing is one of the coolest things about angular testing. Hence, just like unit testing, End-To-End testing starts with karma. Then, Karma launches the browser. Only, difference here is karma is not going to load entire app code, rather it will just use scenarios mentioned to get tested. Since, we are going to depend ng-scenarios, hence I need to install the same as shown below in the screen shot.

Getting Started with Angular JS

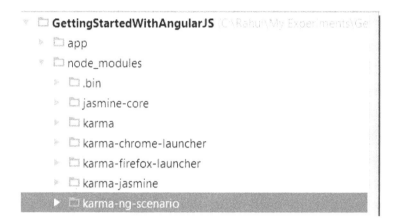

```
Microsoft Windows [Version 6.3.9600]
(c) 2013 Microsoft Corporation. All rights reserved.

C:\WINDOWS\system32>cd\

C:\>cd rahul\my experiments\gettingstartedwithangularjs

C:\Rahul\My Experiments\GettingStartedWithAngularJS>npm install karma-ng-scenario --save-dev_
```

Once, it installed successfully, it will reflect in **node_modules** folder as shown below

- **GettingStartedWithAngularJS** C:\Rahul\My Experiments\Ge
  - app
  - node_modules
    - .bin
    - jasmine-core
    - karma
    - karma-chrome-launcher
    - karma-firefox-launcher
    - karma-jasmine
    - ► karma-ng-scenario

In addition, I have configured different configs file for E2E test, as I need to kick these things manually. Below, is the config file for the same.

```
module.exports = function(config){
  config.set({

    basePath : '../',

    files : [
      'test/e2e/**/*.js'
    ],

    autoWatch : false,

    browsers : ['Chrome'],

    frameworks: ['ng-scenario'],

    singleRun : true,

    proxies : {
      '/': 'http://localhost:8000/'
    },

    plugins : [
      'karma-junit-reporter',
      'karma-chrome-launcher',
      'karma-firefox-launcher',
      'karma-jasmine',
      'karma-ng-scenario'
```

Chapter 6: Testing Angular

Getting Started with Angular JS

```
    ],

    junitReporter : {
      outputFile: 'test_out/e2e.xml',
      suite: 'e2e'
    },


  })}
```

Moreover, I have written one bat file and placed the same in scripts folder. This does nothing but launch the karma with E2E config file. Hence, the first thing is launch the server using server.bat as shown below in the screen shot.

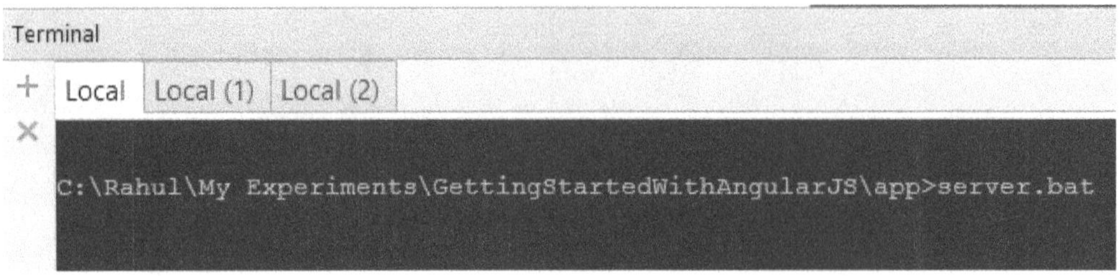

Terminal

```
+   Local   Local (1)   Local (2)
×

    C:\Rahul\My Experiments\GettingStartedWithAngularJS\app>server.bat
```

Once, the same get started successfully, and then we need to run the test either from terminal window or from the command prompt as shown below.

```
Administrator: Command Prompt

C:\Rahul\My Experiments\GettingStartedWithAngularJS\scripts>e2e-test.bat
```

Once, you run the same, then it will produce the below shown result.

```
Administrator: Command Prompt

C:\Rahul\My Experiments\GettingStartedWithAngularJS\scripts>e2e-test.bat
21 08 2015 23:48:35.040:WARN [config]: "/" is proxied, you should probably change urlRoot to avoid conflicts
21 08 2015 23:48:35.111:INFO [karma]: Karma v0.13.3 server started at http://localhost:9876/
21 08 2015 23:48:35.117:INFO [launcher]: Starting browser Chrome
21 08 2015 23:48:37.947:INFO [Chrome 44.0.2403 (Windows 8.1 0.0.0)]: Connected on socket E8KN17vMqb9wmIn6AAAA with id 14638091
Chrome 44.0.2403 (Windows 8.1 0.0.0): Executed 0 of 0 ERROR (0.021 secs / 0 secs)

C:\Rahul\My Experiments\GettingStartedWithAngularJS\scripts>_
```

It says, it executed **0 of 0,** as I have not written any test file. Now, let me go ahead, write some tests, and execute the same. If you see the below screen shot, here we can test couple of things

Getting Started with Angular JS

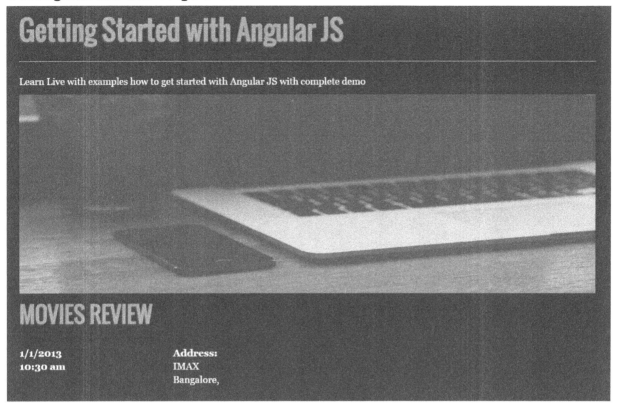

Like heading of the page, then sub heading, paragraph and many other things. Let us go ahead and start with simplest test as shown below in the snippet.

```
/**
 * Created by Rahul_Sahay on 8/21/2015.
 */

describe('Movie Review App',function(){

  describe('movies',function() {

    beforeEach(function () {
      browser().navigateTo('/MovieDetails')
    });

    it('Should Display Home Page',function(){
      expect(element('h1:first').text()).toContain('Getting Started');
    });
  });
})
```

Here, in the above snippet, it tries to match the sub string "**Getting Started**" in first **h1** tag. In addition, one point to notice here, since we are doing HTML test, hence it has dependency on page rendering and that to home page. This is where **browser** method comes into picture. With the above change in place, when I go ahead and run the page, it will display the following message.

Getting Started with Angular JS

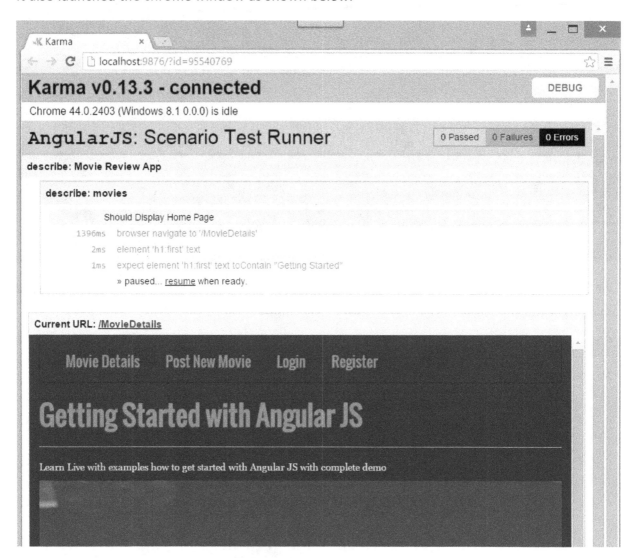

It also launched the chrome window as shown below.

Here, I have used the **pause** keyword, so that I can show the IFRAME, window at least which is launching while running the test. Similarly, we can write some other tests like shown below.

```
/*
 * Created by Rahul_Sahay on 8/21/2015.
 */

describe('Movie Review App',function(){
```

Getting Started with Angular JS

```javascript
describe('movies',function() {

  beforeEach(function () {
    browser().navigateTo('/MovieDetails')
  });

  it('Should Display Home Page',function(){
    expect(element('h1:first').text()).toContain('Getting Started');
  });

  it('Should Display Paragraph',function(){
    expect(element('p:first').text()).toContain('Learn Live with examples');
  });
});
})
```

With the above change in place, it will produce the below output.

Therefore, this was just the glimpse different kinds of test, you can write with angular. You can go ahead and write as much test you, even for click handlers and many other stuffs. You can explore more about writing Unit Test or End-To-End test on jasmine website.

DEBUGGING TIPS:-

In this section, I am going to provide few tips for debugging any angular app. Many a time, we land up in a situation, wherein we need to debug or troubleshoot the production code where you do not have the flexibility of your favorite editor. In these cases, I rely on chrome extensions. First extension, which I am going to talk about, is the **ng inspector** as shown below in the screen shot.

ng-inspector for AngularJS   0.5.10   ✔ Enabled

Inspector pane for AngularJS apps

Details

ID: aadgmnobpdmgmigaicncghmmoeflnamj

Inspect views: background page (Inactive)

☐ Allow in incognito   ☐ Allow access to file URLs

Getting Started with Angular JS

As soon as this extension gets installed, then it will create one **A** symbol on the URL bar as shown below.

moviereview.rahulsahay.com/#/

Then, once you launch any angular app as if http://moviereview.rahulsahay.com/ and then you click on **A** link, then it will popup one complete list with angular scopes and values for a particular page like shown below.

Getting Started with Angular JS

Getting Started with Angular JS

I have already explained the same in detail on my blog @ http://myview.rahulnivi.net/angular-tidbits/. You can refer the same for more details.

YEOMAN:-

In this section, we are going to look around one shortcut technique to create controllers, views, services and many other stuffs with scaffolding template provided by yeoman. You can learn more about Yeoman at http://yeoman.io/. Let us create one new app, just to give glimpse for the same.

Chapter 6: Testing Angular

Getting Started with Angular JS

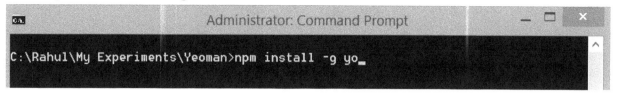

```
C:\Rahul\My Experiments\Yeoman>npm install -g yo_
```

After installing yeoman, you can then install generators. These generators will help create project templates for you. Many generators have generators embedded in it. However, let us go ahead and install the yeoman first. Since, I have already installed node. Hence, I am skipping this step. Therefore, first step is installing node, then yeoman. As, you can see that I am installing the same from command line and installing yeoman as a global so that we can use the same from command line.

```
— titleize@1.0.0
— array-uniq@1.0.2
— figures@1.3.5
— user-home@1.1.1
— opn@1.0.2
— humanize-string@1.0.1 (decamelize@1.0.0)
— sort-on@1.2.2 (arrify@1.0.0, dot-prop@2.2.0)
— async@1.4.0
— yeoman-character@1.0.1 (supports-color@1.3.1)
— findup@0.1.5 (commander@2.1.0, colors@0.6.2)
— repeating@1.1.3 (is-finite@1.0.1)
— meow@3.3.0 (object-assign@3.0.0, minimist@1.1.3, indent-string@1.2.2, camelc
— chalk@1.1.0 (escape-string-regexp@1.0.3, supports-color@2.0.0, ansi-styles@2
— string-length@1.0.1 (strip-ansi@3.0.0)
— root-check@1.0.0 (sudo-block@1.2.0, downgrade-root@1.1.0)
— update-notifier@0.5.0 (is-npm@1.0.0, latest-version@1.0.1, semver-diff@2.0.0
— configstore@1.2.1 (os-tmpdir@1.0.1, object-assign@3.0.0, graceful-fs@4.1.2,
— yosay@1.0.5 (ansi-regex@1.1.1, ansi-styles@2.1.0, word-wrap@1.1.0, strip-ans
— package-json@1.2.0 (registry-url@3.0.3)
— npm-keyword@1.2.0 (registry-url@3.0.3)
— got@3.3.1 (lowercase-keys@1.0.0, timed-out@2.0.0, is-stream@1.0.1, is-redire
d-all-stream@3.0.1)
— fullname@1.1.0 (npmconf@2.1.2)
— cross-spawn@0.4.1 (lru-cache@2.6.5, spawn-sync@1.0.13)
— yeoman-environment@1.2.7 (log-symbols@1.0.2, escape-string-regexp@1.0.3, dif
— insight@0.6.0 (object-assign@2.1.1, async@0.9.2, lodash.debounce@3.1.1, os-n
— lodash@3.10.1
— yeoman-doctor@1.4.0 (object-values@1.0.0, log-symbols@1.0.2, semver@4.3.6, e
— inquirer@0.8.5 (ansi-regex@1.1.1, cli-width@1.0.1, through@2.3.8, readline2@
```

Then, you need to install bower with the below shown command.

Getting Started with Angular JS

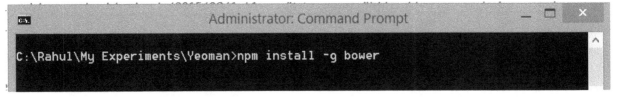

After that, Grunt needs to be installed.

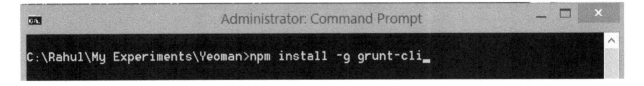

Now, the next thing is installing angular as shown below.

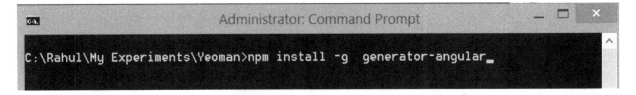

At this stage, installation is completed. Now, I can launch yeoman as shown below.

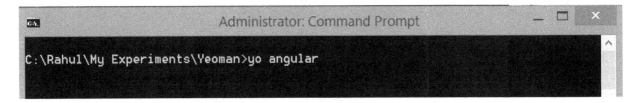

Upon, successful launch it will show the below confirmation message and will start a questionnaire session, for other required components.

Getting Started with Angular JS

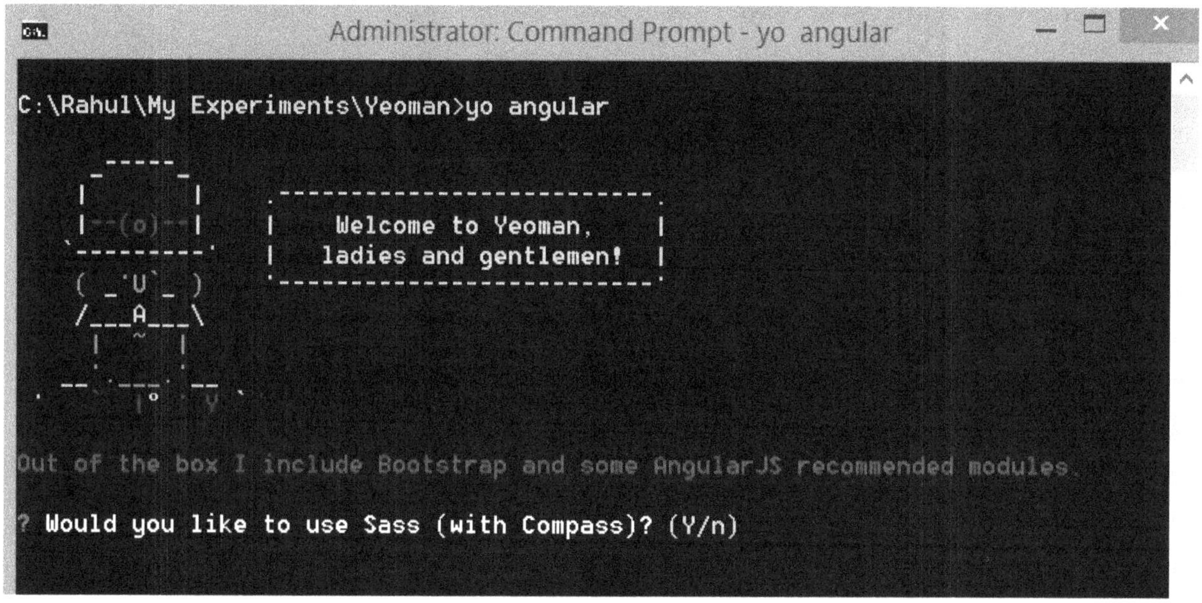

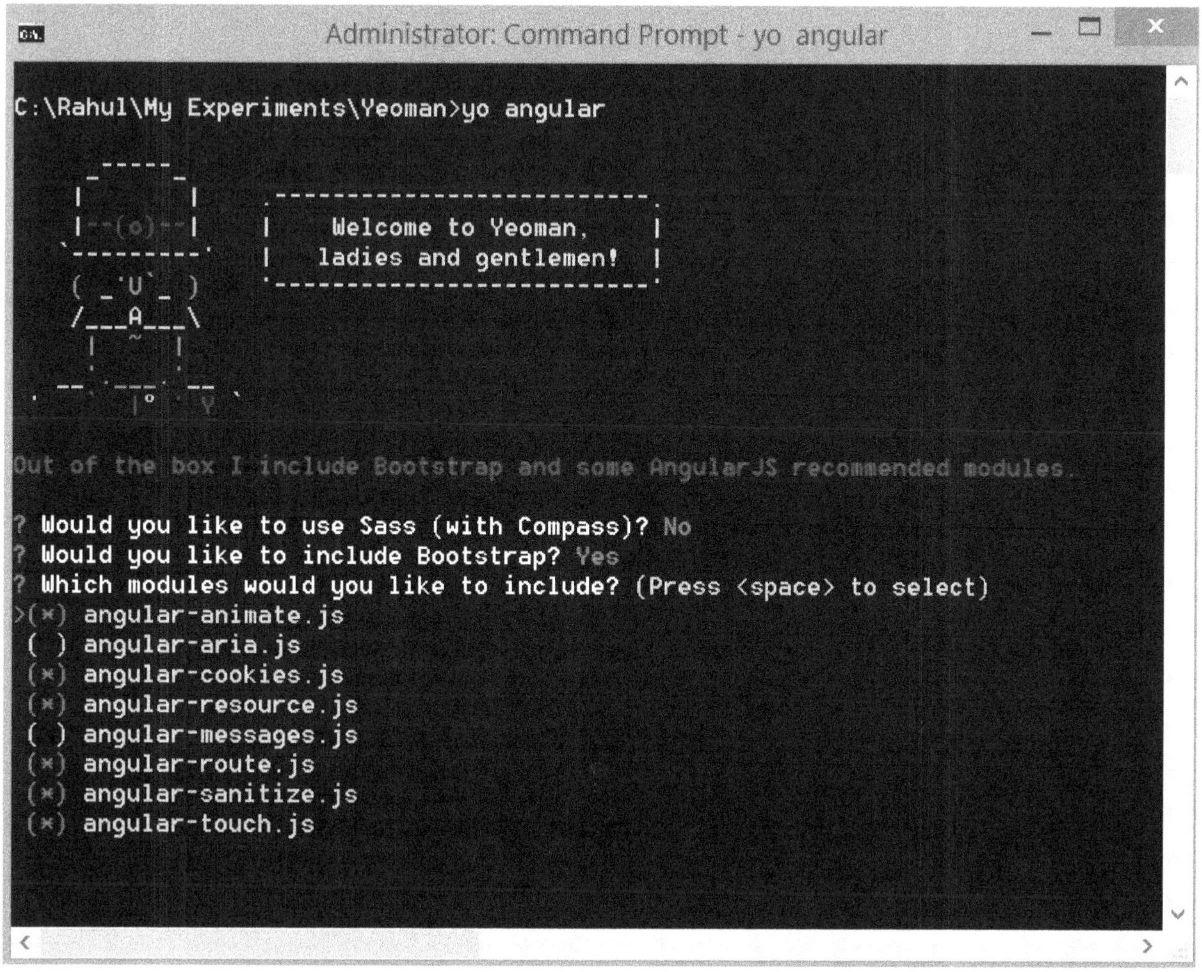

I said ok means I am ok with default selection and hit enter. Then, it started installing all the required stuffs as shown below.

Chapter 6: Testing Angular

Getting Started with Angular JS

Upon successful installation, it will show below message.

Getting Started with Angular JS

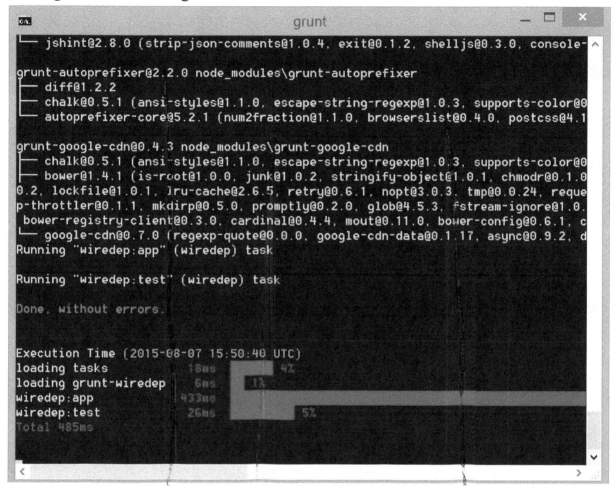

At this stage, everything is installed. Hence, I can launch the template with grunt command as shown below.

Getting Started with Angular JS

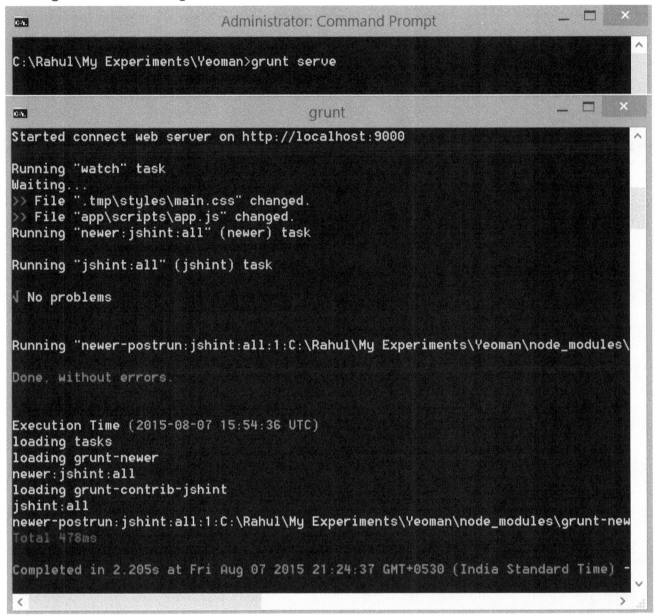

After doing initial check, it will launch the same in browser as shown below.

Getting Started with Angular JS

yeoman   Home   About   Contact

'Allo, 'Allo!

YEOMAN

Always a pleasure scaffolding your apps.

HTML5 Boilerplate

HTML5 Boilerplate is a professional front-end template for building fast, robust, and adaptable web apps or sites

Angular

AngularJS is a toolset for building the framework most suited to your application development

Now, let us open the project created in webstorm. It will display the below project structure.

Getting Started with Angular JS

Getting Started with Angular JS

```
▹ 🗀 .tmp
▶ 🗀 app
▹ 🗀 bower_components
▽ 🗀 node_modules (library home)
    ▹ 🗀 grunt
    ▹ 🗀 grunt-angular-templates
    ▹ 🗀 grunt-autoprefixer
    ▹ 🗀 grunt-concurrent
    ▹ 🗀 grunt-contrib-clean
    ▹ 🗀 grunt-contrib-concat
    ▹ 🗀 grunt-contrib-connect
    ▹ 🗀 grunt-contrib-copy
    ▹ 🗀 grunt-contrib-cssmin
    ▹ 🗀 grunt-contrib-htmlmin
    ▹ 🗀 grunt-contrib-imagemin
    ▹ 🗀 grunt-contrib-jshint
    ▹ 🗀 grunt-contrib-uglify
    ▹ 🗀 grunt-contrib-watch
    ▹ 🗀 grunt-filerev
    ▹ 🗀 grunt-google-cdn
    ▹ 🗀 grunt-newer
    ▹ 🗀 grunt-ng-annotate
    ▹ 🗀 grunt-svgmin
    ▹ 🗀 grunt-usemin
    ▹ 🗀 grunt-wiredep
    ▹ 🗀 jit-grunt
    ▹ 🗀 jshint-stylish
    ▹ 🗀 time-grunt
▹ 🗀 test
  🗎 .bowerrc
  🗎 .editorconfig
  🗎 .gitattributes
```

Getting Started with Angular JS

As you can see in the above screen shot, everything is organized pretty well. Therefore, this is the benefit of using scaffolding template. It will give you all the boilerplate code to get started. Hence, let us suppose you want to create movies view template, then you need to use the below shown command.

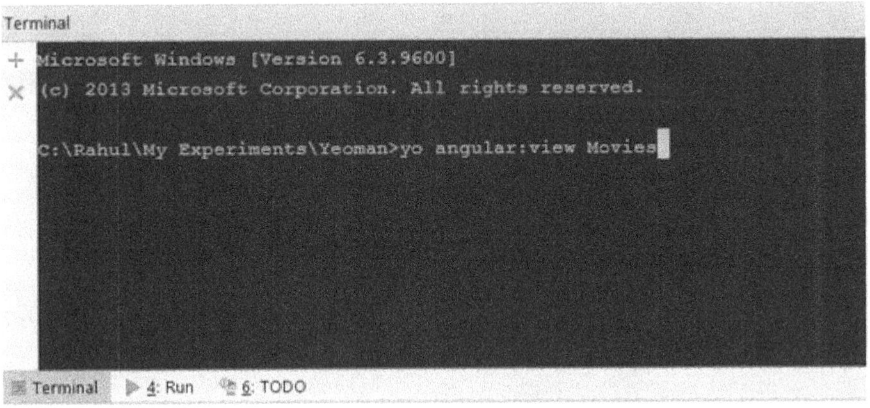

Upon successful creation of template, it will give the below confirmation message.

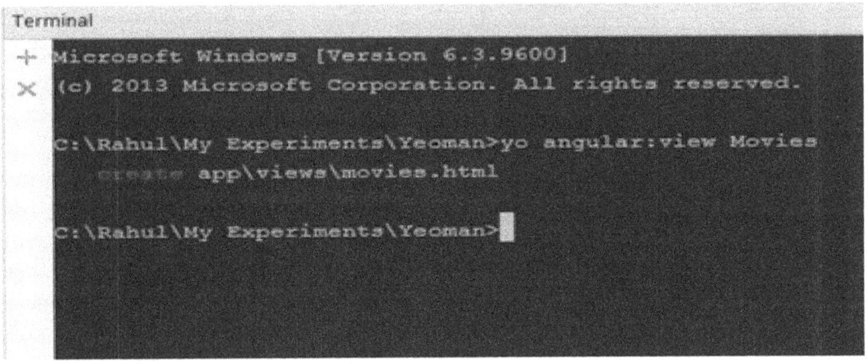

You can also verify the same in folder structure as shown below in screenshot.

Getting Started with Angular JS

- ▼ 🗀 **Yeoman** (C:\Rahul\My Experiments\Yeoman)
  - ▶ 🗀 .tmp
  - ▼ 🗀 app
    - ▶ 🗀 images
    - ▶ 🗀 scripts
    - ▶ 🗀 styles
    - ▼ 🗀 views
      - 📄 about.html
      - 📄 main.html
      - 📄 movies.html
    - 📄 .buildignore
    - 📄 .htaccess
    - 📄 404.html
    - 📄 favicon.ico
    - 📄 index.html
    - 📄 robots.txt

Now, if you open the template, it will be like plain simple template. Then, you need to define the route for the same and other required stuffs that we have already learnt in previous chapters.

However, I have done little improvisation to this template, just to make it look bit lucrative. Below are the sample snapshots for the same.

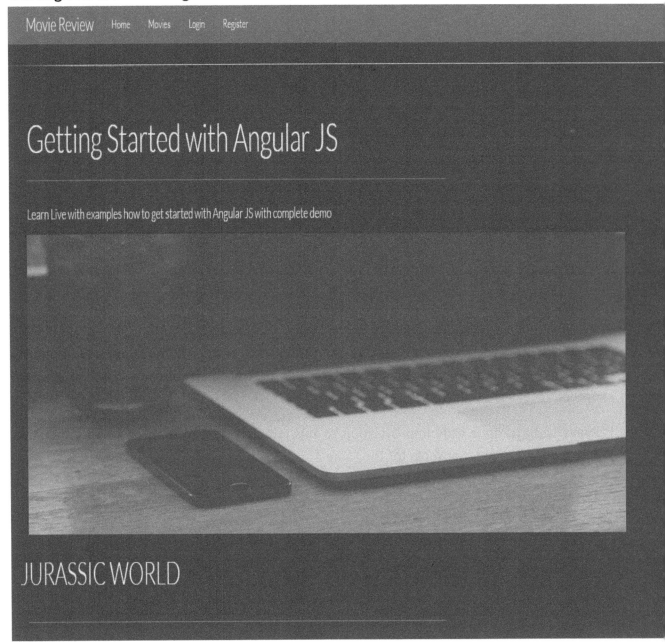

Getting Started with Angular JS

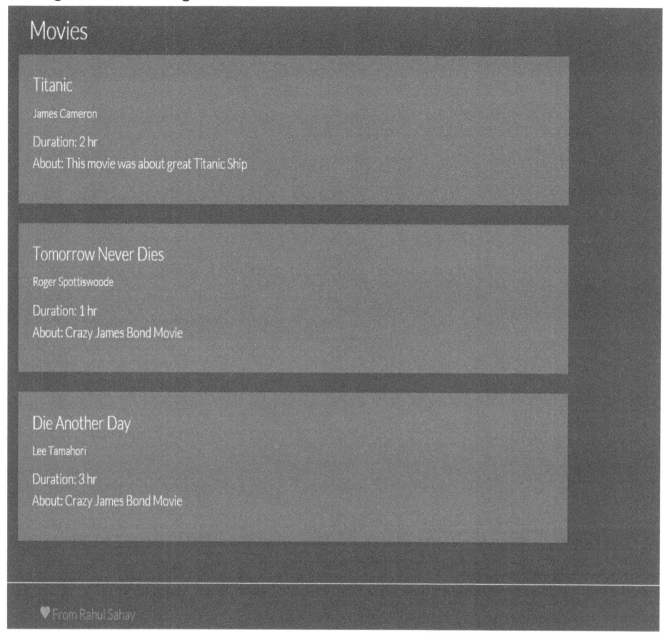

Getting Started with Angular JS

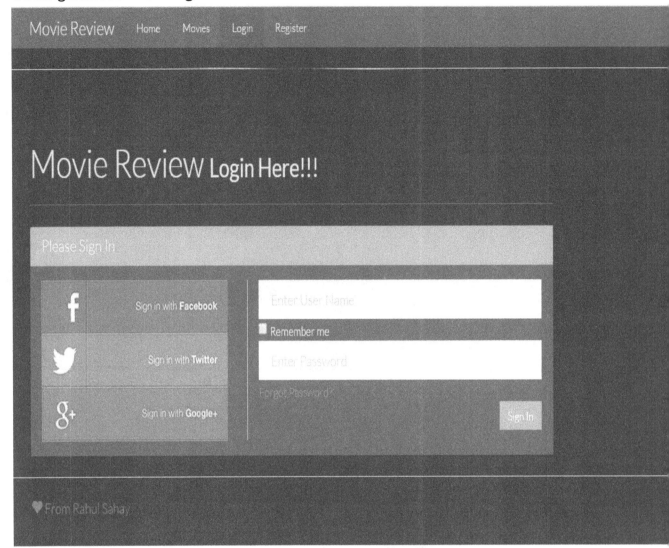

Getting Started with Angular JS

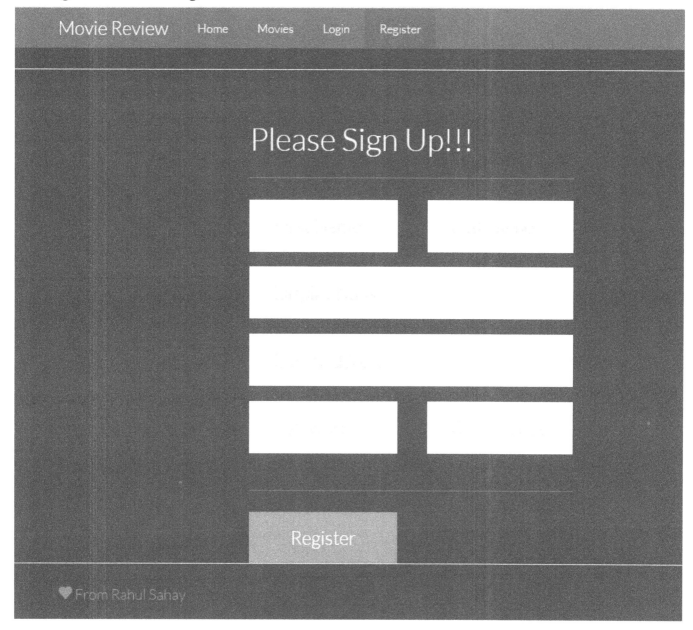

I hope you have enjoyed this glimpse of yeoman for building full-fledged angular app with backend in place.

SUMMARY:-

In this chapter, we have covered variety of techniques to write different kind of test cases. We started with first by installing test runner, which is karma. Then, we also installed jasmine testing framework for writing test cases. We also saw how to initialize the karma configs file with all specs in place. Then, for example, we have covered several testing scenarios by writing

Chapter 6: Testing Angular

Getting Started with Angular JS

different test cases. In the end, I also shared the some debugging and troubleshooting techniques.

Getting Started with Angular JS

WHAT DO you find in this CHAPTER?

- Introduction
- Features
- Creating New Project
- Creating Components
- Embedding Components
- Using Babel
- Using TypeScript
- Using TypeScript With Angular
- Configuring TypeScript in WebStorm
- Configuring File-Watcher
- Creating Angular App
- Summary

INTRODUCTION:-

In this section, we are going to see the glimpse of Angular 2.0. Angular 2 is getting released coming December 2015. This release is going to bring some major path breaking changes like major performance improvements and feature enhancements. In more than 400 commits, google has fixed more than 100 bugs and added around 30 additional features. These stats are just the initial stats and final list will have many more features. However, I thought it would be great, if I can provide a brief snapshot around the same. AngularJS 2 is for mobile apps. It is for desktop as well, but major focus is on mobile. With this, let us go ahead and look at the complete list of features.

FEATURES:-

- **Mobile First**: - Angular Team, at ng-conf made it clear they will go for mobile first approach. I think this is bold and brilliant step around that. These days, demand is very adaptive. Hence, if you can fit perfectly in mobile environment then I think desktop apps will be cakewalk.

Getting Started with Angular JS

- **Loosely Coupled Modules**: - Angular Team has been detaching from its several core versions now. At the same time, community started offering very interesting modules like ui-router. Both, angular team and community have successfully built an ecosystem, which keeps on increasing. You can find more details around the same @ http://ngmodules.org/.

- **Modern Browsers**: - The set includes Chrome, Firefox, IE10/11, Opera, Safari and all latest mobile browsers support.

- **ECMA Script 6**:- All code in AngularJS is written entirely in ES6. Since, ES6 don't run in browsers today, hence google is testing the same using traceur-compiler to generate ES5 script which runs everywhere. Do not worry if you do not want to upgrade to ES6, you can still write entire angular 2 in ES5.

- **Change Detection**: - Faster change detection is one key elements of Angular 2 design. The speed of AngularJS app is hugely dependent on data binding happening internally in the application. **Object.observe()** is a low level API that let you add listener to be notified whenever a JavaScript object changes state. If you want to explore more about Change Detection, you can refer the link here.

- **Dependency Injection**: - Dependency Injection is still a key differentiator between AngularJS and other client side frameworks in eliminating much of application's wiring code and making testability-by-default. Based on ES6, it provides less complex syntax, declarative annotations and lazy loading.

- **Templating & Directives**: - The ability to specify template directly in HTML and extend its syntax are like cakewalk in AngularJS. In Angular 2, this process has become more simplified. It also boosts performance.

- **Touch Animations**: - Angular team is working on touch animations to make the performance on mobile devices much better than ever before. The main goal here is creating a module that implements usage patterns using native browsers features.

- **Router**: - The initial angular router was designed just to handle simpler use cases. As AngularJS grew, Angular team added tons of new features to it to extend it further.

- **Persistence**: - There was always a room between fetching the data from the server and fetching the data from local storage like from browser. Mobile apps need to work on the same lines. Angular team is working on the same to provide higher level of abstraction. Apart from these there are many other features which are getting added by angular team.

Getting Started with Angular JS

CREATING NEW PROJECT:-

In this section, we are going to create a new Sample Angular 2 project. Here, I will simply get started with ES5 syntax and later on explain different components and new syntax structure with ES5 and ES6. ES5 does not need any transpiler like Typescript, Babel or Traceur. However, we do need this for ES6, as currently, we do not have any browser, which supports ECMA Script 6. Hence, without wasting time let us get started with new project creation.

In the above screen shot, as you can see that I have created a blank project and then pasted the downloaded Angular 2 scripts from google site in my lib folder. Now, I will be referring these scripts throughout the application. Now, let us go ahead and add plain HTML file with required dependency in there.

```html
<!DOCTYPE html>
<html lang="en">
<head>
  <meta charset="UTF-8">
  <script src="lib/angular2.sfx.dev.js"></script>
  <script src="js/app.js"></script>
  <title></title>
</head>
<body>
<helloAngular></helloAngular>
</body>
</html>
```

As you can see in the above snippet, I have added one Angular 2 script reference and another script file reference, where I will be writing my logic to display data on the page. Apart from this, I have also added one custom tag, which we will code in a next section.

Getting Started with Angular JS

CREATING COMPONENTS:-

In this section, we will go ahead and write the required component in ES5 style to display the data on the page. Here, we will also understand new syntax required for Angular 2 style coding. Below, in the screenshot, as you can see that WebStorm is helping with new syntax structures which is expected in Angular 2.

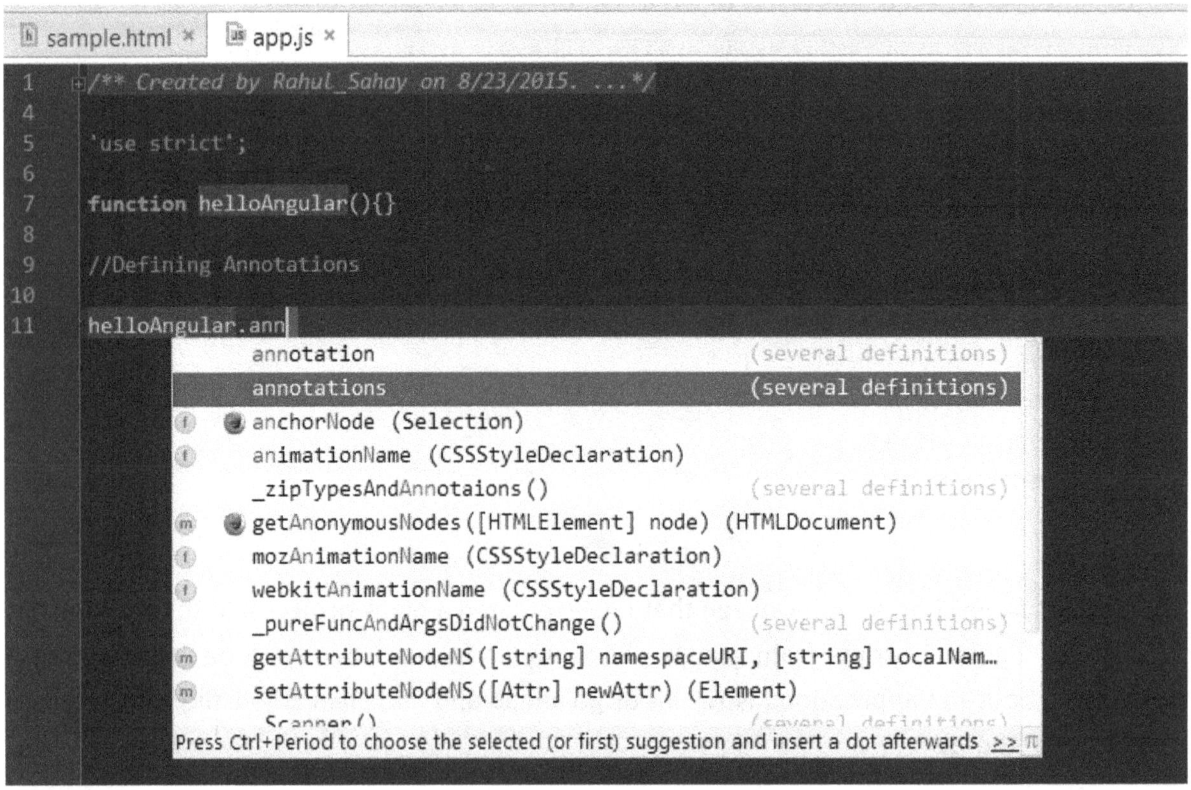

```js
/**
 * Created by Rahul_Sahay on 8/23/2015.
 */

'use strict';

function helloAngular(){}

//Defining Annotations

helloAngular.annotations=[
  new angular.Component({
    selector:"helloAngular"
  }),
  new angular.View({
    template:"<div><h1>Hello Angular 2</h1></div>"
  })
];

//Bootstrapping Components

document.addEventListener("DOMContentLoaded",function(){
```

Getting Started with Angular JS

```
angular.bootstrap(helloAngular);
});
```

Let me explain the snippet here. Here, I have added the new helloAngular function and there I have added new constructor and kept the same blank. You can obviously go ahead put properties inside that as well. However, I prefer to use annotations property here, which is just an array. Moreover, inside the array, we have passed two things component annotation and a view annotation.

Inside, the component annotation, I have defined my selector that I kept on the sample html page. In addition, then I defined my view annotation where in I defined my simple custom template. Last but not the least; I have bootstrapped my component explicitly. However, here I have wrapped this call inside DOM ready event. With the above changes in place, when I go ahead and run the app, then it will produce the below output.

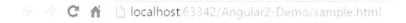
localhost:63342/Angular2-Demo/sample.html

Hello Angular 2

EMBEDDING COMPONENTS:-

In this section, I am going to create another component and then I will embed the same in my parent component, which I have created in previous section. Below, is the completed snippet for the same.

```
/**
 * Created by Rahul_Sahay on 8/23/2015.
 */

'use strict';

function Tagline(){}

Tagline.annotations=[
  new angular.Component({
    selector:"message"
  }),
  new angular.View({
    template:"<div><h2>Getting Started With Angular 2!!!</h2></div>"
  })
];

function helloAngular(){}

//Defining Annotations

helloAngular.annotations=[
  new angular.Component({
```

Getting Started with Angular JS

```
    selector:"helloAngular"
  }),
new angular.View({
  directives:[Tagline],
  template:"<div><h1>Hello Angular 2</h1><message></message></div>"
  })
];

//Bootstrapping Components

document.addEventListener("DOMContentLoaded",function(){
  angular.bootstrap(helloAngular);
});
```

Now, let me go ahead and explain the snippet a bit. As you can see that, I have created another function with the name Tagline and added similar selectors and view to it. However, I have used the same as directive in my parent tag and in the parent tag, I have used the new custom tag. Hence, this way I never have to bootstrap another component; it will be taken care by the parent one. With the above change in place, when I go ahead and run the app, it will produce the below result.

Hello Angular 2

Getting Started With Angular 2!!!

You can download this sample @ https://github.com/rahulsahay19/Angular2-Demo.

USING BABEL:-

In this section, we are going to go through one of the Transpilers available. Here, we will write ES6 code, which will eventually get converted into equivalent JavaScript code, which we can use in our angular app. Here, I will go @ https://babeljs.io/. Below is the default page for this site.

Getting Started with Angular JS

Now, here I will go ahead and click on the **Try it out** link. Moreover, this will look like as shown below.

Therefore, in the left window, I will write my movie class which will eventually get converted into corresponding JavaScript code which I can use anywhere in any application as this is ES5 generated code.

```
1 ▾ class Movie{
2      directorName;
3      movieName;
4      releaseYear;
5      noOfReviews
6      constructor(directorName,movieName,releaseYear,noOfReviews)
7 ▾    {
8        ///define the props
9        this.directorName=directorName;
10       this.movieName=movieName;
11       this.releaseYear=releaseYear;
12       this.noOfReviews=noOfReviews;
13     }
14     }
15     var movie = new Movie('James Cameron','Avatar','1997','200');
16
17     console.log(movie);
```

Getting Started with Angular JS

Below is the corresponding JavaScript generated code.

```
1    'use strict';
2
3    function _classCallCheck(instance, Constructor) { if (!(instance instanceof Constructor)) { throw new TypeError('Cannot call a class as
4
5    var Movie = function Movie(directorName, movieName, releaseYear, noOfReviews) {
6      _classCallCheck(this, Movie);
7
8      ///define the props
9      this.directorName = directorName;
10     this.movieName = movieName;
11     this.releaseYear = releaseYear;
12     this.noOfReviews = noOfReviews;
13   };
14
15   var movie = new Movie('James Cameron', 'Avatar', '1997', '200');
16
17   console.log(movie);
```

This also produced me the required output at the bottom of the screen in JSON format.

```
{"directorName":"James Cameron","movieName":"Avatar","releaseYear":"1997","noOfReviews":"200"}
```

USING TYPESCRIPT:-

In this section, I am going to achieve the same thing, but with a different transpiler and that is TypeScript. Hence, when I go @ http://www.typescriptlang.org/Playground link, it will again produce the similar kind of playground what we saw with Babel.

Here, you can make enjoy the boilerplate code example of different types as shown below in the dropdown list.

Getting Started with Angular JS

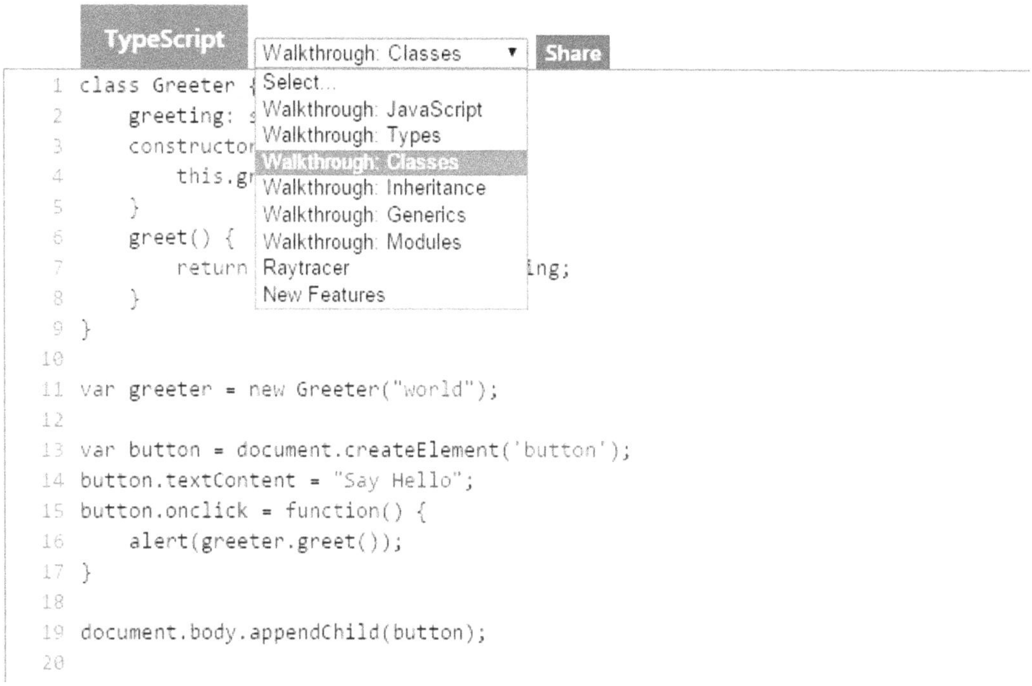

```
        TypeScript    Walkthrough: Classes    ▼  Share
                       Select...
  1  class Greeter {   Walkthrough: JavaScript
  2      greeting:     Walkthrough: Types
  3      constructor   Walkthrough: Classes
  4          this.gr   Walkthrough: Inheritance
  5      }             Walkthrough: Generics
  6      greet() {     Walkthrough: Modules
  7          return    Raytracer              ing;
  8      }             New Features
  9  }
 10
 11  var greeter = new Greeter("world");
 12
 13  var button = document.createElement('button');
 14  button.textContent = "Say Hello";
 15  button.onclick = function() {
 16      alert(greeter.greet());
 17  }
 18
 19  document.body.appendChild(button);
 20
```

Now, when I write my movie class as shown below in the screen shot

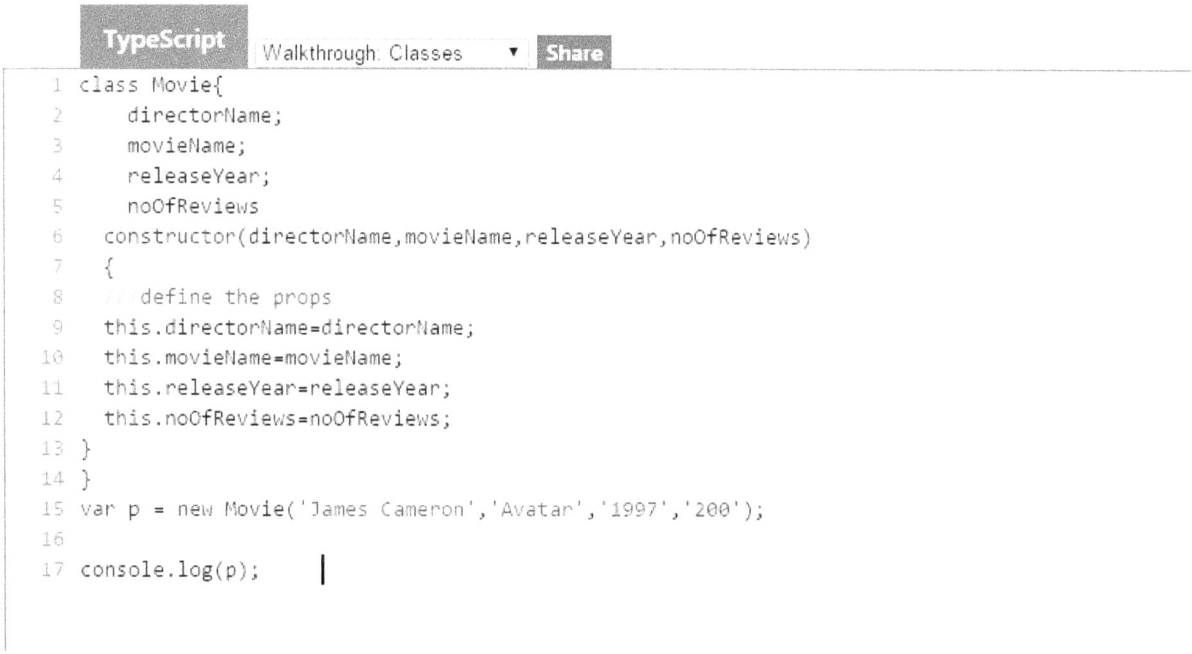

```
        TypeScript    Walkthrough: Classes    ▼  Share
  1  class Movie{
  2      directorName;
  3      movieName;
  4      releaseYear;
  5      noOfReviews
  6    constructor(directorName,movieName,releaseYear,noOfReviews)
  7    {
  8      //define the props
  9    this.directorName=directorName;
 10    this.movieName=movieName;
 11    this.releaseYear=releaseYear;
 12    this.noOfReviews=noOfReviews;
 13  }
 14  }
 15  var p = new Movie('James Cameron','Avatar','1997','200');
 16
 17  console.log(p);        |
```

It will produce the corresponding JavaScript.

Getting Started with Angular JS

```
   1 var Movie = (function () {
   2     function Movie(directorName, movieName, releaseYear, noOfReviews) {
   3         //define the props
   4         this.directorName = directorName;
   5         this.movieName = movieName;
   6         this.releaseYear = releaseYear;
   7         this.noOfReviews = noOfReviews;
   8     }
   9     return Movie;
  10 })();
  11 var p = new Movie('James Cameron', 'Avatar', '1997', '200');
  12 console.log(p);
  13
```

However, when I click on the Run as shown above in the screenshot, it will open a new blank window and in there when I click F12 and inspect the console, it will produce the following output.

```
🔍 🗌  Elements  Network  Sources  Timeline  Profiles  Resources  Audits │Console│ AngularJS Graph
🚫 ▽  <top frame>  ▼ ⬜ Preserve log
 ▼ Movie ⬚
    directorName: "James Cameron"
    movieName: "Avatar"
    noOfReviews: "200"
    releaseYear: "1997"
  ▶ __proto__: Movie
>
```

This is obviously very small demo around ES6, but it gives you a good insight of what is happening in ES6 and how you can make advantage of classes and related types in ES5.

USING TYPESCRIPT WITH ANGULAR:-

In this section, I am going to use TypeScript with angular. Here, I will create different project and install TypeScript in it. Nevertheless, before that let us go ahead and look at the TypeScript workflow flow for any angular project briefly.

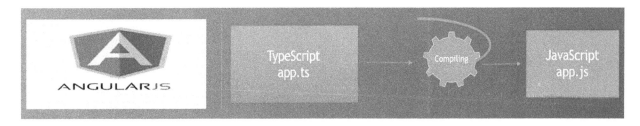

Getting Started with Angular JS

Therefore, we will have one Angular project wherein we will install TypeScript using node package manager and write our typescript code. Then, TypeScript compiler will come into picture and compile the same into corresponding JS file. We will go through the process in a moment.

Below is the project, which I have created with my usual angular 1.x library, which I have used while writing Movie Review app and other dependencies.

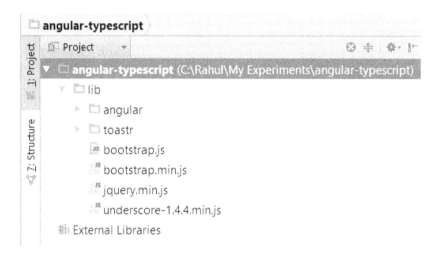

Now, I will go ahead and use the npm command to install the TypeScript in my project as shown below.

Terminal

```
Microsoft Windows [Version 6.3.9600]
(c) 2013 Microsoft Corporation. All rights reserved.

C:\Rahul\My Experiments\angular-typescript>npm install -g typescript
```

Once, installation is complete, and then we can go ahead and verify the installed version of TypeScript compiler with the following command as shown below.

Terminal

```
C:\Rahul\My Experiments\angular-typescript>tsc -version
message TS6029: Version 1.5.3

C:\Rahul\My Experiments\angular-typescript>
```

Getting Started with Angular JS

Next, we need to install TypeScript definition files. Nevertheless, before that let us talk about the significance of **tsd** files. Below are few benefits of tsd files.

- Allows Strongly Typed definitions
- It defines the types, which is defined in external libraries.
- You can recognize this kind of file by with the extension **.d.ts**
- These files are not used for deployment rather only for development and compiling.
- Editors use this file to help with tooling.

We already have one dedicated site http://definitelytyped.org/. At this site, you can find tsd files for all popular JavaScript libraries.

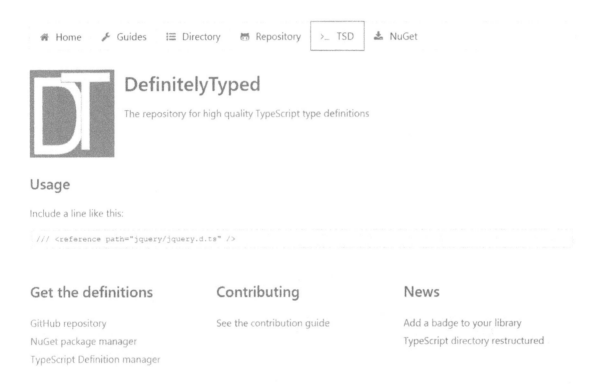

As shown in the above screenshot, I will go ahead and click on the link **TSD**.

Getting Started with Angular JS

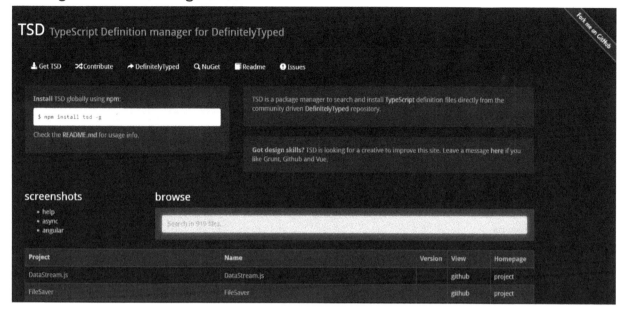

As you can see that, there is a command to install the TypeScript Definition Manager explicitly. Let us go ahead and install the same.

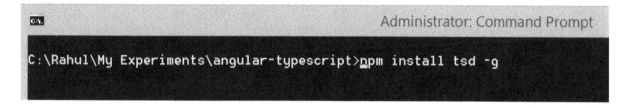

CONFIGURING TYPESCRIPT IN WEBSTORM:-

In this section, we are going to enable TypeScript in WebStorm. It may happen that by default this feature is disabled. In order to enable it, you need to open the settings page either by pressing the combination **CTRL+ALT+S or File → Settings**. There, in Language and Framework section, Select TypeScript from the left pane and enable the checkbox as shown below.

Getting Started with Angular JS

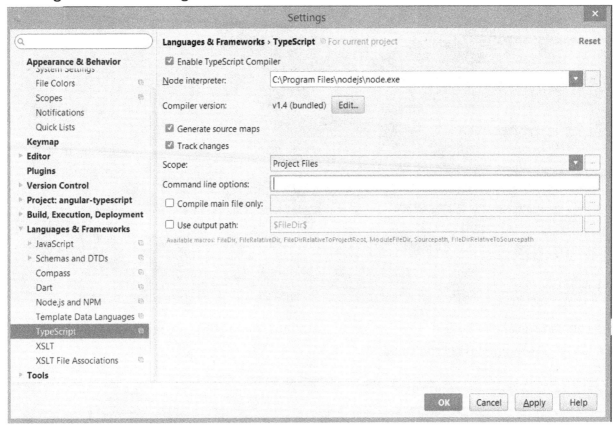

Then, click on apply and say ok.

CONFIGURING FILE-WATCHER:-

In this section, we are going to configure file watcher for TypeScript. File-Watcher will automatically create exactly same directory structure based on TypeScript Directory structure as shown below

When, I click on ok button, it will create the following directory structure.

Getting Started with Angular JS

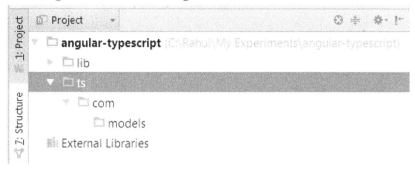

In addition, here I have created my TypeScript file as shown below.

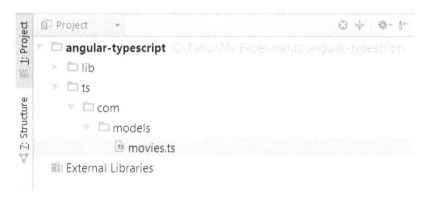

```
/**
 * Created by Rahul_Sahay on 8/25/2015.
 */

class movie{
    directorName;
    movieName;
    releaseYear;
    noOfReviews;

    constructor(directorName,movieName,releaseYear,noOfReviews){
        //define the props
        this.directorName=directorName;
        this.movieName=movieName;
        this.releaseYear=releaseYear;
        this.noOfReviews=noOfReviews;
    }
}

var mov = new movie('James Cameron','Avatar','1997','200');

console.log(mov);
```

Now, let us go ahead in File-Watcher as shown below.

Getting Started with Angular JS

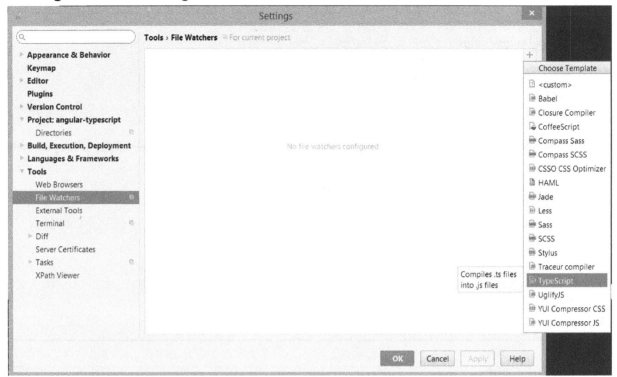

Then, here while configuring arguments; we can take help of macros as shown below in the screenshot.

Getting Started with Angular JS

Finally, argument will look like this.

--out $ProjectFileDir$/js/$FileDirPathFromParent(ts)$$FileNameWithoutExtension$.js $FileName$

Hence, now when I do any change in TypeScript file and synchronize, it will produce the corresponding directory structure.

It also created the corresponding folder structure with the required JS file in there.

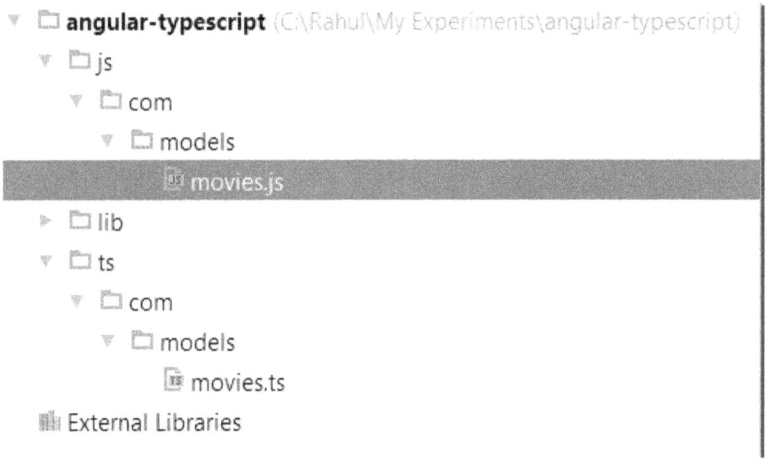

Getting Started with Angular JS

```
▼ 🗀 angular-typescript (C:\Rahul\My Experiments\angular-typescript)
   ▼ 🗀 js
      ▼ 🗀 com
         ▼ 🗀 models
                🗋 movies.js
   ▶ 🗀 lib
   ▼ 🗀 ts
      ▼ 🗀 com
         ▼ 🗀 models
                🗋 movies.ts
▮ External Libraries
```

JavaScript file will look like as shown below.

```javascript
/**
 * Created by Rahul_Sahay on 8/25/2015.
 */
var movie = (function () {
    function movie(directorName, movieName, releaseYear, noOfReviews) {
        //define the props
        this.directorName = directorName;
        this.movieName = movieName;
        this.releaseYear = releaseYear;
        this.noOfReviews = noOfReviews;
    }
    return movie;
})();
var mov = new movie('James Cameron', 'Avatar', '1997', '200');
console.log(mov);
```

In order to run this file, we need to have HTML file in place. Hence, let us go ahead and create one sample file as shown below.

```html
<!DOCTYPE html>
<html lang="en">
<head>
  <meta charset="UTF-8">
  <script src="js/com/models/movies.js"></script>
  <title></title>
</head>
<body>

</body>
</html>
```

With the above change in place, when I run the file and open the console, then it will produce the same output as shown below.

Getting Started with Angular JS

Q   Elements Network Sources Timeline Profiles Resources Audits Console AngularJS Graph

⊘ ▽ <top frame> ▼ ☐ Preserve log

```
▼ Movie
     directorName: "James Cameron"
     movieName: "Avatar"
     noOfReviews: "200"
     releaseYear: "1997"
   ▶ __proto__: Movie
>
```

CREATING ANGULAR APP:-

In this section, we are going to build angular module with TypeScript. Here, I have created new folder structure for module as shown below.

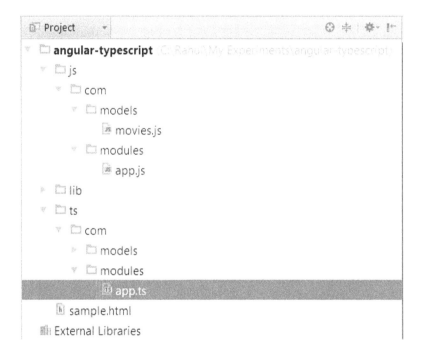

Now, following snippet in TS file is giving me error.

```
/**
 * Created by Rahul_Sahay on 8/25/2015.
 */

angular.module("app",[]);
```

```
cmd.exe /D /C call C:/Users/Rahul_Sahay/AppData/Roaming/npm/tsc.cmd --out "C:\Rahul\My Experiments\angular-typescript/js/com/modules/app.js" app.ts
app.ts(5,1): error TS2304: Cannot find name 'angular'.

Process finished with exit code 2
```

Chapter 7: Getting started with Angular2 & Typescript

Getting Started with Angular JS

With the below command, it will resolve the angular issue

```
Terminal

C:\Rahul\My Experiments\angular-typescript>tsd install angular --save

 - angularjs / angular

>> running install..

>> written 1 file:

   - angularjs/angular.d.ts
```

TypeScript Compiler   ▶ 4: Run   6: TODO   Terminal

In addition, creates the subsequent JavaScript file in corresponding JS folder as shown below.

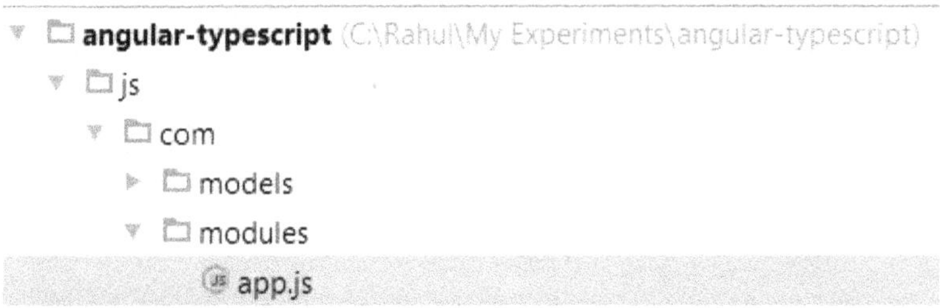

▼ ☐ **angular-typescript** (C:\Rahul\My Experiments\angular-typescript)
  ▼ ☐ js
    ▼ ☐ com
      ▶ ☐ models
      ▼ ☐ modules
        ⬚ app.js

```
/**
 * Created by Rahul_Sahay on 8/25/2015.
 */
angular.module("app", []);
```

Now, let us go ahead and add some angular stuffs in **TS** file and use the same via **JS** file. Now, let us go ahead and controller here

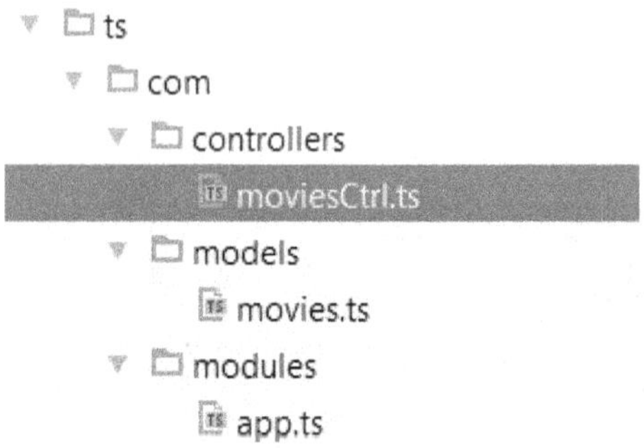

▼ ☐ ts
  ▼ ☐ com
    ▼ ☐ controllers
      ⬚ moviesCtrl.ts
    ▼ ☐ models
      ⬚ movies.ts
    ▼ ☐ modules
      ⬚ app.ts

```
/**
 * Created by Rahul_Sahay on 8/25/2015.
 */

interface IMoviesModel {
```

Getting Started with Angular JS

```
movieName:string;
directorName:string;
releaseYear:number;
noOfReviews:number;
}
```

As you can see the above snippet, here I have created one interface, which has all the properties that I want to use the same in my controller. Since, I have created the interface, hence, now I have to implement the interface using class. Below is the snippet for controller class that implements the interface.

```
/**
 * Created by Rahul_Sahay on 8/25/2015.
 */

interface IMoviesModel {
    movieName:string;
    directorName:string;
    releaseYear:number;
    noOfReviews:number;
}

class moviesCtrl implements IMoviesModel{
    movieName:string;
    directorName:string;
    releaseYear:number;
    noOfReviews:number;
}
```

Next, I need to create the constructor that will inject the value in the controller.

```
18        constructor(){
19            this.movieName="Avatar";
20            this.directorName="James Cameron";
21            this.releaseYear="1997"
```
error TS2322: Type 'string' is not assignable to type 'number'. more... (Ctrl+F1)

In the above screenshot, while writing the code, I passed in release year as string, which I earlier defined as number. Hence, compiler started complaining. So, this is the power of TypeScript, It keeps warning you if you do anything wrong. One more point to notice here, that I am writing JavaScript with Object Oriented Programming notion. Therefore, those people who have OOPs background, can write these stuffs very quickly.

```
/**
 * Created by Rahul_Sahay on 8/25/2015.
 */

interface IMoviesModel {
    movieName:string;
    directorName:string;
    releaseYear:number;
    noOfReviews:number;
```

Getting Started with Angular JS

```
}

class moviesCtrl implements IMoviesModel {
    movieName:string;
    directorName:string;
    releaseYear:number;
    noOfReviews:number;

constructor() {
    this.movieName = "Avatar";
    this.directorName = "James Cameron";
    this.releaseYear = 1997,
    this.noOfReviews = 200
    }
}
```

With the above change in place, corresponding JavaScript file got generated.

```
▼ 🗀 angular-typescript (C:\Rahul\My Experiments\angular-typescript)
   ▼ 🗀 js
      ▼ 🗀 com
         ▼ 🗀 controllers
              📄 movies.js
              📄 moviesCtrl.js
         ▶ 🗀 models
         ▼ 🗀 modules
              📄 app.js
```

```
/**
 * Created by Rahul_Sahay on 8/25/2015.
 */
var moviesCtrl = (function () {
    function moviesCtrl() {
        this.movieName = "Avatar";
        this.directorName = "James Cameron";
        this.releaseYear = 1997,
            this.noOfReviews = 200;
    }
    return moviesCtrl;
})();
```

Next thing is I need to register the controller with the module. Below is the corresponding TS and JS snippets for the same.

```
/**
 * Created by Rahul_Sahay on 8/25/2015.
 */

interface IMoviesModel {
    movieName:string;
    directorName:string;
    releaseYear:number;
    noOfReviews:number;
}
```

Chapter 7: Getting started with Angular2 & Typescript

Getting Started with Angular JS

```
class moviesCtrl implements IMoviesModel {
    movieName:string;
    directorName:string;
    releaseYear:number;
    noOfReviews:number;

constructor() {
    this.movieName = "Avatar";
    this.directorName = "James Cameron";
    this.releaseYear = 1997,
    this.noOfReviews = 200
    }
}


//Registering the controller with the module
angular.module("app").controller("moviesCtrl",moviesCtrl);
```

```
/**
 * Created by Rahul_Sahay on 8/25/2015.
 */
var moviesCtrl = (function () {
    function moviesCtrl() {
        this.movieName = "Avatar";
        this.directorName = "James Cameron";
        this.releaseYear = 1997,
            this.noOfReviews = 200;
    }
    return moviesCtrl;
})();
//Registering the controller with the module
angular.module("app").controller("moviesCtrl", moviesCtrl);
```

Then, I need to reference all JS stuffs in my HTML file as shown below in the snippet.

```
<!DOCTYPE html>
<html lang="en">
<head>
  <meta charset="UTF-8">
  <link rel="stylesheet" href="css/bootstrap.superhero.min.css"/>
  <title></title>
</head>
<body ng-app="app">
<div class="container">
  <div class="navbar">
    <div class="navbar-inner">
      <ul class="nav">
        <li><a href="#">Movie Details</a></li>
        <li><a href="#">Post New Movie</a></li>
        <li><a href="#">Edit Profile</a></li>
        <li><a href="#">Cache Demo</a></li>
      </ul>
    </div>
  </div>
  <div ng-controller="moviesCtrl as vm">
    <h1>Movie Name: {{vm.movieName}}</h1>

    <h2>Director Name: {{vm.directorName}}</h2>
```

Chapter 7: Getting started with Angular2 & Typescript

Getting Started with Angular JS

```
    <h3>Release Year: {{vm.releaseYear}}, Reviews: {{vm.noOfReviews}}</h3>
  </div>
</div>
<script src="lib/angular/angular.js"></script>
<script src="lib/angular/angular-route.min.js"></script>
<script src="js/com/modules/app.js"></script>
<script src="js/com/controllers/moviesCtrl.js"></script>
<script src="lib/bootstrap.min.js"></script>
</body>
</html>
```

One point to notice here, that I have not used **$scope** object in controller, rather I am using as syntax here in markup with controller. Using as syntax does not require $scope object. With the above change in place, when I go ahead run the app, it will produce the below output as shown below.

You can download the source code for this small demo from here http://bit.ly/ng-type-demo.

VISUAL STUDIO CODE GLIMPSE:-

In this section, I am going to introduce one new and fancy editor from Microsoft, **Visual Studio Code**. Initially, this topic was not in the scope of this book. However, during ng-conf, I found that all the Google folks were using Visual Studio code for demoing different features. Hence, thought to include this as well, wherein I will show, how to get started with Visual Studio Code, in terms of app setup. You can download this tool from here @ http://visualstudio.com

Getting Started with Angular JS

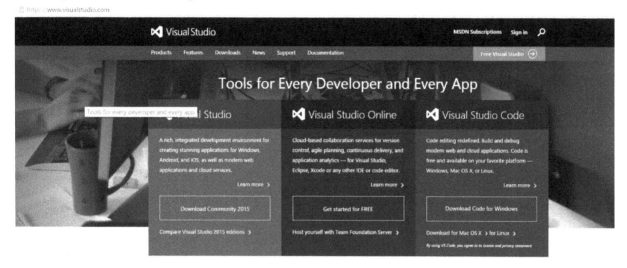

One thing to note here, Visual Studio Code is open source editor that runs on all Operating Systems. Therefore, you can download your choice of version from here. Once, installed successfully, let us go ahead and open the editor.

As you can see in the above screenshot, fairly simple, very lightweight, ideal editor for writing any angular or node app. Off-course, you can write .NET projects as well and that is well supported by it out of the box. Nevertheless, .NET is not in the scope of this book. Hence, I am skipping this piece. Conceptually, VS-Code is folder based, hence you can open any app folder here and it will list the files as it is.

Therefore, it is very easy to explore. I would recommend John Papa's blog (http://bit.ly/Jpapa-vscode) on systematic Visual Code setup and other high-level stuffs like git, debugger, intellisense and many more out of the box settings. Let us go ahead and create one sample folder as shown below from the command line.

Getting Started with Angular JS

Now, let us open the folder using VS-Code.

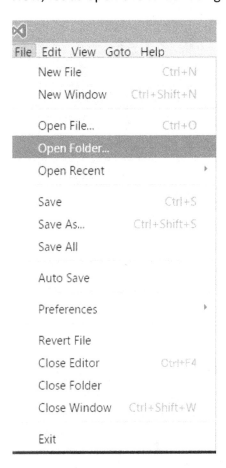

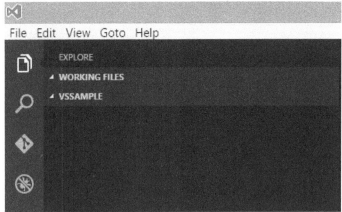

Let us go ahead and add new file here.

Getting Started with Angular JS

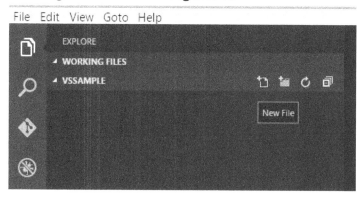

As, you can see in the below screen shot, I have created new TS file and as soon as I started writing my function, editor started providing suggestions.

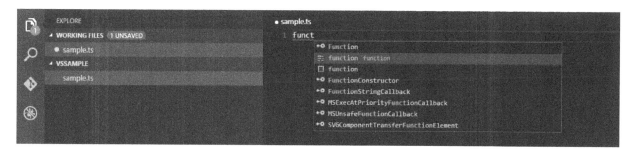

```
sample.ts
 1  class movie{
 2      directorName;
 3      movieName;
 4      releaseYear;
 5      noOfReviews;
 6
 7
 8      constructor(directorName,movieName,releaseYear,noOfReviews){
 9          //define the props
10          this.directorName=directorName;
11          this.movieName=movieName;
12          this.releaseYear=releaseYear;
13          this.noOfReviews=noOfReviews;
14      }
15  }
16
17  var mov = new movie('James Cameron','Avatar','1997','200');
18
19  console.log(mov);
20
```

Now, in order to compile this TypeScript code, I need to configure the compiler option. Here, I need to create one JSON file (tsconfig.json) as shown below. Notice, while setting Compiler

Getting Started with Angular JS

options also, editor is helping at every step. This is why I love Microsoft tools as it really speeds up the development activity.

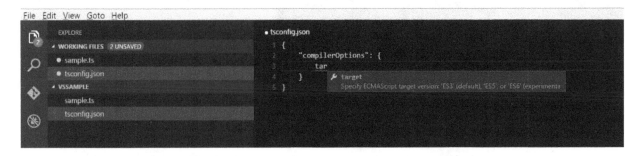

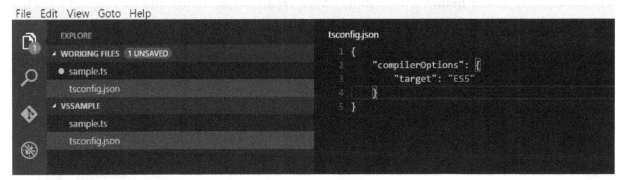

Now, I will go ahead and press CTRL+Shift+B to compile the project or CMD+Shift+B for MAC. As soon as, I did the same, it said, "No Task runner configured".

In order to configure the same, let us go ahead and click the button **Configure Task Runner**.

Getting Started with Angular JS

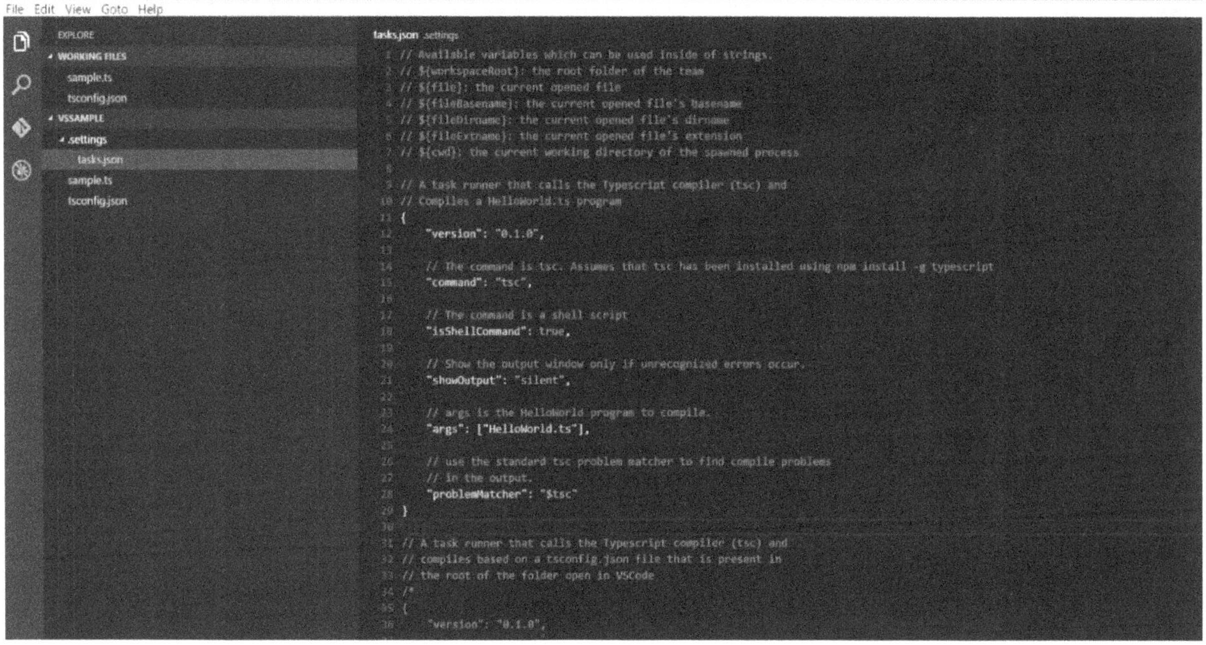

As soon as I clicked on the button, it configured all the required stuffs and created new file tasks.json. Now, here in the args section, I will specify my file name as shown below.

```
// args is the VS-Sample program to compile.
"args": ["sample.ts"],
```

With the above change in place, when I go ahead and compile again, it will produce the corresponding JS file as shown below.

```
sample.js
 1  var movie = (function () {
 2      function movie(directorName, movieName, releaseYear, noOfReviews) {
 3          //define the props
 4          this.directorName = directorName;
 5          this.movieName = movieName;
 6          this.releaseYear = releaseYear;
 7          this.noOfReviews = noOfReviews;
 8      }
 9      return movie;
10  })();
11  var mov = new movie('James Cameron', 'Avatar', '1997', '200');
12  console.log(mov);
13  |
```

We can also go ahead and open the TS and JS files side by side as shown below.

Getting Started with Angular JS

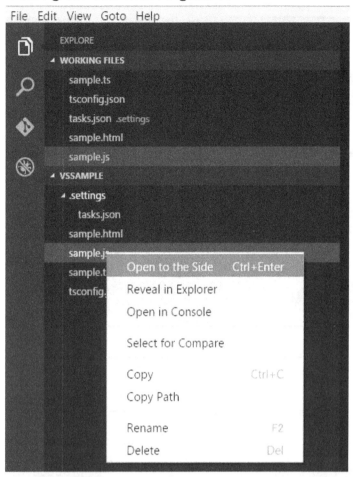

This is one of the great features of this editor to compare line by line. However, I have not done anything fancy in the above example, but that is ok, you understand the intent here. In order to run the same, we need to add one simple HTML file as shown below.

Getting Started with Angular JS

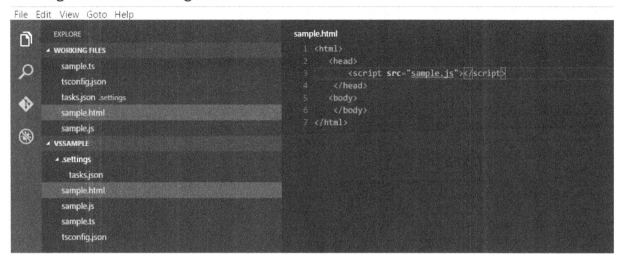

Now, in order to run the same, we need to install the server for the first time in the project and then, we can go ahead and start the server as shown below. Here, I need to select the html file and select open in console.

Then type the following command as shown below

Getting Started with Angular JS

```
C:\WINDOWS\system32\cmd.exe                        — □ ×

Microsoft Windows [Version 6.3.9600]
(c) 2013 Microsoft Corporation. All rights reserved.

c:\Rahul\My Experiments\VSSample>npm install -g http-server_
```

This will install the HTTP server.

```
C:\WINDOWS\system32\cmd.exe                        — □ ×

Microsoft Windows [Version 6.3.9600]
(c) 2013 Microsoft Corporation. All rights reserved.

c:\Rahul\My Experiments\VSSample>npm install -g http-server
C:\Users\Rahul_Sahay\AppData\Roaming\npm\hs -> C:\Users\Rahul_Sahay\AppData\Roam
ing\npm\node_modules\http-server\bin\http-server
C:\Users\Rahul_Sahay\AppData\Roaming\npm\http-server -> C:\Users\Rahul_Sahay\App
Data\Roaming\npm\node_modules\http-server\bin\http-server
http-server@0.8.0 C:\Users\Rahul_Sahay\AppData\Roaming\npm\node_modules\http-ser
ver
├── opener@1.4.1
├── corser@2.0.0
├── colors@1.0.3
├── http-proxy@1.11.1 (eventemitter3@1.1.1, requires-port@0.0.1)
├── union@0.4.4 (qs@2.3.3)
├── portfinder@0.4.0 (async@0.9.0, mkdirp@0.5.1)
├── optimist@0.6.1 (wordwrap@0.0.3, minimist@0.0.10)
└── ecstatic@0.7.6 (url-join@0.0.1, mime@1.3.4, he@0.5.0, minimist@1.2.0)

c:\Rahul\My Experiments\VSSample>_
```

Once, the same get installed successfully, then type the below shown command.

Getting Started with Angular JS

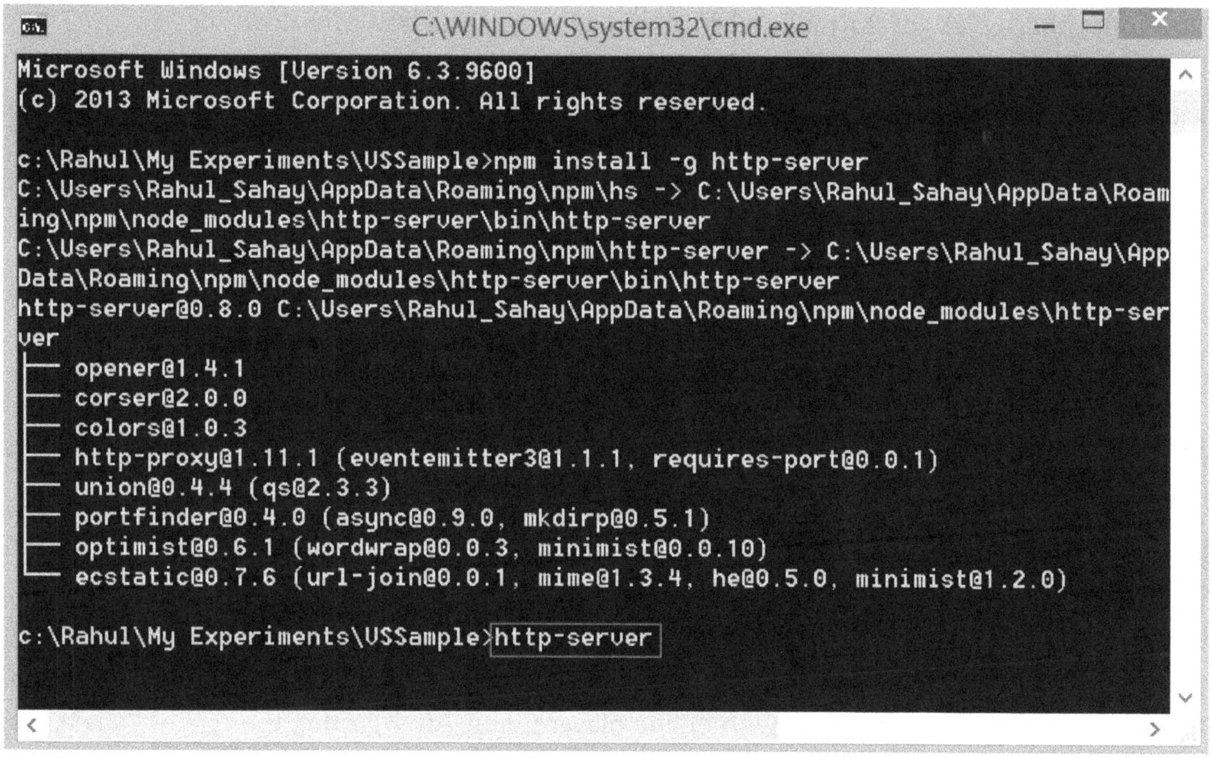

This will launch the server as shown below.

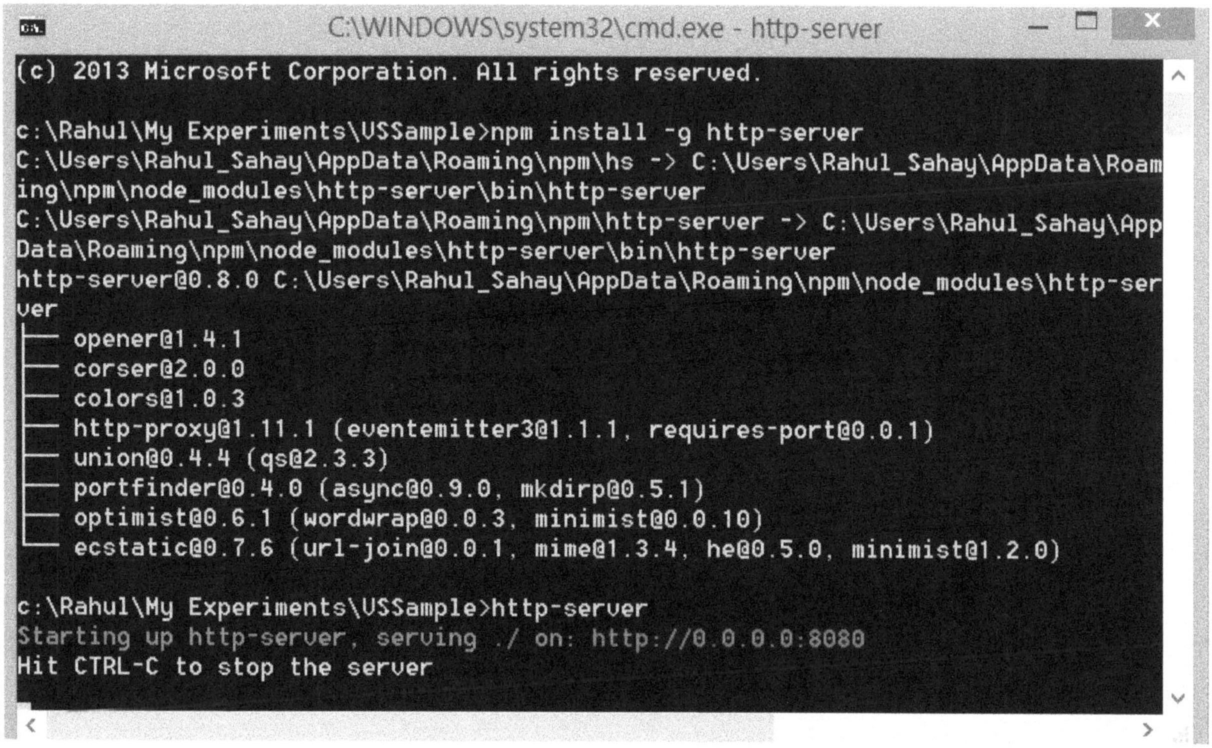

Getting Started with Angular JS

Now, once the server got started, we can go ahead and navigate to
http://localhost:8080/sample.html. In addition, then we can inspect the output in console
window as shown below in the screenshot.

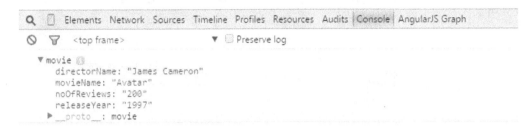

Similarly, you can go ahead and write angular app. With this, I would like to wrap the stuffs
here. I hope you have enjoyed this angular journey.

SUMMARY:-

In this section, we have seen all new upcoming features in a nutshell. We have initiated the
chapter with Angular2 version features. We have seen some Angular2 components in action.
Then, we have started TypeScript with online playgrounds. After getting the feel of TypeScript,
we have implemented one small project using TypeScript and Angular. Here, I have left this
code unfinished as an exercise for readers to re-write the entire project that we built earlier in
TypeScript way.

Getting Started with Angular JS

Rahul Sahay is a software developer living in Bangalore, India. Rahul has been working in various aspects of the software development life cycle since 8+ Years, focusing on **Google** & **Microsoft** technology-specific development. He has been part of the development in different applications, ranging from client applications to web services to websites.

Rahul is a Senior Consultant at **Capgemini**. But he works for Capgemini's client **Dell R&D**, on their premier e-commerce portal("_http://www.dell.com/account_"). His roles and responsibilities at this project are very tech-oriented like analyzing exiting use cases and taking the new requirements to add features on the existing segment. Prior to Capgemini, he has been associated with Mindtree and TCS. He is also active blogger; his writings can be viewed at _http://myview.rahulnivi.net_. You can also refer his professional profile @ http://rahulsahay.com